DAD.
HELP ME PLEASE

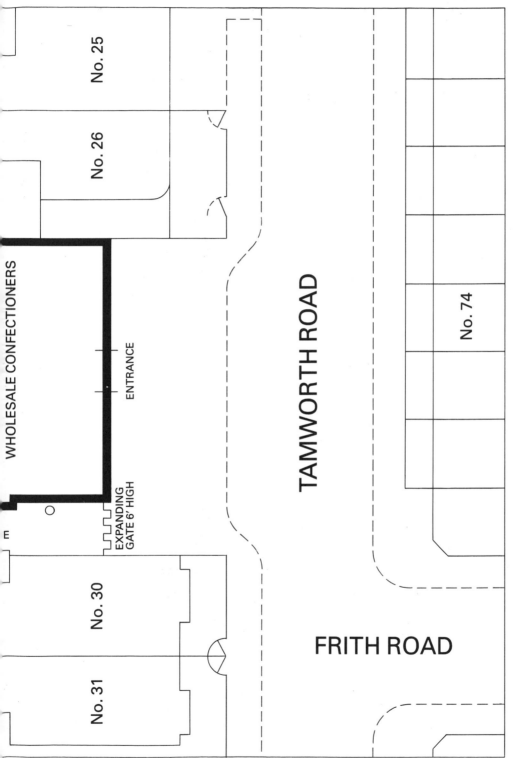

Plan of the warehouse roof and nearby buildings.

DAD, HELP ME PLEASE

Christopher Berry-Dee

Robin Odell

W H ALLEN

First published in Great Britain 1990 by
W. H. Allen & Co Plc
Sekforde House, 175/179 St John Street, London EC1V 4LL

ISBN 1-85227-131-0

Printed and bound in Great Britain by
Mackays of Chatham PLC, Chatham, Kent

Contents

Acknowledgements   vii

Preface   ix

1   *'Shan't be long, Mum'*   1

2   *'Let him have it, Chris'*   10

3   *'I did not know he was going to use the gun'*   25

4   *'You never know how little things can get you into trouble'*   30

5   *'Everybody knows I didn't kill Mr Miles'*   54

6   *'I'm not afraid to die because I am innocent'*   74

7   *'I've got nothing on my conscience'*   98

8   *'Dad, help me, please help me'*   111

9   *'See you tomorrow...'*   128

10   *'The truth of this story...'*   150

Appendix I Firearms evidence   165

Appendix II Dr Matheson's report on Derek Bentley   178

Appendix III The Lord Chief Justice's
    summing-up and charge to the jury   184

Appendix IV Judgment delivered at the Court
    of Criminal Appeal   194

Selected Bibliography   198

Index   199

Acknowledgements

The authors wish to express their grateful thanks to Iris Bentley and Rae Bradbury (Rita) for their help in providing details concerning Derek Bentley's personality and family background.

For information and advice on the medical, legal and police aspects of the Craig and Bentley case we are indebted to the following: Lord Lane, Lord Chief Justice; B. M. Birnberg & Company, Solicitors; R. W. Stone, Editor of *The Criminologist*; Professor Derrick J. Pounder; Dr Anthony Harbott; His Honour Judge Francis Cassels; Bill Waddell, Curator of the Black Museum at Scotland Yard; The Law Society; The Lord Chancellor's Department; HM Prison Service; The Home Office; The Metropolitan Police; The Metropolitan Police Forensic Science Laboratory; and The Maudsley Hospital.

For historical background and social details we are grateful for the help given by Harry Allen; Clive Wilkins; John Lee; The Rt Hon Gerald Kaufman MP; *The Croydon Advertiser*; The Lord Mayor of Croydon; Croydon Library; Croydon Health Authority; The Public Records Office; The London Transport Museum; The London Ambulance Service; The London Fire Brigade and The Fire Brigade Society. We wish to record special thanks to those citizens of the Borough of Croydon who came forward to provide reminiscences and anecdotal material; Mrs Johnson, Mrs Sherman, Mrs Savage, Mrs Pickett (née Ware), Mr Brown, Mr Lawrence, Mr Eason and Mr Carter.

Thanks are due to Frazer Ashford of Crystalvision Production Limited, and Peter Watson-Wood and Timothy Woolford of Film-screen Productions, for their interest in the dramatic potential of the Derek Bentley story, and also to David Cox, who helped with the research, and Eric Dobby, Derek Johns and Susanne McDadd of the Harrap Publishing Group, for their guidance. Lastly, but by no means least, we express our appreciation to Patrick Dee and Tracey Berry-Dee for their help and encouragement at all stages and Minna Fryman who processed all the words.

Preface

Derek William Bentley, a dull-witted, nineteen-year-old youth with a history of epilepsy, was executed in 1953 for a murder he did not commit. The official file on the case of Christopher Craig and Derek Bentley, who were tried for the murder of Police Constable Sidney Miles, is held under 'Extended Closure' until the middle of the next century. Iris Bentley, the executed youth's sister, has struggled for over thirty-six years to obtain access to these papers with a view to clearing his name, but all her representations have met with refusal.

However, while researching another case at the Lord Chancellor's Department, Christopher Berry-Dee was allowed to see the papers on the tragic case, and was permitted to photocopy them. Realising later that an error had been made, the Lord Chancellor's Department immediately replaced them under Extended Closure. This book is thus the first to be published that has drawn extensively on the documents and papers contained in that file. Many appear here for the first time, including letters that Derek dictated during his last days in his cell. The authors believe it is time that the record on this case was set straight.

The passage of time has distorted many of the issues surrounding Bentley's execution. A number of theories aired in the Press, in books and on television – such as the presence of a third man on the Croydon warehouse roof on that fateful night, or the suggestion that the luckless PC Miles was killed by a stray police bullet – have not been substantiated. The present authors have certainly found no evidence to support either of these hypotheses.

It would have been easy when compiling research for this book to have relied on the Press accounts of the day and on subsequent books and articles, but many of these were coloured by plain error, or by intense emotions of anger and indignation. The killing of a police officer on duty is no small matter, and neither is the execution of a feeble-minded teenager; both require the benefit of a proper perspective. The authors have spent hundreds of hours interviewing men and women who knew the Bentleys well and all the major protagonists in the case who are alive today. Christopher Berry-Dee learnt more about the Bentley case than Iris Bentley could ever have hoped to learn in her fight to clear her brother's name. Dozens of people who were involved in the events of 1952 and 1953 came forward to provide detailed and moving personal accounts and wherever possible, these first-hand accounts have been woven into the text. The witnesses each told their own often painful story, and we thank them all.

Although Britain abolished the death penalty in the wake of Derek Bentley's execution, it is a sobering thought that, at the time of writing, over thirty young people await execution on America's Death Row. Several are under the age of eighteen, and some suffer the same mental impairments as young Bentley.

As the book neared completion, we had to make a decision about its title, and there seemed to be two possibilities. On the one hand, there was the unfortunate remark made by Frank Cassels, one of the two defence counsel, at a pre-trial conference between counsel, 'I think both little bastards ought to swing'. On the other, were the words that fell from Derek Bentley's trembling lips during a conversation in the condemned cell with his devastated father, 'Dad, help me, please'. We chose Bentley's own poignant words, and dedicate this book to his memory, and in the hope that justice will finally prevail.

Christopher Berry-Dee
Curdridge, Hampshire
Robin Odell
Sonning Common, Oxfordshire

1

'Shan't be long, Mum'

The year 1952 was a momentous one for Britain. In February the nation grieved with the Royal Family over the death of King George VI at Sandringham after a painful illness. Tragedy also visited a number of ordinary families throughout the kingdom in the form of an official telegram carrying news of the death of a son or a husband in military action. Despite the end of the Second World War seven years before, Britain was still very much a nation at war. Members of the armed forces, many of them National Service conscripts, fought and died with the regular forces during the Malayan Emergency, and also in the Korean War.

In October the mushroom cloud of Britain's first atomic test explosion off the coast of Australia showed the shape of things to come. In many ways Britain was in the grip of the sort of disillusionment which often follows a great victory. Large numbers of men were in uniform in the Army occupying Germany, or serving their country elsewhere in the quickly receding days of imperial power. Rationing of some foods was still in force, and with it racketeering and a thriving Black Market. Crime was also on the increase, and robbery took on a new edge with the use of firearms. This was not surprising in view of how many had been trained to use firearms during the War, and the ready availability of handguns afterwards. Many servicemen had brought weapons home with them as souvenirs and prized trophies of overseas campaigns.

The public had been shocked in 1947 when Alec de Antiquis, the father of six children, was shot dead in a London street by armed raiders. He had carried out his citizen's duty by attempting to frustrate their escape, and was left dying in the gutter for his pains. Of the three robbers, two were hanged for murder and the third, aged seventeen, being too young to hang, was sentenced to be detained at His Majesty's Pleasure. It was a depressing incident that

1

pointed towards an increasing spiral of violence. The only satisfactory outcome was that the police hunt for the killers was so intense that many gun-owners discarded their weapons in dustbins or on rubbish-tips.

The growth of armed crime was underlined in the following year when Police Constable Nathaniel Edgar was shot and killed by an Army deserter. Edgar stopped and questioned George Thomas in a London street in connection with inquiries he was making about burglaries in the neighbourhood. Thomas drew a Lüger pistol and fired three times at the officer before fleeing. Edgar had written his assailant's name and address in his notebook, a routine piece of police work which the dying man handed to his colleagues.

When Thomas was traced a copy of an instructional book, *Shooting to Live with the One-hand Gun*, was found among his possessions. Although he was convicted of murder, he escaped execution because the death penalty had been suspended for a trial period. The availability of handguns and ammunition fuelled the ambitions of petty criminals and dangerously excited the curiosity of delinquent teenagers.

The 1950s proved to be the precursor of a more sinister decade which from 1955 saw an annual growth of about ten per cent in Britain's crime rate. The rising crime rate was accompanied by the use of firearms on an unprecedented scale – what Peter Gladstone Smith, Crime Correspondent for the *Daily Telegraph*, called 'The New Face of Crime'. A particularly worrying feature of this phenomenon was the increased proportion of juvenile crime. A Home Office report referred to the 'delinquent generation' – young people whose childhoods had been spent at a time when their fathers were absent from home on military service and parental supervision was at a low ebb. This age group created a prominent peak in official statistics on juvenile offenders.

Rising crime trends resulted in a record one million serious offences committed in Great Britain in the early to mid-1960s, of which 'The Great Train Robbery' in 1963 was the most sensational. The seeds of violence laid down in the years following the Second World War were to create a bitter harvest especially among juvenile offenders. Truancy, vandalism, theft, arson and drug-taking all erupted on the social scene and the years between 1963 and 1973 saw an eighty per cent rise in the number of young people brought before the courts.

The year 1952 was also one in which a great injustice was

perpetrated. On 11 December, the last day of his trial at the Old Bailey, a nineteen-year-old youth was sentenced to hang for murdering a police officer; his name was Derek William Bentley. He did not pull the trigger of the gun that fired the fatal shot – he was under arrest at the time – and by any reasonable assessment he was not fit to stand trial. He was the victim of a miscarriage of justice, and his execution was a painful reminder that the due process of the law can be fallible. He was also the victim of a mistaken idea that his execution would act as a deterrent to others who might be tempted to break the law. The premise was wrong, as subsequent events have proved, and in his case it was practised without regard for either fairness or objectivity and, more culpably, it ignored the facts.

The Bentley family, like many working-class households which survived the War, was a close-knit unit. They had suffered their share of trials and tribulations, having been bombed out of their house in Walworth, south-east London, by a German V-1 rocket bomb in 1944. Derek, eleven years old at the time, had been dragged from the wreckage, but the family was safe. In June 1945, after the War in Europe had ended, William and Lilian Bentley moved with their children to Norbury, in south-west London. Their house in Fairview Road gave them more space than they had had before and, as William Bentley put it, provided 'a slight lift-up in social scale'.

Lilian Bentley was a shy woman, her reticence possibly being due to a spinal deformity which left her with a slightly hunched back. She made routine visits to the shops to buy the necessities of life but otherwise her domain was really limited to her home and she chose not to be overly familiar with the neighbours. William Bentley, an ex-serviceman with a good sense of humour,was a practically-minded man, clever with his hands and with a gift for repairing things which defeated other people. He smoked, but drank little and, like his wife, was content to enjoy life at home and to watch the world go by.

The Bentleys had three surviving children. The eldest was Iris, a bright outgoing girl, who was to be a tower of strength to her parents and her two brothers Derek and Denis. Of the three, it was Derek who, from his early life as a weak child through his troubled teenage years to his death as prescribed by the law at the age of nineteen, was the source of anxiety and heartache. Iris, three years Derek's senior, was used to shielding her brother. Indeed, when they were both pupils at Edgware during the Blitz, Iris was allowed to sit with her brother in the boys' class to help him overcome his nervousness.

3

While his sister was always out and about enjoying the company of her friends, Derek seemed to have inherited his parents' shyness. He was a backward child and at the age of eleven still could not read or write. This made him a target for the taunts of his schoolfellows and his life was made a misery. Derek was essentially a loner and his lack of intelligence drove him more and more into a world of his own. He had few friends and tended to gravitate towards the younger age groups. He spoke very little to anyone and what he did say was usually in short, disjointed sentences. For all these reasons, Derek was a vulnerable boy open to the temptation of being easily swayed by others.

Derek's withdrawn nature and evident unhappiness worried his parents. They tried hard to find an avenue that would offer their son some success and his father built a small workshop at home to encourage him to develop some craft skills. He was also useful with his hands and helped his father with simple radio and television repairs in his spare time. The boy was undoubtedly spoilt by his parents who realised that he suffered some serious shortcomings and their indulgence was an attempt to compensate.

Derek was extremely fond of animals, to the extent that his parents allowed him to keep twenty-four cats, three dogs, several rabbits and a solitary chicken. He would not eat meat because it upset him to think he was eating some poor animal. His father was later to make much of Derek's love of animals, which betrayed, he believed, a gentle nature. To the whole world Bentley would not hurt a fly. Bearing in mind the stringent times in which they lived, his menagerie perhaps said something also about parental indulgence.

Derek was beginning to show some promise and his parents were optimistic that he would find a job in which he would be able to use his mechanical skills when he left school in the summer of 1948. However, their hopes were shattered when he was ordered by the Juvenile Court to spend three years in an Approved School for alleged theft. His parents were shocked by the turn of events, but resiliently determined that he should make the best of it. They hoped that exposure to firm but kindly discipline would benefit him.

The shy youth was treated sympathetically at Kingswood Training School, near Bristol, and he responded by behaving well and making some progress in his mental abilities. But, when he was sent for an IQ test, he was rated sixty-six, with a reading age of four and a half. Sixty-six was a very low rating indeed, equivalent to that of an eleven- or twelve-year-old child, and put him in the category of 'feeble-minded'. There were also ominous signs of incipient ill health. Derek suffered a number of fits during his short life, the first one occurring after a bad fall when he was four years old, and while he was at Kingswood he experienced persistent headaches and had several blackouts. A medical examination at that time recorded he was suffering from *petit mal*. This is the lesser type of epileptic seizure in which there is momentary loss of consciousness due to fluctuations in the brain's electrical activity. There may be loss of concentration – sometimes explained as daydreaming – when the conversation is broken or the subject may stagger slightly when walking. *Petit mal* is confined to the sudden arrest of consciousness for short periods of 15 to 20 seconds and does not involve convulsive spasms. The onset of epilepsy is usually before the age of five, and although there may be an hereditary disposition, other factors such as injuries to the head, sudden fright or prolonged anxiety may be precipitating causes.

There is no doubt that Derek's antecedents were poor on his mother's side. There was a family history of epilepsy, and Mrs Bentley's cousin had died during an epileptic fit. Moreover, his twin brother had died at birth and another born with Down's Syndrome died as an infant.

Apart from suffering fits or experiencing relatively minor loss of consciousness, the epileptic does not particularly suffer ill health. In some cases it is recognised that there is a gradual deterioration of wellbeing due mainly to the social attitudes which sufferers of epilepsy have to face. There may be feelings of rejection resulting from difficulties in securing employment, and the subject may tend towards dullness, irritability and forgetfulness.

Derek was released fourteen months early from the Approved School, and returned to live with his family. It was a listless, pasty-faced youth who arrived home in July 1950. His mother thought he was ill, and set about building him up by providing a good diet and loving care, but neither she nor her husband could shake him out of the depression into which he had sunk. He worked first for a furniture removal business and then for Croydon Corporation as a dustman and later as a road-sweeper. He seemed to have shaken off some of his lethargy, and began to take an interest in life. However, in July 1952, he was dismissed from his job as a road-sweeper for unsatisfactory service and from then on was unemployed.

Physically, Derek Bentley was a fine, good-looking lad; tall, with fair, wavy hair. He was the sort of young man who in other circum-stances, would probably have benefited from compulsory conscription to the armed forces. In February 1952 he reported for the medical examination undergone by all those eligible for National Service. The doctor found him mentally sub-normal and placed him in the lowest grade, Grade IV, which made him unfit for National Service. His family doctor had provided the authorities with a certificate stating that Derek Bentley was subject to *petit mal*.

Derek was addicted to cinema-going and his evening life largely centred on 'going to the pictures', hanging around in the street waiting for the cinema to open and engaging in good-natured larking about afterwards. His sister, Iris, worked as an usherette at the Astoria Cinema in Streatham and still retained her sisterly super-vision of Derek, keeping an eye on him and the people with whom he associated. Derek met the one girl in his life at the cinema in Streatham where she also worked as an usherette. He treated her warmly and generously, but more like a sister than a girlfriend; their brief encounters had no sexual content.

Towards the end of 1951, Derek, who had no close friends, befriended Christopher Craig, a boy three years younger than him-self whom he had first come into contact with at Norbury Manor School in about 1948. Craig presented himself as a young thief full of bravado, and he quickly made himself *persona non grata* with William Bentley. Mr Bentley, ever mindful of Derek's previous encounter with the law and his spell at Approved School, advised his son against seeing Craig again. This proved difficult, as Craig persisted in pressing his friendship with Derek and the older youth found it impossible to resist.

Without doubt, Craig manipulated the weak-minded Bentley. They had been drawn together by their devotion to the make-believe world of toughness, which they enjoyed on the cinema screen. There was no contest of wills between the forceful boy from a middle-class back-ground and the weak-minded lad from a working-class home. Craig dominated the weaker personality and used him for his own ends. For his part, Derek probably found confidence in his new friendship with an arrogant, street-wise lad who feared nothing. He developed a cocky attitude and lied to his parents about his activities. All that Derek had achieved was to exchange his reliance on his parents for dominance by a stronger personality. He did not have the intelligence to understand what was happening and probably all that mattered to him was that he saw a way of escaping a cosseted life and embracing some excitement and adventure.

Just before the Bentley family sat down to Sunday lunch on 2

6

November 1952, there was a ring on the doorbell. Derek answered, and with his ten-year-old brother Denis at his heels, spoke to the caller. Sixteen-year-old Christopher Craig spoke to him in a low voice, sharing a confidence of some kind, and then left. Derek's father was not amused to learn the identity of the caller, for he had not changed his unfavourable opinion of Craig and had tried to dissuade him from seeing his son. He sensed that Derek had been asked to do something against his better judgement and inquired what was going on. 'It's nothing, Dad, it's nothing,' said Derek. 'The bloke's barmy.'

The family sat around after lunch reading the Sunday newspapers and talking. At about 5 p.m. Derek left the house, telling his mother that he was going to the cinema to see a Betty Grable film, which was on at the Astoria. He returned earlier than expected at about 7.20 p.m., saying that he had a bad headache and had left before the programme finished. Knowing their son, whose ill-health they had coped with since he had suffered his first epileptic fit at the age of four, the Bentleys attributed his headache to a mind troubled by Christopher Craig.

Derek nevertheless enjoyed a large tea, and afterwards the family settled down to watch television. Derek declared that he was staying in for the evening as he wanted to watch the *Old Time Music Hall*, one of his favourite programmes. This scene of quiet domesticity was disturbed by the doorbell. Mrs Bentley answered, and when she came back to the sitting-room explained that the caller was Craig, wanting to know if Derek was in. She had told him that her son was not in, and Derek seemed to approve of her actions. 'If you keep on telling him I'm not in, he'll get sick of it,' he said.

About a quarter of an hour later, at around 8.30 p.m., the doorbell rang again. Mrs Bentley went to the door and after a few minutes she returned to tell Derek that two boys named Norman Parsley and Frank Fazey wanted to know if he would go out for a walk with them. The Bentleys did not know sixteen-year-old Parsley, and asked Derek about him. 'He's a good bloke,' was the answer and this was borne out by the well-dressed and well-mannered youth who assured Mr Bentley that they would not be out for long. Fazey was equally polite. With the promise that he would be back soon, Derek put on his coat and briefly embracing his mother, told her, 'All right. Shan't be out long, Mum.'

Thus was the first step taken towards the tragedy. Parsley and Fazey were Craig's stooges and as soon as they were out of sight of the Bentley house, Craig appeared on the scene. Parsley and Fazey, their job completed, were sent packing, and Craig and Bentley fell into conversation. One of the reasons for Derek's tension and head-ache during the afternoon was that he had in his possession the keys to a butcher's shop in West Croydon, which had been stolen with the intention of staging a later break-in. That moment had now arrived.

Christopher Craig came from a respectable background. His father, Niven, was an educated man, large and portly, who worked in the Norbury branch of Lloyd's Bank as chief cashier, a responsible position. He had served in the Army during the First World War, being promoted to captain by the age of twenty-two, and mentioned in dispatches. In the Second World War, he had been a Home Guard Commander. His wife, Edith, was a gentle and sensitive woman, with a great love of poetry. She took an active part in social work and on one occasion, rather ironically, had given a talk on the wireless on juvenile delinquency. The Craigs' large semi-detached house lay in a quiet street just off the main Norbury road.

However, Christopher, the youngest of nine children, had fallen into delinquent ways, which echoed those of his eldest brother. On 30 October, just three days before the night of events leading to Bentley's and Craig's convictions, Niven Craig had been sentenced at the Old Bailey to twelve years' imprisonment for armed robbery. Mr Justice Hilbery's remarks before passing sentence had a prophetic ring for the Craig family. 'I believe that you would shoot down, if you had the opportunity to do so, any police officer who was attempting to arrest you,' he told Niven Craig. It was a sad moment for his parents, and perhaps especially poignant for his father.

As he stood on the pavement with Bentley on that rainy Sunday evening, Christopher Craig, unknown to his friend, carried a loaded .455 Colt service revolver in his pocket and no small amount of hatred in his heart. He had his own criminal record of sorts, having been fined in September 1951 for possession of a firearm, and had carried out a number of robberies, the most recent a mere two weeks previously when he and Parsley robbed an elderly greengrocer at gun-point. Like Bentley, he had been to the cinema on that Sunday afternoon, when he had seen a French film involving the killing of a policeman.

Wearing wide-brimmed hats and long overcoats and looking rather like extras for a James Cagney film, Bentley and Craig waited in the rain for their transport. This was not to be a limousine that would whisk them on squealing tyres to the crime scene but a No. 109 London Transport bus. They boarded it, and bought tickets to West Croydon Station. As they went through the wet streets, which glistened with the lights reflected from shops and passing vehicles, the two teenagers discussed their plan.

The intention was to break into the butcher's shop in Tamworth Road, the keys of which were in Derek's pocket. Both lads carried knives, and Craig gave his companion a home-made spiked knuckle-duster which he had fashioned in the garage where he worked. Derek's possession of this weapon would later be a matter of great controversy, but as they sat together on the top deck of the bus the knuckleduster was no more to them than a token of their shared adolescent ideas about gangsterism.

Far more sinister was the loaded revolver carried by Craig. He was fascinated by guns, and had been in the habit of carrying one since his early teens, and probably before. Despite the show of shared violence, it was understood that Derek Bentley balked at the idea of carrying a gun. Christopher Craig later admitted that Derek would not have gone along with him that night if he had thought he had a gun in his pocket.

The pair alighted at West Croydon and made their way to the butcher's shop, where they planned to gain easy access using their stolen keys. To their disappointment they saw a light in an upstairs window, and concluded that the proprietor was still on the premises. They turned away, but not wishing to be thwarted, decided to try their luck at a nearby electrical shop. Again they were stymied, this time by a courting couple in the alleyway which gave access to the premises.

Determined to succeed, they elected to force an entry at Barlow & Parker, a confectionary wholesalers in Tamworth Road. Finding the main doors at the front of the building locked and impenetrable, they walked round to the side, where they were confronted by a six-foot high gate constructed of spiked iron railings. First Craig and then Bentley climbed over the gate and landed softly on the other side in their stout, crepe-soled 'brothel creepers'. The time was just on 9.15 p.m. A woman in a house across the street at 74 Tamworth Road was called into the front bedroom by her nine-year-old daughter, who had spotted the two men furtively reconnoitring the side entrance at Barlow & Parker. As the intruders were looking for a way of getting into the building, Mrs Ware told her husband to call the police.

9

2

'Let him have it, Chris'

Unaware that they had been spotted by the Ware family (whose house at No. 74 Tamworth Road permitted a slightly angled but unobstructed view across the street to the warehouse), Craig and Bentley illegally entered the premises of Barlow & Parker. It was raining steadily as the intruders found themselves in a narrow passageway between the side of the two-storey warehouse and a neighbouring fence. The side doors of the building were firmly secured, and there seemed to be no other means of getting into the building.

At the point when this third attempt to effect a breaking and entering that evening seemed doomed to failure, Craig had an inspiration. Ascending the wall of the warehouse were several stout metal drainpipes. He indicated his intention to scale one of these in order to reach the roof. As Bentley later told the police, 'Chris then climbed up the drainpipe to the roof and I followed.' Window-ledges and wall brackets provided hand and foot holds and Craig, a fearless sixteen-year-old, soon reached the flat roof of the building just over twenty-two feet above ground-level.

Bentley succeeded in reaching the roof on his second attempt, being less adept than his companion and feeling giddy about three-quarters of the way to the top. Urged on by Craig, he scrambled over the guard-rail, which ran along the side of the warehouse roof, and on to the asphalt roof. Crouching in the semi-dark, the intruders took stock of their surroundings in the intermittent illumination afforded by the partially obscured moon.

Immediately to their left was a brick structure with a door, which opened on to a stairway leading down into the warehouse. In line with the stairhead, and in the centre of the roof, were four large roof-lights. These were glazed structures with rigid roofs standing four and a half feet high at the middle.

10

To the far left, beyond the roof-lights, was the head of the lift shaft, a brick structure standing eleven and a half feet above roof-level and measuring about six feet by eight at its base. Behind the lift-head, the flat roof gave way to a long, sloping, factory-style section constructed of glass panels and asbestos sheets. The battle that occurred in the wake of the pair's arrival on the roof took place to the left of their point of access. The area of the roof to their right was an open, asphalted expanse leading to the front of the warehouse overlooking Tamworth Road.

While the pair had been making their perilous ascent into the unknown, events well beyond their control were happening on the ground. Edith Ware in her house across the street watched as first one climbed over the gate and then his companion followed. John Ware, who had been shaving, hastily dried his face and ran out of the house to a police telephone box some fifty yards down the street and dialled 999.

Until then it had been an evening of calm routine at Croydon Police Station. The telephone call from Scotland Yard, informing the local CID of a possible breaking and entering on their manor, altered all that. But the message 'suspects on premises, Tamworth Road, Croydon', carried no real portent of life or death. Detective Constable Frederick Fairfax (known to his colleagues as 'Fairy') left in the typewriter his report on a case involving theft from a gas meter and ran out into the station yard. It was about 9.25 p.m. when he rounded up Police Constable Norman Harrison and two other officers, and drove off in the station's black Morris van, heading for Barlow & Parker in Tamworth Road, about a mile away.

A radio message from Scotland Yard referring to 'suspects on roof proceed at once, other officers on their way' was received by police car 7Z, which was patrolling in the area. Police Constable James Christie McDonald, the radio operator in the Wolseley, timed the message at 9.25 p.m. His driver, Police Constable Sidney Miles, put his foot down, and they sped through central Croydon towards Tamworth Road.

The two police vehicles arrived practically at the same time, and after a brief discussion with Mr and Mrs Ware, McDonald and Fairfax climbed over the metal gate at the side of the warehouse and surveyed the wall and its several drainpipes. None of the police officers was armed, and in the best tradition of the Force, their approach to whatever lay ahead of them can best be described as fearless.

11

Fairfax (as he put it later in the matter-of-fact style of his deposition) said, 'I then climbed up a drainpipe at the western wall of the premises.' The pipe – which had already borne the strain of two climbers – felt none too safe. Recalling the moment afterwards, he said, 'I didn't know whether to pray to God or to curse the plumber who'd put it there.' Having reached the roof, he saw two men standing about fifteen yards in front and to the left of him.

From the rooftop Craig and Bentley had heard the police cars arrive, and picked up the buzz of conversation in the street below. If at that point they had elected to curse their luck at having been found out and had yielded to the law, no hurt would have resulted other than that to their pride. As it was, Craig – his hand comfortingly round the butt of the revolver in his pocket – decided on defiance. They were standing between the roof-lights and the lift-head building when Fairfax approached to within six feet. 'I am a police officer; come out from behind that stack,' he said.

Craig replied, 'If you want us, fucking well come and get us.'

'All right,' said Fairfax, and he dashed behind the lift-shaft and grabbed hold of Bentley. He pulled him out into the open, and Craig darted to the opposite side of the brick structure.

As events on the warehouse roof rapidly approached flash-point, Fairfax alone faced the two youthful intruders. His colleague PC James McDonald, a heavily-built man, was defeated in his first attempt to scale the drainpipe. When he was about six feet short of the roof he was forced to go back down and make another attempt. Meanwhile, PC Norman Harrison, a quick-thinking, agile man, had made his way round to Upper Drayton Place, which ran along the rear of the warehouse. He climbed a fence that gave access to the garden of No. 24 Tamworth Road, then scaled a six-foot wall and clambered on to the roof of the 'Blue Star' confectioners building at No. 25. Dropping into the garden of No. 26, a private house, he emerged into Tamworth Road. Quickly assessing the options open to him, he returned to the garden of No. 26, from where he climbed on to the roof of No. 25 again and made his way along its length to the point where it joined the roof of Barlow & Parker's premises. From this position he could clearly see Fairfax, and was in time to observe his fellow police officer take hold of Bentley.

With Bentley momentarily in his custody, Fairfax moved round the lift-head with 'a view to closing in on Craig'. Law officer and teenage robber came face to face at the western corner of the lift-head. At that moment Bentley broke away from Fairfax's restraining hold,

12

and as he did so was alleged to have shouted out, 'Let him have it, Chris!' The words were heard by PC McDonald, who was descending the drainpipe after his abortive endeavour to reach the roof, and by PC Harrison, standing on the roof at a point some fifty to sixty feet from the three moonlit figures at the lift-head.

A loud report rang out in the night, and there was a flash. Fairfax was spun round by the impact of a bullet hitting him in the right shoulder, and he fell to the floor. He was not seriously wounded, and as he struggled to regain his feet he saw one of the intruders move to his left and the other to the right. He rushed at the figure on his right (who turned out to be Bentley) and struck him with sufficient force to knock him to the ground. There was a second shot, and Fairfax dived to the ground, pulling Bentley down in front of him as a shield.

Fairfax searched Bentley and removed the knuckleduster and knife that he was carrying. Pushing the youth in front of him, he worked his way to the safety of the roof stairhead. By this time PC McDonald had made it to the roof at his second attempt, although (in an incident bordering on the farcical) he required assistance from Fairfax to clamber over the guard-rail. Bentley was left to his own devices while this was going on, but once McDonald was safely on the roof both officers seized him and he was searched again. Referring to the knuckleduster and knife Bentley said, 'That's all I've got, guv'nor. I have not got a gun.' He warned, 'He'll shoot you.'

Fairfax shouted to Craig, 'Drop your gun.'

Back came the reply, 'Come and get it.'

PC Harrison was now also on the roof, close to the chimney-stack, which belonged to No. 25 Tamworth Road. He started to move along the sloping roof section at the rear of the warehouse by the precarious method of lying on his back and digging his heels into the gulley where the sloping section joined the flat roof. When he was about halfway along he saw a figure come to the edge of the flat roof. As Harrison recalled later in his statement, 'He said something about "a copper" and then raised a revolver in his right hand and fired.' The shot struck the roof behind the police officer, who began edging his way back to the chimney-stack, dropping his torch as he went. Another shot rang out which also missed, striking the brickwork of the chimney. McDonald shouted to Fairfax, 'What sort of gun has he got, "Fairy"?'

Bentley volunteered the information, 'He's got a .45 Colt and plenty of bloody ammunition for it too.' The youth was also alleged to have said, 'I told the silly bugger not to use it.'

As the drama on the roof unfolded a scene of confusion was developing in the street below. Police swarmed round the alleys and backyards, and two fire engines and an ambulance announced their arrival with clanging bells. The street was cordoned off to keep the hundreds of inquisitive bystanders at bay, while firemen set up a gas floodlamp to illuminate the warehouse. The atmosphere crackled with tension and stories of robbers engaged in an armed battle with police on the rooftops gained currency.

With one officer wounded by a defiant gunman and without firearms themselves, the police were at a distinct disadvantage. At this point Fairfax heard the encouraging sounds of police reinforcements coming from the other side of the stairhead door. He shouted out his position to them, and warned that the gunman was located to their left. Suddenly PC Sidney Miles forced the locking bar on the inside of the stairhead door and burst out on to the roof. He moved only a few steps before being felled by a bullet that struck him between the eyes. Fairfax immediately went to his assistance. He seized his dead colleague by the shoulders and, with help from McDonald, dragged him behind the stairhead wall. PC Harrison, who had left his earlier position on the roof and entered the warehouse at ground level, had been following Miles. He saw his colleague fall, and Craig came into full view holding his revolver with both hands. Another shot rang out and hit the brickwork of the stairhead.

Retaliating in the only way he could, Harrison crouched in the doorway and flung his truncheon at Craig, and then a milk bottle and a block of wood, the only missiles which came to hand. The gunman called out, 'I am Craig. You have just given my brother twelve years. Come on, you coppers. I'm only sixteen.' Harrison joined Fairfax and McDonald, and the three policemen decided to take Bentley – who seemed mesmerized by the speed of events – off the roof in order to isolate Craig. Further reinforcements arrived in the form of PCs Robert Jaggs and Stuart Stanley Lowe, who had successfully climbed the drainpipe to reach the roof. They helped escort Bentley downstairs; he shouted out, 'Chris, they're taking me down.'

Another shot was fired and Craig called, 'Are they hurting you, Derek?' He was also alleged to have shouted, 'Come on, you brave coppers. Think of your wives.'

Bentley warned his custodians, 'You want to look out, he will blow your heads off.'

Fairfax took Bentley to the bottom of the stairs and handed him over to Inspector Bodley. In exchange for his prisoner he was given a police automatic pistol,[1] and no doubt feeling that he could now compete on equal terms, he returned to the roof. Only one other handgun was issued from the gun cabinet at Croydon Police Station. PC Lowe had stayed at ground-level, and by clambering over some garden fences and into a yard was able to secure a vantage-point from which he could clearly observe the roof. Craig was sitting on the guard-rail, and was holding a gun in both hands. When Fairfax re-emerged from the stairhead he called out, 'Drop your gun, I also have a gun.'

Back came the answer, 'You are going to make a shooting match of it, are you? Come on, then, copper, let's have it out then.'

The policeman moved round the skylights towards Craig and fired twice. Craig attempted to shoot back, but his revolver misfired. No doubt realizing that the game was up, Craig, a veteran of countless shoot-outs in gangster films, ran to the edge of the roof shouting, 'Well, here we go, give my love to Pam,' and jumped over. He plunged downward a distance of some 22 feet 3 inches, striking a greenhouse on the way and crashing to the ground. He fractured his spine, dislocated his breastbone and broke his left wrist, but still had enough strength to say, so it was alleged, 'I wish I was fucking dead. I hope I've killed the fucking lot.' As he fell the revolver dropped from his grasp and smashed through the glass of the greenhouse, where it was later retrieved by Sergeant Edward Roberts. The time was 10.05 p.m. and the drama was over; what remained were degrees of grief and a great many questions.

Christopher Craig was found on the ground where he had fallen. PC Lowe removed a sheath knife from the teenager's belt before he was put into an ambulance and taken to Croydon General Hospital. PC Fairfax, who with his colleagues had faced an armed intruder with little more than his courage and sense of duty, travelled to hospital in the same ambulance as Craig. Fairfax was examined at about 10.30 p.m. by Dr Nicholas Jaswon, who found what he termed as 'a searing wound over the skin on his right mid-clavicular region'. This was the medical description of a wound caused by a bullet which had struck his body in the collarbone region, and which had passed across the skin without penetrating the flesh or causing a fracture. He was bruised and shocked, but otherwise not seriously injured. While he was at the hospital he discovered the bullet that had injured him in

[1] This was the first time for four years that police in the London area had been armed.

the waistband of his trousers, where it had become lodged during his exertions on the roof.

Craig was examined in the casualty ward by Dr Douglas Freebody, who made an initial assessment of his injuries. He believed they would keep the youth on his back for a month. At about 12.45 a.m. Craig was put into a private room where police surveillance could be maintained throughout the night. At 2.15 a.m. he received his first medication in the form of two Codeine tablets to relieve his pain.

The body of PC Miles was taken to the Croydon Borough Mortuary (also known as the Mayday) for post-mortem examination the next day, and Derek Bentley was taken by police car to Croydon Police Station. After he was taken off the warehouse roof Bentley was handed over to Sergeant Edward Roberts. The officer cautioned him, and explained that he would be taken to Croydon Police Station where he would be detained 'in connection with the shooting of Police Constable Miles'.

Bentley said, 'I didn't have the gun. Chris shot him.' He was put in the back of the police car between Roberts and PC James Leslie Alderson; the driver was PC Henry Stephens. Both Roberts and Stephens recorded in their depositions made on 17 November that Bentley had said, 'I knew he had a gun but I didn't think he would use it. He's done one of your blokes in.' This remark that he had prior knowledge of Craig's possession of a firearm was an obviously injudicious one, and prompted Sergeant Roberts to issue a second caution. In view of the weight later attributed to this remark, it was interesting that the third police officer present, PC Alderson, made no deposition. These depositions, which are quoted throughout the book, have never been released before. We are the first researchers to have had full access to them.

Once inside Croydon Police Station, Bentley was required to turn out the meagre contents of his pockets – a comb, a handkerchief, cigarettes and keys. His mind was probably numbed by the speed and decisiveness of the incident to which he had been party. Now, in the confines of the police station, he was part of a world that he had previously seen only on celluloid. Bentley was asked a few questions, but was not expected to make a statement until the following day. At around 10.15 p.m. he was shut up in a police cell.

At about the time Bentley was being deprived of his liberty, Detective Chief Inspector John Smith, accompanied by Detective Sergeant Stanley Shepherd, took their first look at the scene of the rooftop battle. From there they travelled to the mortuary for the grim task of viewing the body of their dead colleague, PC Miles. The law required that the dead man be properly identified before they could fulfil their next task. Other officers had the unwelcome responsibility of informing Mrs Miles that her husband had been killed in the course of carrying out his duty. She was given news of the tragedy at about 11.25 p.m.

Meanwhile Smith and Shepherd went to Croydon General Hospital, where they talked first to Fairfax and then to Craig. 'I am Chief Inspector Smith,' announced the senior man. 'I have seen the dead body of Police Constable Miles at Mayday Mortuary. I charge you, as a result of the inquiries I have made, with being concerned with Bentley in murdering him.'

After being cautioned, Craig asked, 'He's dead, is he? What about the others?' The Chief Inspector declined to answer but informed Craig that he would remain under arrest until such time as he was fit to be removed from hospital.

Detective Sergeant Shepherd stayed by Craig's bedside during the small hours of the night. He reported that at about 2.10 a.m. he was asked, 'Is the policeman I shot in the shoulder still in hospital? I know the one I shot in the head is dead.' He gave no reply. Later he was asked, 'What do you get for carrying a knuckleduster? Bentley had mine.' Again no reply was given. A few minutes later in this one-sided conversation came the question, 'Did you see the gun I had? It was all on the wobble so I took it to work and sawed two inches off the barrel.'

Thus did the excitement of that evening subside into the banal, but an emotional avalanche was about to burst on the quiet of the Bentley household at 1 Fairview Road. William Bentley had gone to bed early as he had been suffering from fibrositis in his shoulder. He was joined later by his wife, but both were awakened at around midnight by their daughter Iris expressing her concern that Derek had not returned home. It was supposed that he might be staying at the house of his new friend Norman Parsley, but Iris, for so long her brother's guardian, was not reassured. She went downstairs to read and to make a cup of tea. Eventually, she drifted off to sleep in an armchair.

The serenity of the house was rudely shattered at about 1.30 a.m. by violent knocking on the front door. Knowing that Derek had a key, Iris called out, 'Who are you? What do you want?'

'Open that door! We're police officers,' was the response. She opened the door and three men dressed in plain clothes led by Detective Inspector Close burst into the house. 'Who are you?' one of them asked.

'Iris Bentley.'

'Where's your father?'

'Upstairs in bed. He's not well.'

By this time William Bentley, wakened by the commotion, had come down. 'I'm Mr Bentley. What do you want?' he asked.

Back came the grim reply, 'Your son has killed a man.'

Those six words changed the lives of the Bentley family for ever. Lilian Bentley collapsed at the news and was comforted by her tearful daughter. William Bentley said later, 'I was in a sort of trance,' and he hardly heard a police officer telling him: 'We shall have to search the house.' No search warrant was produced nor was one strictly necessary in the case of a search for firearms in the wake of a serious crime.

His mind numbed with shock, William Bentley followed the police officers from room to room while they searched cupboards, looked behind pictures on the wall and turned over the everyday items of the family's existence. At this moment of crisis, as in others that had preceded it during the War, Bentley acted with dignity. He did his best to calm his wife and daughter and at the same time to deal courteously with questions put by the police search team. 'Is there a loft in this house?' he was asked.

'Yes.'

'Show us.'

He took them up to the attic and watched in silence as everything was turned out and examined.

Next the search switched to Derek Bentley's bedroom, which he shared with his Uncle Albert. The sleepy-eyed man sat up in bed and watched in blinking incredulity as the cupboards, washstand and wardrobe were ransacked, with William Bentley helplessly standing by. 'I'll explain later,' was all he could say. Derek's Bible lay on his bedside table and there was a cross above his pillow. Among Derek's childhood toys stored in the wardrobe, the searchers found a sheath knife, which he had bought to remove the upholstery from old furniture in his first job with a local removal firm. The officer who made the discovery held the knife in one hand while continuing to sort through the toys. With the finding of the sheath knife the search of the Bentley's home appeared to have ended. 'We shan't use it in evidence,' said one of the policemen to Lilian Bentley when leaving. Asking where his son was, Bentley received the curt reply, 'Croydon Police Station'. The searchers departed, taking the knife but leaving its sheath behind.

At about the same time that the peace of the Bentley home was being shattered, Detective Chief Inspector Smith and Detective Sergeant Shepherd were searching Christopher Craig's home. They arrived at 9 Norbury Court Road at around 1.15 a.m. Here the search was more profitable. In the sixteen-year-old's bed Shepherd found a .45 bullet, and beneath a floorboard in the attic above the bedroom he found part of a barrel sawn off a .45 revolver together with a tin box containing an assortment of ammunition. There were .303 and .22 rifle rounds and revolver ammunition for .32, .38, .31 and .45 weapons, along with some .303 blanks and a quantity of air-gun pellets.

Having elicited from the officers searching his house where Derek was being held, William Bentley made an attempt to see his son. It was to prove one of many disappointing and fruitless representations that he would make in the months to come. Accompanied by his brother, Albert, he found a taxi to take them to the police station. He identified himself to the duty sergeant and asked if Derek Bentley was being held under arrest. 'Yes,' was the reply.

'I'd like to see him if possible,' said Bentley.

'You won't see your son tonight,' answered the sergeant.

Frantic for information, Bentley appealed to the officer's better nature, 'Put yourself in my position,' he implored. 'If you're a father you must know what it means to me.'

'There's nothing I can tell you except that a policeman has been murdered. Shot.'

'Is my son accused of it?'

'I've told you all I've got to say,' was the cold response.

Making their way home, the two men felt there must be a mistake as they firmly believed Derek was innocent as he did not possess a gun. Mr Bentley may have considered contacting a solicitor at this stage, but he was probably unsure of his son's legal rights. It is only relatively recently that the police have been obliged to tell people under detention that they have a right to see a solicitor and that they don't have to say anything or make a statement before they've seen one.

To complete an exhausting night's work, Smith and Shepherd returned to Croydon Police Station at around 4 a.m. to talk to Derek Bentley. The youth said, 'I didn't kill him, guv, Chris did it.' Smith cautioned him and then took his statement, which was hand written by Shepherd and dated 3 November 1952.

STATEMENT OF: DEREK WILLIAM BENTLEY, age 19

1 Fairview Road, London Road,

Norbury

Electrician

who saith:

I have been cautioned that I need not say anything unless I wish to do so, but whatever I do say will be taken down in writing and may be given in evidence.

(Signed) Darek Bentley

Derek Bentley

I have known Craig since I went to school. We were stopped by our parents going out together, but we still continued going out with each other – I mean we have not gone out together until tonight.

I was watching television tonight [2 November 1952] and between 8 p.m. and 9 p.m. Craig called for me. My mother answered the door and I heard her say that I was out. I had been out earlier to the pictures and got home just after 7 p.m.

A little later Norman PARSLEY and Frank FAZEY called. I did not answer the door. Mother told me that they had called and I then ran out after them. I walked up the road with them to the paper shop where I saw Craig standing. We all talked together and then Norman Parsley and Frank Fazey left. Chris Craig and I then caught a bus to Croydon. We got off at West Croydon and then we walked down the road where the toilets are – I think it is Tamworth Road. When we came to the place where you found me, Chris looked in the window. There was a little iron gate at the side. Chris then jumped over and I followed. Chris then climbed up the drainpipe to the roof and I followed. Up to then Chris had not said anything. We both got out on to the flat roof at the top. Then someone in a garden on the opposite side shone a torch towards us. Chris said, "It's a copper, hide behind here." We hid behind a shelter arrangement on the roof. We were there waiting for about ten minutes. I did not know he was going to use the gun.

A plain clothes man climbed up the drainpipe and on to the roof. The man said, "I am a police officer – the place is surrounded." He caught hold of me and as we walked away Chris fired. There was nobody else there at the time. The policeman and I then went round a corner by a door.

A little later the door opened and a policeman in uniform came out. Chris fired again then and this policemen fell down. I could see that he was hurt as a lot of blood came from his forehead just above his nose. The policeman dragged him round the corner behind the brickwork

20

entrance to the door. I remember I shouted something but I forgot what it was. I could not see Chris when I shouted to him – he was behind a wall. I heard some more policemen behind the door and the policeman with me said, 'I don't think he has many more bullets left.' Chris shouted, 'Oh yes I have,' and he fired again. I think I heard him fire three times altogether. The policeman then pushed me down the stairs and I did not see any more.

I knew we were going to break into the place, I did not know what we were going to get – just anything that was going. I did not have a gun and I did not know Chris had one until he shot. I now know that the policeman in uniform that was shot is dead.

I should have mentioned that after the plain clothes policeman got up the drainpipe and arrested me, another policeman in uniform followed and I heard someone call him 'Mac'. He was with us when the other policeman was killed.

tis as be

This statement has been read to me and it is true

Signed Derk

      Derek W Bentley

Statement taken by me [Smith], written down by Detective Sergeant Shepherd, read over and signature witnessed by J. Smith, Detective Chief Inspector.

The curious words 'tis as be' resulted from Smith's attempt to make Bentley write 'This statement has been read to me and is true.' The illiterate youth stumbled over the words and, turning to the officer, said, 'I cannot do it, you do it.' His failure was rectified by Shepherd, and his faltering signature was witnessed by Smith.

At about 5.30 a.m. Bentley was told that he would be charged 'with being concerned with Craig in the murder of PC Miles'. He was formally cautioned and replied, 'Chris shot him. I hadn't got a gun. He was with me on the roof and shot him between the eyes.' He was then formally charged, but made no reply.

As the pale light of a new day dawned, Christopher Craig continued to exude hatred from his bed at Croydon General Hospital. A succession of police officers had been on duty throughout the night. When PC John Smith came on duty he was told, 'You are coppers. Ha! The other one is dead with a hole in his head. I'm all right. All you bastards ought to be dead.' Probably drifting in and out of consciousness as a result of pain and shock, Craig woke at around 6.30 a.m. and asked PC Vincent Denham, 'Is he dead?'

'Who?' said the officer.

'That copper. I shot him in the head and he went down like a ton of bricks.'

As the people of Britain went to work on the morning of 3 November the national newspapers carried sensational headlines about the previous evening's shooting. 'PC Shot Dead in Roof Gun Battle' and 'PC Shot Dead, CID Man Hit in Roof Siege' were among the more mild; 'Chicago Gun Battle in London – Gangsters with Machine Gun on Roof Kill Detective, Wound Another' was one of the more sensational. The *Mirror* carried a carefully posed picture of Pearl Edith Ware, the girl who raised the alarm, photographed with her father as 'he continued his interrupted shave after the battle'. It was from the dramatic and in many cases unreliable sources of the national newspapers that the Bentley family was to learn the reasons for Derek's arrest.

The gravity of the incident on the rooftop was captured in Dr David Haler's post-mortem examination of PC Miles. This was carried out at about 5 p.m. in the presence of Detective Chief Inspector Smith. In his subsequent deposition the doctor stated:

> I found that this was a well-built, well cared for, muscular man in perfect health. He was five feet eleven inches high. There were two wounds in his head. One was at the inner side of the left eyebrow and was a typical wound of entry of a large calibre bullet. The other, slightly to the right at the back of the head, was the wound of exit of the same bullet. This wound had killed him. Death would have been virtually instantaneous.

Earlier in the day the police had been busy at the scene of Miles's death on the roof of Barlow & Parker's warehouse. A detailed plan was made of the rooftop and its structures, and the torch dropped by PC Harrison when Craig fired in his direction was retrieved. A careful search was made of the roof to recover any spent cartridge cases and bullets. Three spent .45 cases were found near the lift-head, and a spent .45 bullet on the eastern corner of the roof.

Detective Chief Inspector Smith examined Craig's Colt .45 revolver, which had been retrieved from the greenhouse where it fell when he jumped from the roof. There were two live rounds in the chamber, which had been struck by the weapon's firing-pin but had not discharged, and four spent cartridge-cases.

On Monday morning, 3 November, Derek Bentley appeared before

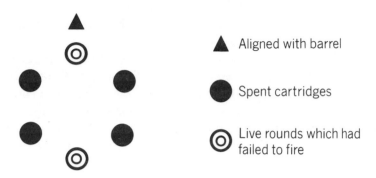

▲ Aligned with barrel

● Spent cartridges

◉ Live rounds which had failed to fire

the magistrates at Croydon. A large crowd had gathered to see one of the gangsters alluded to in the newspaper reports. He was formally charged with the murder of PC Miles, to which he answered, 'Not me, sir.' His partner in crime did not appear in court, as he could not be moved from his hospital bed. Bentley was remanded in custody for a week and taken to the Medical Wing at Brixton Prison for medical reports. The whole proceedings took about a minute, and his father caught only a distant glimpse of his son: there was certainly no opportunity to speak to him.

By the end of that day, the first shock to the three families most affected was perhaps beginning to subside into dull, aching grief. The police officer's widow quite properly had the benefit of public sympathy; her husband had, after all, died in the service of the community. The Craig family had now lost two sons to violent crime, and in addition to their own private shame they had to bear the brunt of public opprobrium. In both cases the pain and shock were administered suddenly, but at least the extent of their grief was known – Miles was dead and Craig was beyond the hangman's reach. The Bentleys' ordeal had only just begun, and they were to be subjected to a kind of continuous torture over the next eleven weeks. What made their plight less bearable was the ultimate injustice they were made to suffer.

As events moved on after the high drama of that Sunday evening in Croydon, the apparent simplicity of a criminal act involving the death of a police officer began to take on a more subtle quality. To begin with, as the law stood the two teenagers accused of murder would be treated differently. Christopher Craig, who fired the shot, was aged sixteen and therefore too young to face a capital sentence. Derek

Bentley, on the other hand – three years older and known not even to possess a firearm, let alone to have fired one at the police – was old enough to be hanged if found guilty of complicity in an act of murder.

Great debate would ensue over the intention in Bentley's mind when he shouted to Craig during the gun battle, 'Let him have it, Chris.' Was this a piece of sensible advice from the older youth, telling his companion to surrender his weapon to the police, or was it stereotyped incitement drawn from the culture of the gangster film to shoot to kill? There would be less debate over the state of Bentley's mind and his fitness to stand trial. Indeed, the lack of proper discussion on this important matter amounted to an omission which ultimately led to a miscarriage of justice.

3

'I did not know he was going to use the gun'

William Bentley eventually succeeded in talking to his son at Brixton Prison at about 7. p.m. on Monday evening, 3 November. Together with his wife and daughter, he sat waiting on the visitors' side of the long table which separated the prisoners from their loved ones and the outside world. When Derek appeared he smiled at his parents and sister. 'Hello, Mum. Hello, Dad. Hello, Iris,' he greeted them. One side of his face was bruised and swollen, but any answer to his father's question as to the cause was prevented by a warder. Bentley was told that prison regulations prohibited such questions.

Derek was cheerful, and his mood lifted his family's spirits. He talked about what he planned to do when he was released from prison, and it is probable that neither he nor his parents had a grasp of the peril he faced. This is borne out by the effect on Lilian Bentley of a remark by the warder that Derek would be able to scrub floors really well when he got home. The thought that even so lowly an official hinted at Derek coming home kept her spirits up for many weeks, according to her husband. However naive her belief, she could not be faulted for holding to one of the greatest human virtues — hope.

Derek was granted the equivalent of today's legal aid and his father engaged John Stevens, a Croydon solicitor, to begin the task of building a defence against a background of hostile public opinion. Anxieties about increasing lawlessness in Britain were naturally fuelled by the killing of a police officer, and it was not surprising that bitter feelings should be focused on Craig and Bentley. There were many who wished to fan the flames, and the newspapers were filled with talk of hanging and of the reintroduction of flogging.

In this emotional climate, the ranks of law and order closed in solidarity. Mr J.W. Bennet, who conducted the Coroner's Inquest on PC Miles, adjourned the court in view of the impending trial, but had felt obliged to call Mrs Miles to say that she had identified her husband's body at the mortuary. She need not have been put through this harrowing experience, which served only to prejudice public opinion against the accused. In concluding the inquest, the Coroner referred to the brave and fearless men in the police service who safeguarded the public and spoke of the untimely death of one of their number in the performance of his duties.

Such feelings were widely shared and sympathy for Mrs Miles was felt in ordinary households throughout Britain. What the Coroner had contributed to was the contamination of the man-in-the-street's sense of justice and fair play. The tidal wave of indignation broke four days after the rooftop battle when PC Miles's funeral was attended by 1,200 mourners. It was a massive demonstration of public sympathy in which the Home Secretary, Sir David Maxwell Fyfe, took part. It meant that the chance of an objective and unbiased trial for the two accused was practically negligible.

Craig was discharged from hospital at 9.30 a.m. on Tuesday 11 November. He was taken by ambulance to Croydon Magistrates' Court where a large group of people eagerly awaited his arrival in order to vent their anger. He was carried into court on a stretcher after running the gauntlet of the hostile crowd shouting such insults as 'He ought to swing.' It was the mentality of the lynch mob, and the police had a hard time protecting Craig. His appearance before the magistrates was brief, and he was remanded for seven days.

On Monday 17 November Bentley and Craig appeared in court together, the younger lad lying on a stretcher in the well of the court. In addition to the charge of murdering PC Miles, they were now also charged with the attempted murder of Detective Constable Fairfax. The charges read:

(1) On the 2nd day of November 1952, in the County Borough of Croydon, did murder, Sidney George Miles Contrary to Common Law.
(2) On the 2nd day of November 1952, in the County Borough of Croydon, feloniously did shoot at Frederick Fairfax with intent thereby feloniously to murder the said Frederick Fairfax. Contrary to Section 14 of the Offences Against the Person Act, 1861.

Each defendant replied, 'I call no witnesses here. I plead not guilty and reserve my defence.' Asked whether they wished to give evidence on their own behalf or intended to call witnesses, each answered, 'No.' What followed was a procession of police officers – eighteen in all, including those most intimately involved in the incident on the rooftop.

Craig's hate-filled remarks made to various police officers while he was in hospital were repeated. He was also alleged to have referred to his gun in comments made on 5 and 6 November. To PC Thomas Sheppard he asked, 'Did you see the gun I had? It was all on the wobble so I took it to work and sawed two inches off the barrel.' He expanded on this theme the following day to PC Ernest Brown: 'If I hadn't cut a bit off the end of the barrel of my gun I would probably have killed a lot more policemen. That night I was out to kill because I had so much hate inside me for what they done to my brother. I shot the policeman in the head with my .45. If it had been the .22 he might not have died.'

Shocking though Craig's words were, he was protected from their full consequences by his age. This privilege did not extend to Bentley. His shouted remark on the roof, interpreted as an instruction to Craig, 'Let him have it, Chris', was testified to by Fairfax, McDonald and Harrison. This was taken to prove his incitement to Craig, and his remark when he had been arrested, testified to by Sergeant Roberts and PC Stephens, 'I knew he had a gun but I didn't think he would use it. . . .', was used to counter later suggestions that he did not know Craig was armed.

Lewis Nickolls, Director of the Metropolitan Police Laboratory, gave his findings regarding the firearms evidence. He stated that the .45 Colt revolver[1] retrieved from the scene of the crime was in good working order with a normal trigger pull. He confirmed that its barrel had been shortened and that the sawn-off piece of barrel found at Craig's home matched the weapon.

Several of the police witnesses were cross-examined by John Stevens on behalf of Bentley and also by Craig's solicitor. At the conclusion of the evidence, the Chairman of the Magistrates, Mr R. L. Richardson, committed the two defendants for trial at the Old Bailey during the first week of December. Cases went to trial much more quickly then than they do today and this timescale was not particularly unusual, although it is likely the public interest in *Regina v. Bentley and Craig* did influence the Court Calendar to some extent. It allowed exactly twenty-one days in which to prepare a defence for the two teenagers, one of whom would be fighting for his life. There

[1]Nickolls was in error in his description of the revolver; its calibre was .455, not .45.

was no question of bail being applied for in view of the seriousness of the crime.

The rush to judgement had begun. At this stage guilt seemed so self-evident, with both defendants having made incriminating state-ments, that the meticulous regard for detailed evidence, which is a feature of the English trial system, seemed to lapse. One aspect of the evidence to fall victim was that regarding Craig's revolver and the other, even more crucial, was the mental status of Derek Bentley.

There is an extended discussion of the firearms evidence in Appendix I, plus an explanation of some of the principles involved, which clearly shows that, in the gathering momentum to place Bentley and Craig in the dock, the normal painstaking procedure that should have ensued to establish a full scientific account of the shooting did not take place. There were shortcomings in the evidence which were simply glossed over and gaps which might have been exploited by the defence if the whole affair had not been rushed. Certainly, there was a failure on the part of the professionals involved in not tying up the loose ends of the firearms evidence and in neglecting to question Craig about the point at which he loaded his revolver.

It also became clear at the trial that neither the judge nor the prosecution understood this most important aspect of the case. Lord Goddard twice made mistakes in his summing-up over which shot killed Miles and prosecution counsel made similar mistakes. Such gross errors were really unforgivable in a trial for murder at which a man's life was at stake.

The fatal bullet that killed PC Miles was never recovered and matters were further complicated by the inaccuracy of Craig's gun, which had lost some of its rifling in the piece of barrel he had sawn off. This gap in the linkage of evidence was later exploited by David Yallop in his book *To Encourage the Others* with his contention that Miles was shot and killed by a fellow police officer.

While Bentley and Craig waited in their cells for the trial to begin a detailed examination of the firearms evidence should have been in progress. Instead, minds were being exercised on the likely meaning of some of Bentley's remarks, and not a few contradictions which arose. Apart from the ambiguous shouted instruction to Craig, 'Let him have it, Chris', other remarks allegedly made by Bentley directly pertaining to the gun were being examined for their damage potential.

Perhaps by then Bentley realized something of the jeopardy he was in, although according to various police statements, his written denial was already too late. When PC McDonald inquired of Fairfax what sort of weapon Craig had, it was Bentley who was reported as volunteering the information that it was a .45 Colt and that his companion had plenty of ammunition for it. For perfectly understandable reasons the lad might simply have been confused. His father stated that Bentley was incapable of either writing or dictating the statement taken from him at Croydon Police Station at four o'clock in the morning on 3 November. He would not have known the meaning of many of the words used, nor would he have been capable of constructing many of the phrases. It is a matter of record that the statement was taken by one policeman and written down by another. However scrupulous this exercise may have been, there was every danger that two well-intentioned officers might put words into the mouth of a teenager whom they may have regarded as dim, but who was in fact retarded and had a mental age of eleven. In this light, apparent contradictions take on a new significance.

But, as matters stood in the days leading up to the trial, on the crucial question of whether Bentley knew Craig was armed on the night of their killing escapade, the balance of evidence was against him. Three police officers had made sworn statements to the effect that he knew his friend had a gun and the anomalies in his statements also went against him. His later denial, supported by both his father and Craig, did not combine with such effective force as the testimony of three police officers.

If there had been oversights in analysing the firearms evidence in preparation for a murder trial of major interest to the public, there were greater omissions to be perpetrated in considering Bentley's mental status and his fitness to stand trial.

4

'You never know how little things can get you into trouble'

When he arrived at Brixton Prison on 3 November Derek Bentley became '8664 BENTLEY, Derek William, aged 19 years. . . No. 27 in the Calendar'. He was examined by Dr J.C.M. Matheson, the Principal Medical Officer (PMO), who found no evidence of old or recent disease and described him as 'loosely built and his body muscles are poorly developed'. The doctor put him 'under close mental observation' in the Prison Hospital, where he was seen daily either by the PMO or by one of his colleagues.

The purpose of this surveillance, to which Craig was also subjected, was to provide the Director of Public Prosecutions with reports on the mental condition of the two teenagers, including an opinion on whether they were fit to stand trial. These reports were required by law to be submitted to defence counsel as well as to the prosecution and the trial judge. Sadly, this requirement was not carried out and the assessment of Bentley's mental health, which should have been a major element in his trial for murder, was overlooked if not even suppressed.

That Bentley's defence counsel was not given a copy of the report to which he was entitled by law was a grave enough omission on its own. But what was unforgivable was the failure of the judge (who did see the report) to afford the court's protection to the accused by ensuring that all relevant evidence was placed before the jury. On this occasion, and uncharacteristically for British justice, the judge also wanted to be the jury. From start to finish, the assessment of Bentley's mental status was flawed with errors, omissions and professional misjudgements.

Dr Matheson, having had a month in which to observe Bentley and call for all the medical and family background information he required, submitted his report to the Director of Public Prosecutions on 5 December 1952 – four days before the trial at the Old Bailey. On

26 November he sent Bentley to the Maudsley Hospital for an electroencephalogram (EEG) to be carried out.

The basis of the EEG is to measure the changes in electrical potential in the brain, which arise from the rhythmic discharge of energy by nerve cells. Characteristic patterns are produced by the brain in the working state and during sleep. These are distinguished from the abnormal patterns which arise as the result of impairment of brain function caused by diseases such as epilepsy. The electroencephalograph is an instrument for measuring the pattern of electrical activity in the brain, and the pen-recordings traced on paper are used to help medical diagnosis. Normal alpha waves occur with a frequency of ten per second when the subject is resting with the eyes closed. Abnormal responses with a frequency of seven or less per second are known as delta waves, and occur in epileptics.

This was a routine examination at the time in the case of a person accused of a capital crime. As was customary, Dr Matheson sent a letter to his colleague at the Maudsley, Dr (later Sir) Denis Hill. In it he made reference to the 'Croydon Murder' and spoke of the 'murdered' policeman. This perhaps said more about the doctor's state of mind than his patient's. After all, the purpose of the trial was to determine whether a murder had been committed, and by whom. These unfortunate statements prejudged the entire court proceedings. The letter of introduction also included several errors concerning Bentley's medical history and that of his family.

HM Prison
Brixton SW 2
26.11.52

Dr Denis Hill, MB, FRCP
The Maudsley Hospital
Denmark Hill SE5

Dear Hill,

       8664 BENTLEY, Derek William, aged 19 years
Herewith a history of the above-named who is going to the Maudsley tomorrow for an EEG examination. He is involved in the Croydon Murder case where a policeman was murdered and another policeman injured. Bentley had no active part in the shooting which was done by his co-defendant, Craig, a boy of 16. Craig I am not sending for an EEG, because he has a crush fracture of the 7th dorsal vertebra, a fracture dislocation of the sternum and a fracture of the left radius.

If, however, you think that such disabilities would not be insurmountable in the taking of an EEG I would send him along to you. It would, of course, have to be in the near future, as the trial may commence on the 3rd of next month, ie a week today. I will 'phone you sometime tomorrow when you have read this letter and get your views.

As regards Bentley. No morbid family history has been elicited. Personal History. When Bentley was 24 hours old, his father tells me, he was sent to Guy's Hospital suffering, he says, from bronchial pneumonia. He had blood transfusions and was nursed in an oxygen tent.

In infancy, the father states, he had one or two falls on the head but apparently they were not serious.

During the War he was buried once when the house was struck. Again, the father says, most of the rubble was on his head. (The father is, in my opinion, an extremely poor informant.)

There is a history of fits; the first one when he was aged between 3 and 5 years. He was sitting at a meal when he said he was not feeling well and asked permission to leave the table. He arose from the table and then, the father says, he collapsed – his head shook first, then his jaw clenched and then he stiffened. He did not lose control of his sphincters on this occasion. He had four subsequent fits all of the same nature; the last fit it is stated took place when he was aged 8 years.

He went to school when he was aged 5. His behaviour at school was very bad; he truanted a lot and quarrelled with the pupils and with his teachers. In consequence he was shifted to another school where he remained for two years. Then he was transferred back to his first school which he left in March 1948. He was in the top class of the inferior group when he left.

In 1948 he was before a Juvenile Court for store-breaking and stealing and was bound over for 2 years. Six months later he was again in Juvenile Court for store-breaking and stealing and on this occasion was sent to an approved school. At this approved school it was found that his IQ was 66 and that he had a reading age of $4\frac{1}{2}$ years. The school authorities felt that he was being encouraged by his father to make complaints about his treatment so that he would be granted an early licence. At all times he gave the impression at the school that he conserved his energy only for eating and talking; that he was self satisfied; indifferent to training and content to let others do all the work.

In June and July of 1949 he attended the department of Psychological Medicine at Guy's Hospital where he was given small tablets to take twice a day. I have written to Guy's Hospital for a report but have not yet received it. The school authorities, however, say that Guy's Hospital considered that the boy was influenced by his father and therefore tended to be unco-operative. While at the school an EEG was done at the Burden Neurological Institute. The result was as follows:

There was nothing abnormal in any area while resting. The patient was unco-operative and would only perform hypernoea[1] for one minute but this evoked some low potential theta activity. Photic stimulation[2] evoked several 'single wave and spike' discharges spreading from the occipital lobe. This finding is diagnostic of *petit mal*.

A.L. Winter
Assistant Electroencephalographer

He was finally licensed from the school in July 1950, and then passed into the care of a Home Office Welfare Officer. A report of this Welfare Officer states:

Materially the home is reasonably good and well kept. However, his parents have no influence upon him at all. There is an older sister and a younger brother, neither of whom apparently have been any trouble. The parental attitude is inconsistent and over-indulgent and there was little or no family training. Since leaving the school he has had little work and has been allowed his own way in everything. He had one period of employment with a removal contractor for seven months and his employers state that his character was very satisfactory. He then was employed by the Croydon Borough Council at first as a dustman, from which job he was demoted on account of being unsatisfactory, to a road-sweeper. He then was dismissed from his job because he was unreliable and was a bad time-keeper.

The Welfare Officer reports that early this year he developed a very 'spivish' style in dress and was very truculent and arrogant in manner.

While in custody here he has shown himself to be a very immature, careless adolescent. He blames his co-defendant, Craig, for all the trouble, and is frightened at the position in which he now finds himself. When he came in his hair, as it still is, was marcel-waved and he was wearing a very gaudy flowery pattern shirt.

He cannot read. He says that when he first went to school he tried to

[1]Hypernoea is rapid breathing.
[2]Photic stimulation is a means of observing the brain's response to light.

learn but then, on account of shifting, he gave up the effort and nobody, apparently, bothered about him. It would appear that by the time he reached the approved school his lazy habits were so strong that they could not teach him how to read.

Mental tests, however, show him on the Wechsler scale, to have a verbal IQ of 71; Performance IQ 87; Full Scale IQ 77.

On the Kent oral tests he reaches – on the mid-scale 11 years; and on the upper scale 12 years.

Although of low intelligence it cannot be said, I think, that he is certifiable as a feeble-minded person as the defect is probably an educational one.

There has been no evidence of any epileptic manifestation while he has been in custody here.

I have not yet seen the depositions but from the Press reports it appears that he knew quite well that Craig was armed when they set out to break into the warehouse for the purpose of stealing money.

While there is little good to be said about this lad, in fairness to him I think it should be pointed out that his parents, especially his father, are largely, if not wholly, responsible for his present situation. His mother, I understand, is a small woman and crippled, and the prisoner could easily hold her off when she attempted to inflict corporal punishment. The father who is employed at the Electricity Works at Croydon is, as I indicated earlier in this report, a poor type. He is very satisfied with himself, very confident and will not admit that there is anything evil in his son. Last year, he bought an old Rover motor car for about £200 and gave it to his son. For what purpose it is hard to imagine unless to keep the boy quiet.

Physically there is nothing abnormal except that there is a history of double otorrhoea[1] but his ears at present are clean.

Yours sincerely,
J.C.M. Matheson
Principal Medical Officer

On receiving Matheson's letter, Dr Denis Hill asked the Burden Neurological Institute at Bristol for the records of the two previous EEG examinations carried out on Bentley. He also performed his own examination, and taking all the findings together, reported to Matheson in very clear terms: '. . .the evidence of these three EEGs is certainly compatible with and suggestive of a diagnosis of epilepsy'.

Having referred Bentley for an expert opinion, and after keeping

---

[1]Double otorrhoea is a discharge from the ears due to infection.

him under close observation in prison hospital for a month, Dr Matheson prepared his report for the Director of Public Prosecutions. Despite well-attested indications to the contrary, he concluded:

> I have been unable to find any genuine loss of memory or degree of mental confusion which occurs during an epileptic manifestation.
>
> I do not consider that he is a feeble-minded person under the Mental Deficiency Acts.
>
> I am of the opinion that he is:
>
> (1) sane
>
> (2) fit to plead to the indictment
>
> (3) fit to stand his trial
>
> J.C.M. Matheson
Principal Medical Officer

Thus was Bentley's mental status officially summed-up in a document (reproduced in its entirety in Appendix II) which in any event saw limited light of day only. It was not discussed during the trial and hence was not challenged. Defence counsel, who might have exploited its weaknesses and the differences of opinion held by the doctors, were not privileged to see it, and the judge, who was given sight of it, chose not to complicate the proceedings by introducing any doubts that might favour the accused.

Derek Bentley's birth was accompanied by grief as well as pain. In June 1933 William and Lilian Bentley and their two-year-old daughter Iris, lived in a couple of rented rooms in a dilapidated house in Blackfriars. Their eldest child, Joan, who was six, had been sent to live with her grandmother in the borough. Lilian, aged thirty-one, spent her confinement at home. At about midnight on 30 June her husband sent for the midwife, and half an hour later she gave birth to Derek William, her first son.

Some two hours after delivery, Lilian called out in distress to her husband who was sleeping in a chair by her bedside. She had pains that experience taught her signalled the imminent arrival of another baby. William Bentley, with natural good sense and the benefit of his training in the St John Ambulance Brigade, delivered a second boy. But Derek's twin brother survived a mere two hours, so that the Bentleys' joy at the birth of Derek was marred by the sadness of his brother's death. Distressed and exhausted, Lilian Bentley awaited the arrival of the doctor.

The family doctor, on learning of the night's events, turned immediately to the new arrival, and lost no time in deciding that the infant needed hospital care. He put the baby into his car and drove to Guy's Hospital, where the baby was placed in an oxygen tent after bronchial pneumonia was diagnosed. The child teetered on the edge of death for a week, and doctors advised the parents to baptize him at once.

The infant won his fight for life and developed into a normal child. He was strongly attached to his mother, and appeared to be afraid of other children. When Derek was two years old he moved with his family to a better flat in Webber Street, Blackfriars. Friar Street Elementary School was close by, and at the age of three he started nursery school.

The adventure of attending school did not appeal to him, and he screamed uncontrollably, calling for his sister Iris who attended a senior class at the same school. After several days of this behaviour the patience of the teachers was worn down and they asked his father to call at the school and discuss the situation. The solution agreed was that Iris should be transferred from her class so that she could sit next to her brother. This calmed the boy, and brother and sister were allowed to sit together throughout his early schooling.

When he was four Derek suffered a seizure which was described at the time as an epileptic fit. The boy had been playing with other children on a lorry carrying reels of newsprint, which had stopped in the neighbourhood on its way to Fleet Street. Apparently he fell about fifteen feet to the ground from the top of one of the huge paper-reels. Iris, ever in close attendance, rushed to fetch her father, who was at home on that Saturday morning. The child was taken indoors with a bleeding nose and abrasions to the head. He would not be comforted, and appeared to be suffering convulsions. He was taken by ambulance to Guy's Hospital, where he was eventually calmed and his head-wound dressed. According to William Bentley, the doctor told him, 'Your son has had an epileptic fit.' He was advised that there might be a recurrence, and was warned to take care and prevent the child receiving any accidental blows to the head.

Derek appeared to make a satisfactory recovery, but his father thought he was quieter than before, and clung even more tenaciously to his mother and sister. William Bentley worried too that his son seemed more withdrawn, and because of his unwillingness to mix readily with other chidren, was a lonely little figure. A second attack occurred about eighteen months after the first. This time there was no specific triggering blow to the head, although it is known that the day before he had fallen down while playing. He collapsed and went into convulsions, struggling to resist those who tried to help him. He had to be forcibly restrained, and on this occasion was taken to Lambeth Hospital where he was detained for several days. Mr Bentley was warned by the doctor that his son's attacks were likely to be repeated periodically.

Tragedy struck the Bentley family during the early months of the air-raids on London. William Bentley was a member of the ARP (Air-Raid Precautions) and elected to stay in London during the bombing to assist the civilian population. He tried to persuade Lilian to take the children to one of the safe evacuation areas but they decided to stick it out in London. An air raid on the London Docks in 1940 resulted in bombs shattering houses and buildings in the Blackfriars area, and an explosion rocked the shelter in which Lilian and the children had taken refuge with other families. Although unhurt, they were all frightened. But worse was to come in a subsequent raid when the shelter accommodating the residents of the Union Street flats took a direct hit. Among the twenty-eight dead pulled from the wreckage were Derek Bentley's grandmother and his twelve-year-old sister, Joan.

Apart from the fear experienced by every child of his age during the terror of the Blitz, Derek was badly affected by the death of his sister. His father thought he was increasingly nervous and fearful, and events conspired to deprive him of regular schooling. Three months were lost when he and his sister Iris were ill first with scarlet fever and then with chicken-pox, which meant they were confined at Tooting Isolation Hospital. When they rejoined their parents' attendance at the Friar Street School was out of the question, as the building had been destroyed in the Blitz, which was now at its peak.

Lilian was finally persuaded to take the children to the safer environs of Edgware, where something approaching normal school attendance was possible. Both children went to Camrose Avenue School, which ran separate classes for boys and girls. This did not suit Derek – now aged eight – who refused to be split up from his sister, and his father negotiated a special dispensation with the headmaster allowing Iris to sit with her brother. Both children attended school at Edgware from August 1941 to December 1943, and unity was restored when Mr Bentley managed to rent a house in the district and lived with his family. During this time the family was enlarged by the arrival of Denis, who was born in 1942.

In the summer of 1944 the whole family had a miraculous escape. Late one evening Lilian made an impulsive decision to visit friends in Edgware and accepted an invitation to stay the night. They awoke to the din of anti-aircraft fire and went with their friends to the air-raid shelter. The following morning when they returned home they found that their house had been demolished by a direct hit from a German V-1 'flying bomb'. Had they been at home the family would almost certainly have been killed. Homeless, and possessing only the few things that Lilian had packed for the overnight stay, they returned to Blackfriars in search of accommodation.

They eventually found a flat at Walworth but, fearful of the bombing raids, spent their nights in the depths of Leicester Square tube station. For several months they endured this routine along with thousands of other Londoners whose fortitude was being severely tested.

A further miserable period followed when William Bentley, then thirty-eight, was called up for military service. The children were understandably upset over his departure – particularly Derek, whom his mother described in a letter as a 'lost soul'. These were hard times for Lilian, with three children to care for on a frugal budget. There were also increasing concerns over Derek. Their son had not suffered any recurrence of his fits since 1941 (although he had complained of headaches and sickness), but his parents had noticed that his skin had a blue appearance, and that his lips and fingernails also had a blueish tinge. Dr McManus, the family practitioner, examined the boy and thought that his ailments were probably due to strain and lack of sleep. Undeniably, he had been fretting over his father's call-up. In view of the length of time that had elapsed since the last epileptic fit, the doctor thought it possible that Derek had grown out of them.

It seemed almost as if the Bentleys were a marked family, for in the autumn of 1944 their Walworth house was hit by a flying-bomb while the family lay asleep. Amid the confusion, Lilian seized baby Denis, and found Iris who was unhurt. Derek was trapped under debris from the roof – which had caved in – but he was quickly dug out by rescue workers, dazed though apparently uninjured. He was examined again by the family doctor, who treated him for shock.

William Bentley recounted the wartime experiences of his family in his book published in 1957, and he wrote: 'I am not singling out the Bentley family for sympathy.' He well understood the sufferings of fellow Londoners but by any criterion his family had been subjected to a traumatic series of events. The effect of these on Derek may be imagined but not measured. He can scarely have escaped unscathed.

With the war mercifully drawing to a close, and life returning to something approaching normality, Derek resumed his schooling. His parents had been concerned at the many interruptions to his education caused by illness and the War. He was sent to the John Ruskin School at Walworth, where the full extent of those months of missed teaching became apparent. After a week at the new school the headmaster called on Lilian Bentley to tell her that her eleven-year-old son was illiterate. This came as a complete shock, and the headmaster was at pains to stress the seriousness of the discovery.

On being informed of this development, William Bentley – who had believed Derek had made good progress in reading and writing while at Camrose Avenue School – told Lilian to take their son to the doctor. This she did, and, against a background in which many London children had missed schooling during the War years, was told that lost time would probably be made good as life returned to normal. The doctor did not examine the child. Thus the wartime phase of the Bentley family ended. No doubt they rejoiced along with their fellow-citizens that the cessation of hostilities would allow them to overcome their losses and enter a more fulfilling age. The main shadow on the horizon (although it is doubtful that either William or Lilian Bentley recognized it clearly) was that after eight years' schooling Derek could neither read nor write.

The second phase of Derek Bentley's short life began with the move to Norbury. In June 1945 William Bentley moved his family to 1 Fairview Road in the residential area south of the River Thames. The house was situated at the end of a terrace of twelve properties and had a large sitting-room, a parlour and a kitchen on the ground floor with three bedrooms above. There was also a backyard with its own access via a side gate. The house was a definite improvement on the family's previous accommodation, and they were in good spirits when they moved in complete with Derek's large menagerie of cats, dogs, rabbits and a chicken.

Iris Bentley left school at the age of fourteen and started work, leaving Derek to face the prospect of attending school on his own. He went to Norbury Manor School, where his shortcomings set him up as a target for taunts and bullying. This twelve-year-old boy, who had not mastered elementary reading and writing, was mocked by his fellow-pupils. When it was discovered that the tall, fair-haired youth was also a mother's boy, subject to tearful behaviour, and that he lacked the instinct to stand up for himself, his life became a misery. The wretched time he had at school tended to reinforce his isolation from others of the same age. He did not make friends, played truant when he could and clung ever closer to the protection of his mother.

At this time William Bentley was still serving in the armed forces and Lilian had the sole burden of running the home and managing family affairs. It was only when his father was demobilized that the extent of Derek's unhappiness was revealed. He was urged to stand up for himself, but the depth of his torment persuaded his parents to move him to another school. After an interview with the headmaster at Norbury Manor School, who admitted that Derek was the object of bullying, it was agreed that the boy should be transferred to Ingram Road School at Thornton Heath.

As William Bentley later recorded, 'The change of school did Derek no good.' The mocking and baiting continued, and the boy who stumbled over the simplest questions in a class of thirty was wildly out of his depth. His parents and elder sister tried to help him with his studies at home but the effort lacked determination for, as William Bentley put it, 'my wife and I had forgotten all the little we learned at our Board schools thirty years before'. Observing their unhappy son and concerned over his dejected moods, the Bentleys looked forward to the time when he could leave school and, as they believed, make use of the aptitude he had for practical subjects.

At about this time a further crisis occurred when Derek had another fit following a fall. One morning when he was coming downstairs to breakfast he stumbled and the banister rail gave way. He plunged down into the stairwell and his father rushed out to find him lying unconscious and bleeding from a cut on his head. When he came to he went into convulsions and, as before, had to be sedated. His father linked the attack to the emotional upsets he had suffered at school.

Derek's chances of improving his scholastic abilities were not helped by his truancy. That caused the authorities to intervene, and he became something of a shuttlecock between schools. After spending a few months at Ingram Road School he returned to Norbury Manor, where his attendance was irregular. In order to combat his truancy, the authorities had an order made by a local magistrate specifying Ingram Road as the school that Derek should attend. Against a background of protestations from his father, he went to the school for a period of five months before returning once again to

Norbury. It is hardly any wonder that the teaching staff of both schools had little recollection of Derek Bentley as a pupil in their care who needed special attention. Even allowing for the boy's truancy, it is a severe indictment of the system that this fifteen-year-old could not write his own name.

His father had a sideline business repairing radio and television sets for people in the district. He had a small workshop at home, and encouraged Derek to help him in the evenings in return for additional pocket-money. William Bentley later described the period between 1946 and 1948 as a generally happy one for his son. He saw improvements in the boy's temperament, and his depression seemed to have lifted.

The year 1948 was an eventful one for the Bentley family. In January Lilian gave birth to another son, Roger, who was afflicted with what was then called mongolism and today is termed Down's Syndrome. The child survived for only eleven months. In March Derek lapsed into adolescent crime when he appeared before Croydon Juvenile Court with another, younger boy charged with attempted breaking and entering and with attempting to steal a quantity of bus tickets valued at ten shillings. They were both found guilty and bound over for two years.

At the end of the summer term 1948, Derek left school for good, an event which his father described as 'a happy release for us', and began to look for a job. His father advised him to seek employment where he could use his manual skills, possibly in a garage. The job-hunting lasted for about two weeks, and then real trouble loomed on the horizon. Mr Bentley came home to find Lilian in tears following a visit from the police alleging that Derek had taken some workmen's tools from a building-site. Derek's story was that he and another boy had been playing around on the site, 'shying at a few old tins'. A householder nearby telephoned the police, who rounded up both lads and charged them with the theft of tools valued at eighteen shillings. Derek denied taking the tools, and a police search of his home failed to produce the stolen items.

He was remanded for reports which have apparently perished with the passage of time but before sentencing the youth the magistrate asked him to spell the word 'fluorescent'. If this was an initiative test he failed it, as no doubt would a large percentage of his more literate peers at the time. To the horror of his parents, Derek, along with his friend, was sentenced to three years in an Approved

School. 'We sat together that night in a daze, unable to grasp it,' wrote Mr Bentley later.

This was a severe punishment for so small an offence, and in any event, Derek was ultimately absolved from guilt. The missing tools were recovered from a workman who had apparently taken them home to use. By this time Derek was ensconced at the Kingswood Training School at Bristol and it was judged in his best educational interests to keep him there. Indeed, this period should have been a watershed in his life, because those charged with his supervision had the opportunity to make a proper assessment of his abilities. He was given an IQ test and rated at sixty-six, with a reading age of four and a half years.

By virtually very respected definition of the day, that rating placed him in an underprivileged mental category. Intelligence Quotient (IQ), the ratio of mental age to chronological age, is expressed as a percentage derived from the formula:

$$\frac{\text{mental age}}{\text{chronological age}} \times \frac{100}{1}$$

Mental age is established by various tests, the most widely used being the Stanford-Binet Scale. As with most tests, the difficulties arise in matters of interpretation, especially when it comes to putting labels on an individual's abilities.

The Stanford-Binet scale has been validated over a long period as a means of testing general intelligence. Its principles were first devised by Alfred Binet and Theodore Simon in 1905 as part of an investigation into mentally handicapped children in Paris schools. In 1916 the procedure was revised and elaborated at Stanford University in the United States and soon came into wide use for testing children's intelligence, both in America and Europe. The Stanford-Binet test was used to measure what is now referred to as IQ. Sir Cyril Burt, the London Education Authority's psychologist in the years between the two wars, standardized the test for use in London's schools.

In his book *Juvenile Delinquency*, published in 1952, Dr J.D.W. Pearce, the Physician in Charge of the Departments of Psychiatry at St Mary's Hospital and Queen Elizabeth Hospital for Children, suggested the following guidelines:

Grade	IQ Rating
Superior	125 +
Above average	115 – 125
Average	85 – 115
Dull and backward	70 – 85

Feeble-minded (educationally sub-normal)   50 – 70
Imbecile   20 – 50
Idiot   0 = 20

From this it can be seen that Derek, with an IQ of sixty-six, would have been graded as 'feeble-minded'. While at Kingswood he was visited every month by his parents, and after a few months he was allowed the privilege of seeing them off at the railway station. He appeared to be coping well with the regime at the school, but he complained of persistent headaches and said that he had blacked out on several occasions.

Derek was allowed home on leave in June 1949, and he saw his local general practitioner, Dr Doris Reynolds, about his headaches. She referred him to Guy's Hospital, where he was examined on two separate occasions by Dr James Munroe at the Department of Psychological Medicine. Dr Munroe confirmed what had already been established by the earlier IQ test. 'My impression,' he wrote in his report dated 11 August, 'was that he [Derek] was feeble-minded.' His other conclusions were equally significant:

> The three attacks of unconsciousness he had at the age of eight or nine were probably epileptic fits and these might have been the result of a head injury about age five when he was said to have fallen fifteen feet on his head and been unconscious.
> His father wanted me to arrange that Derek should be at home with him.
> My recommendation was that Derek should return to Kingswood under Mr Collinson's care and in due time be examined at the Bristol Child Guidance Clinic.

Dr Munroe wrote to the principal of Kingswood Training School, Mr J. Adams, giving his opinion: 'There is no doubt that Derek is very backward intellectually and that most of this is the result of congenital lack of intelligence. The father thinks it was quite wrong to commit Derek to an Approved School and he looks forward to having the boy at home to work in his electrician's business. In due time I think this would be a satisfactory solution.' Munroe's assessment was completely different from Dr Matheson's later one that though Bentley was of low intelligence, the defect was an educational one and he was not feeble minded.

When Derek returned to Kingswood he had with him the drugs prescribed for him at Guy's Hospital to control his epilepsy. These were the unspecified 'small tablets to take twice a day' referred to by Dr Matheson in his letter to Dr Denis Hill. It is likely that the prescription was for phenobarbitone, one of the most widely used barbiturate drugs and given as an anti-convulsant. Derek was referred to the Bristol Child Guidance Clinic by the authorities at Kingswood as advised by Dr Munroe. The results of this visit and recommendations, if there were any, are not known.

On 16 November 1949 Derek was sent to the Burden Neurological Institute at Bristol for an electroencephalograph (EEG) examination. The conclusion reached was that 'This finding is diagnostic of *petit mal*.' In other words, that Derek Bentley was prone to the lesser type of epileptic seizure.

The Institute's EEG report on Bentley noted that 'Photic stimulation evoked several "single wave and spike" discharges spreading from the occipital lobe.' This is the effect of light stimulation on the part of the brain related to sight and it was this phenomenon which led to the conclusion that the lad was epileptic. He attended the Burden Neurological Institute for a second EEG on 9 February 1950, and again the reaction to photic stimulation was abnormal.

While he was at Kingswood the School's doctor treated him for an abscess which perforated an ear-drum, and also for a skin rash which affected much of his body. Derek told his father that because of his constant headaches he could not concentrate on his class work, with the inevitable result that he had fallen behind. Mr Bentley wrote later that it was during his visits to his son that 'the look in his eyes was enough to tell us that he was off his balance'. Nevertheless, he thought his behaviour was good and that Derek gave no concern to the school authorities on matters of conduct.

In July 1950 the school wrote to Derek's parents informing them that their son was to be allowed home fourteen months earlier than expected. John Fidoe, the Deputy Headmaster, told them:

> The order of the court was that your son should be detained in an Approved School until 29th September 1951, but I am glad to be able to tell you that the Managers have now decided to release him from the school as from tomorrow, the 28th July 1950.
>
> All boys sent to an approved school for training remain in the care of the Managers for a period of up to three years after the period of detention ordered by the Court. Until the 29th September 1954, Derek will, therefore, be in the care of the School Managers and during this period he should notify the Managers at once of any changes in his

circumstances. Failure to do so, or to behave satisfactorily, may mean that he will be required to return to the school.

We hope Derek will do well, and we shall be glad to see him or hear from him. Please endeavour to see that he writes as often as possible to let us know how he is getting on, and we shall always be glad to see him at Kingswood if he is able to visit the school. Always remember that it is our job to help Derek, and we are anxious to do so.

No reason was given by the school for Derek's early release, but his parents were naturally overjoyed. They travelled down to Bristol to collect him but were worried by his appearance – his father said the life seemed to have gone out of him. Nevertheless, the family was together again, and no doubt Mrs Bentley resolved to build up her lad with home cooking and a few domestic comforts. It was strange that Mr Fidoe in his letter should urge that Derek should write to the school as often as possible with news of his progress. It was, after all, Kingswood Training School that had established Derek's illiteracy beyond doubt by sending him for an IQ test which gave him the equivalent reading age of a four and a half year-old child.

Far from improving at home, Derek seemed to drift and become dangerously withdrawn. He still suffered severe headaches and was not sleeping properly. His doctor continued to prescribe phenobarbitone, but while the drug may have eased his headaches, it did nothing to improve his mental outlook. For a year he refused to leave the house, often following his mother from room to room in aimless fashion. He disliked being left on his own when of necessity his mother left the house to do the family shopping. His refusal to go out in public was based on his feeling that he could not face people in the street who looked upon him as a criminal. His parents tried to rationalize his situation, explaining that even if he had done anything wrong – which, in any case, they disputed – he had served out his punishment. But he would take no heed, preferring to believe that he was still regarded as a criminal.

According to his father, the only time Derek came to life was during the evenings when they worked together repairing radio and television sets. That is, until Uncle Albert came on the scene. Mr Bentley's brother came to live at 1 Fairview Road, and he shared Derek's bedroom. The older man developed a close understanding with the withdrawn teenager and eventually persuaded him to brave the outside world. The day came when Derek accompanied his uncle on a walk to Streatham Common, and over a cup of tea in a café on the way they discussed the desirability of Derek finding a job. This episode cured Derek of his most withdrawn phase, and his general demeanour improved considerably.

The year 1951 began with new promise. Derek found a job with Albert Hutchins, a friend of the family, who ran a furniture-removal business. The work was heavy, but seemingly well within the capacity of a strong seventeen-year-old. Derek was a tall youth, and according to his father took pride in his physical development. He enjoyed his work and gave satisfaction to his employer, who paid him £4 a week. Part of the job was to dispose of old, unwanted furniture, but Mr Hutchins, being a prudent operator, first removed any salvageable material. Covers were torn off padded chairs and settees, for example, in order to retrieve the stuffing. To assist in this task Derek bought a sheath-knife, an act which in the light of subsequent events was to lend an air of criminality to his activities.

In February 1951 he was required to report for a medical examination as part of the procedure to assess his fitness for National Service. At that time all eighteen-year-old males were obliged to serve for two years in one of the armed services. National Service could be deferred to allow a candidate to complete a course of higher education, and exemption was normally permitted only on grounds of ill-health or family dependency.

Derek went to Kingston-on-Thames for his medical, bearing a letter from his general practitioner. Any normal, healthy eighteen-year-old could expect to be passed A1 and fit for the rigours of service life, but Derek Bentley was put into Grade IV, the lowest possible grade, and judged unfit for National Service.

The Ministry of Labour wrote to Mr Bentley informing him of the results of the medical examination.

> When your son was medically examined on 11th February 1952, he brought with him a certificate from his doctor that he was subject to *petit mal*. The doctor who tested his mental capacity decided that he was mentally sub-standard and for those reasons he was placed in Grade IV.

It may be speculated that Derek, had he been fit for National Service, might very well have benefited from the experience, as did many young men of his generation. There have often been arguments about the relative virtues and iniquities of National Service, but there is no doubt that many shy individuals found confidence and self-discipline for the first time in their lives. Derek did not have that opportunity. Instead, if his mind dwelt on it at all, his rejection was confirmation that he was a weak individual, and that weakness set him apart from his contemporaries. It is possible that Bentley may have seen his friendship with Craig as a way of overcoming his weakness.

His life was already balanced on the slide that would plunge him to the depths, and when he gave up his job with the removals firm in March 1952, after just over a year, the descent began in earnest. Derek strained his back while attempting to shift a piano. He was in a great deal of pain, and he spent several days in bed. The family doctor's advice was that he was unsuited to the heavy type of work he had chosen, and that he should seek something less physically demanding. Mr Hutchins was apparently sorry to see Derek leave his employ, and spoke warmly of his character.

Within a few days, acting entirely on his own initiative, Derek took a new job working as a dustman for Croydon Corporation for a weekly wage of £6.15s.0d. Sadly, this new occupation was to be short-lived and after a few months of poor service collecting rubbish he was demoted to the more badly paid job of roadsweeper. Finally, in July 1952, Croydon Corporation considered his work so unsatisfactory that they dismissed him from this most lowly employment. From then on he was unemployed.

It was at this point in his life, having tasted the bitterness of rejection and, from all accounts, still being brought low with regular severe headaches, that Derek was at his most vulnerable. With no objectives, and no meaning to his existence, he was adrift socially. He might have washed up anywhere, but it was his misfortune to be cast up on Christopher Craig's territory.

Although Derek had met Craig at Norbury Manor School in 1948, he first talked openly about him to his parents around Christmas-time 1951. Apprehension flickered in Mrs Bentley's mind. Her son had not long been out of Approved School – indeed, he was still under the supervision of the Welfare Officer for Home Office Schools – and here he was consorting with a fifteen-year-old boy who apparently talked about 'the jobs he had pulled'. While Mrs Bentley fretted, her husband was more inclined to dismiss Craig as a boaster and to believe that they could 'put a stop to it if we notice anything wrong'.

Christopher Craig was a sturdily built, dark-haired youth. He was the youngest in a family of nine, and tended to be impressed by the example of his older brother, Niven. Twenty-six-year old Niven Craig had a history of juvenile delinquency which military service had seemed only to encourage. For unlawfully taking away vehicles at gun-point while serving with the Gordon Highlanders in Italy he spent five years in military prison. When he was released in 1950 he adopted a flashy life-style, wearing fashionable suits and indulging a penchant for large American cars. It is easy to understand that an impressionable younger brother might look up to such an apparently charismatic figure.

By the time that Niven was convicted at the Old Bailey of armed robbery and sentenced to twelve years' imprisonment, young Christopher had already had a brush with the law. A year earlier, in September 1951, he had been found with a twelve-year-old companion at Brighton armed with a revolver and a supply of ammunition. He was fined thirty-five shillings for possessing a firearm without a certificate, and the weapon was confiscated. Young Craig was fascinated by firearms, and ever since he was eleven years old had carried one about with him. He impressed his mates at school by showing them his guns, and even slept with a weapon under his pillow. At one time during his school years he possessed over forty guns, including starting pistols, antique weapons and also modern handguns.

Apart from the admiration for his brother, Craig was also devoted to the cinema and gangster films. In those post-war years, cinema-going was very popular. Many young people queued up once a week on Saturday evenings to see their favourite stars in action. For Craig, though, visits to the cinema were almost a form of addiction; he often went three or four times a week. He emulated the stereotyped American tough-guy on the screen by wearing a wide-brimmed trilby hat and long overcoat, in the pocket of which he carried his 'piece'.

Craig had left school and was working at a garage when he met Derek Bentley again and the two youths became friends. What each saw in the other can only be a matter of speculation. On the face of it, they had little in common; Craig was boastful, daring and self-assured while Bentley was shy, dull and uninteresting. But Craig's escapades may have represented excitement for Bentley, whose record of having been sent to an Approved School impressed the younger boy.

William Bentley took an instant dislike to Craig when he called at the house asking for Derek, who was not home at the time. He thought him arrogant and shifty, although it must be said this assessment was voiced later at a time when his judgement was understandably clouded. Mr and Mrs Bentley questioned Craig about his relationship with Derek, and warned him off. 'Surely you don't think I'll get him into trouble, Mrs Bentley?' he replied. 'I know all about Derek,' he said, 'I know he's been to an Approved School. . . .'

This seemed to incense Mr Bentley, who told the lad to 'keep out of Derek's way' and not to call again at the house.

When Derek returned home his parents advised him not to see Craig in future. Derek said that he didn't want to see him, 'But he keeps pestering me. I can't choke him off.' Mr Bentley spoke later of his uneasy feeling that Craig was using his knowledge of Derek's past to pressurize him. He also said that he had felt the force of Craig's personality, and he must have known instinctively that his weak-willed son was not his equal. The Bentleys had strong suspicions that their son was involved in petty crime, which is why they tried to dissuade him from seeing Craig. But while they may have rebuked him, they tended to draw a veil over his activities.

Despite his parents' warning, Derek continued to consort with Craig, and in May 1952 matters came to a head. A policeman found some empty petrol cans on a stretch of waste ground at the back of Fairview Road, and Craig, Bentley and another boy, Frank Fazey, were questioned at Norbury Police Station. Nothing came of the incident except the clearest possible warning that Derek should break his association with Craig. The station sergeant took Mr Bentley and Derek to one side for 'a friendly word of warning'. The unequivocal message was, 'Keep away from Craig'.

The warning went unheeded, and throughout the summer months Craig and Bentley pursued a life of petty crime. Breaking and entering accompanied by theft was a routine adventure. The crimes were not violent, for it seemed that Derek drew the line at any suggestion of using armed force. But there were times when Craig insisted on being armed, and he usually managed to find a more compliant substitute for Bentley on those occasions. In October, Craig and another youth, Norman Parsley, broke into a green-grocer's shop, but when they found nothing of value they decided to call at the owners' home, reasoning that they must have taken the shop takings with them. Brandishing revolvers, the pair threatened elderly Mr and Mrs Howes and made off with five pounds. Although the crime was reported to the police, the identity of the burglars was not discovered for some time.

According to Mr Bentley, Christopher Craig was beginning to cast an ominous shadow over his family. He had apparently threatened Derek and others at a dance, saying, 'If anyone dances with my girl,

I'll go for them with my knife.' Mr Bentley reported the incident at Norbury Police Station,and urged that something be done to curb young Craig. His protestations met with the polite response, 'Well, we'll certainly keep an eye on him.'

On Saturday, 1 November, Craig called at the Bentley house. Derek was out at the cinema,and Mr Bentley was also away from home. The door was answered by ten-year-old Denis, who told the caller that Derek was out. Craig put his hand in his pocket and withdrew a knuckleduster which he showed the boy. He was still brandishing the implement when Mrs Bentley came to the door, and he told her that he had made it at work. She advised him to get rid of it, but his response was, 'No fear. It'll come in handy one of these days.' Craig allegedly told her, 'We don't like the police – see! They've just given my brother Niven twelve years. Do you think I'm going to let them get away with that? I'm going to get my own back some day – and how!'

Three days previously, Craig had accompanied his mother from Number Two Court at the Old Bailey where Niven Craig had been sentenced to twelve years in prison. As they walked out of the building he heard one of the policemen who had given evidence remark to a colleague, 'Well, we've put that bastard away for a while.' It was a turn of phrase that was to have its echoes in Christopher Craig's own trial a few weeks later.

In the knowledge that he was weak-willed and easily led, it may be argued that Derek Bentley's parents should have taken a stronger line with their son. Equally, it may be said that at precisely the time he was slithering towards disaster, his welfare was under the supervision of the Home Office. Mr G.F. Towes, Welfare Officer for Home Office Schools, visited Bentley's home on thirty-one occasions, and on sixteen of these visits talked to Derek. The Welfare Officer reported his impression that the youth's parents were over-indulgent and that he found it difficult to obtain their, or Derek's, full co-operation. In retrospect, the roots of the ultimate tragedy lay in this lack of communication, for it was during this period that Derek's weak-minded aimlessness was causing concern to his parents.

It is probably fair to say that when the Croydon magistrates invoked The Childrens' and Young Persons' Act 1933 and The Childrens' Act 1948 to send Derek to Approved School they did so not out of a desire to punish him but in recognition of his need for discipline and schooling. By taking control of the lad from his parents and placing him under the guardianship of the welfare authorities and the Home Office they perhaps hoped to effect some improvement of character. Sadly, the follow-up was lax, and all the checks and balances in the system failed to arrest the decline.

The nineteen-year-old youth held in Brixton Prison awaiting trial for murder was therefore known to be an epileptic and of such poor personal attainment that he bordered on feeble-mindedness. Indeed, Dr Munroe at Guy's Hospital had described Derek as feeble-minded, and that was an opinion evidently shared by the Ministry of Labour and National Service when they graded him as mentally sub-standard. How was it, then, that a youth with this background, an IQ rating of sixty-six and a reading assessment of four and a half years, was found fit to stand trial for murder?

It has long been a precept of English law that persons suffering from serious mental disorder amounting to insanity are not held responsible for any crime they may commit. Every person is pre-sumed to be sane and to possess sufficient degree of reason to be held responsible for his acts unless the contrary is proved to the satisfac-tion of a jury. The judicial attitude to the defence of insanity was for over a century influenced by the McNaghten Rules. The rules derived from the trial for murder of Daniel McNaghten in 1843. In that year this Glaswegian shot Edward Drummond, private secre-tary to the Prime Minister, Sir Robert Peel, in a London street. Drummond died five days later, and it became apparent that he had been mistakenly killed by McNaghten whose intended victim was the Prime Minister whom he believed to be persecuting him.

McNaghten was tried for murder at the Old Bailey, when evidence was given regarding his state of mind. His defence counsel argued that he had a background of morbid delusion, and that at the time he committed the murder he did not know that what he was doing was wrong. The jury acquitted McNaghten on grounds of insanity but, immediately afterwards, the House of Lords, in recognition of public concern, exercised its constitutional right to consult the judges on the law relating to insanity in criminal cases. The judges' answers came to be known as the McNaghten Rules, the essence of which is that every person should be presumed sane until the contrary is proved.

In order to establish a defence on the grounds of insanity, it must be shown that at the time of committing the offence the accused was labouring under such a defect of reason – resulting from disease of the mind – as not to know the nature and quality of his act. If he did know it, he did not know that what he was doing was wrong. The chief medical objection to the McNaghten Rules has been that they uncompromisingly divided criminals into those who knew what they were doing, and that it was wrong, and those who did not. By recognizing only mental defects in understanding it has been argued that over the years the McNaghten Rules have sent to the gallows an astonishing number of men and women who by any medical definition were very seriously disturbed although legally they were held to be sane.

Forensic psychiatry was – and to large extent still is – obsessed with definitions of insanity. The McNaghten Rules have come to be looked upon as too rigid and representing a purely fictional 'disorder of the mind' which has no medical status. Various attempts have been made to improve the position of mentally disordered defendants and the tests for insanity, and the emphasis has shifted to consider concepts of responsibility. One result was that the Homicide Act of 1957 permitted pleas of diminished responsibility. But changes in the law are brought about by committing injustices – what happened to Derek Bentley was such a one.

The Mental Deficiency Act 1913 defined the feeble-minded status to which Dr Munroe believed Derek Bentley belonged. Feeble-minded persons were those who had a mental defectiveness which, though not amounting to imbecility, was yet so pronounced that they required care, supervision and control for their own protection or for the protection of others. In the case of children, they involved disability of mind of such a nature and extent as to make them (for the purpose of Section 57 of the Education Act 1944) incapable of receiving education at school. An IQ range between forty and seventy and a mental age between six and eleven years were the flexible guidelines set down.

The Act also defined 'mental defectiveness' as a condition of arrested or incomplete development of mind existing before the age of eighteen, whether arising from inherent causes or induced by disease or injury. The Royal Commission on Capital Punishment (1949–53) also defined the mental defective as 'a person who has never possessed a normal degree of intellectual capacity, whereas in an insane person faculties which are originally normal have been impaired by disease'.

On the question of fitness to plead, the Royal Commission noted that, 'If an idiot or imbecile were charged with murder in England, it is likely that he would be regarded as unfit to plead and found insane on arraignment; and there may be sometimes a similar finding in the case of a feeble-minded person.' On these criteria, there were strong grounds for arguing that Derek Bentley was unfit to plead.

In this case the opinion which mattered most, that of the Principal Medical Officer at Brixton Prison, was that he was both sane and fit to plead. As events progressed to their sad conclusion, Dr Denis Hill – an authority on the diagnosis of epilepsy – would write to the Home Office to ensure there was no doubt in the minds of the officials that Derek Bentley was indeed an epileptic. Derek himself in the last letter he sent to his parents asked them to keep a strict eye on his brother, observing 'you never know how little things can get you into trouble'. In his short life there was a succession of 'little things' and all the telltale signs of trouble to come went unobserved.

5

'Everybody knows I didn't kill Mr Miles'

While the time available to assess the background and mental status of Bentley and Craig – about three weeks – might be described as insufficient, the time allowed to prepare their legal defence was utterly inadequate. Although the defence was paid for by the State under the provisions of the Poor Person's Defence, the magistrates declined to grant the special Defence Certificate applied for by their solicitors. This denied Bentley and Craig the opportunity of having two counsel each to present their case, one of whom could have devoted more time to preparing and researching their defence.

John Stevens, the solicitor acting for Bentley, interviewed his client several times at Brixton Prison and drew up a detailed brief which he offered to Mr. F.H. Cassels, a member of the Middle Temple since 1932. Frank Cassels was the son of Sir James Cassels, a noted barrister who had appeared in some of the famous murder trials of the 1920s and 1930s and retired as a High Court judge in 1961. Frank Cassels was asked to appear on behalf of Derek William Bentley, 'who pleads Not Guilty to the two offences with which he is jointly charged with Christopher Craig'. Cassels accepted the brief, for which he received ten guineas for appearing at the trial and a further eleven for representing his client at the subsequent Appeal.

Craig's solicitors, Edward Davis Nelson and Company, instructed John Parris, an able young Northern barrister and a prospective Labour Party candidate with a reputation for being a maverick. Whereas Cassels represented the Establishment, Parris was a man who challenged conventional wisdom and in due time came to be called the 'Angry Young Man of the Law' by some of the newspapers. Where Frank Cassels in the fullness of time progressed to the Bench, John Parris was eventually disbarred.

John Parris recalled that he was dozing in his armchair after Sunday lunch when his clerk called him on the telephone to say that he had accepted the defence brief for Christopher Craig. Parris, who at the time was heavily involved in a trial at Leeds, had to be reminded that Craig was one of the two teenagers involved in the shooting of a police officer two weeks previously. The brief, when he received it a mere two days before the trial was due to begin, was sparing in the information it provided.'Counsel will obtain all the information he needs from the depositions enclosed herewith and conference with his client.' The fee for Parris's professional services in aid of Craig's defence worked out at $4\frac{3}{4}$d an hour. When these two lawyers, representing opposing strands of the Bar's social fabric, met to discuss their tactics on the eve of the trial, it is substantiated in a number of sources that Cassels greeted Parris with the words, 'I think both little bastards ought to swing'. It was hardly an auspicious start for a fair and objective trial.

In view of his involvement in the case at Leeds Assizes, one of John Parris's first actions was to seek a postponement of Bentley and Craig's Old Bailey trial, which was due to begin on 4 December. Arranging for another counsel to stand in for him at Leeds, he travelled to London for a meeting he had requested with Lord Chief Justice Goddard, who was to try the case. The meeting took place in Lord Goddard's chambers at the Old Bailey and, in addition to Frank Cassels, Mr Christmas Humphreys, counsel for the Crown, was also present. Christmas Humphreys, a senior prosecuting counsel and a practising Buddhist, was, like Cassels, the son of a distinguished judge. Regarding Parris's appointment to the case, he had been heard to remark, 'Oh! he's some young chap who hasn't long been called. . . .' He also alluded to the possibility that Parris was related to Craig's solicitor, which was not the case.

After protracted discussion in chambers, Lord Goddard granted an adjournment of five days until Tuesday 9 December. In the course of a tense meeting he had told Parris that there was no defence in the case of Craig. When Parris disagreed, Goddard – acting with considerable impropriety in view of the presence of prosecuting counsel – elicited from him that Craig's defence would be based on manslaughter. The Lord Chief Justice responded contemptuously, giving no comfort to the defender, who had to rush back to Leeds in a private chartered plane.

Cassels agreed with Lord Goddard that Craig had no defence, and argued that Parris should have his client plead guilty as his age ensured that he could not be hanged. He reasoned that if Craig pleaded not guilty, the boy would have to go into the witness box and in the course of examination might well harm Bentley whose age did not protect him from the ultimate penalty. Against this, Parris maintained that manslaughter was a realistic defence for Craig, and if he succeeded in reducing the charge from murder to the lesser one of manslaughter, Bentley would also benefit because he could not in that event be found guilty of murder. There was no meeting of minds on these crucial matters, and Parris resolved that he would argue a defence of manslaughter based on lack of intent for Craig, who would plead not guilty to murder. Cassels would argue that Bentley was not guilty because there was insufficient evidence to prove either that he knew Craig had a gun or that he incited him to use it.

Thus were the battle lines drawn up, and presiding over the whole proceedings would be the controversial figure of the Lord Chief Justice of England, Rayner Goddard. He had been appointed on the recommendation of Clement Attlee, the Prime Minister, in 1946 and had for a long time previously been regarded as a formidable judge on the Western Circuit, where he was known to his friends as 'Doggy', which was probably just a corruption of his name. Churchill, more forcefully, called him 'Lord God-damn'. At the time of the trial of Bentley and Craig, Lord Goddard, aged seventy-five, was well known for being a Hanging Judge and for his tough attitude towards those who broke the law, and outspoken views on the virtues of corporal punishment and hanging.

Some years later, in 1958, an article by Bernard Levin appeared in *The Spectator* referring, among other things, to the Lord Chief Justice walking 'hand in hand with ignorance on one side of him and barbarism on the other'. His early biographers, Eric Grimshaw and Glyn Jones, wrote that, 'It cannot be said that Lord Goddard in his long and losing fight on behalf of the punitive attitude towards prisoners, has frequently chosen the right and most reasonable arguments.'

Goddard's appointment came at a time of rising crime rates after the Second World War. Theft of all kinds was on the increase, and there was an alarming rise in the involvement of young people, particularly teenagers, in criminal activities. The Lord Chief Justice believed in punishment to fit the crime, and pursued a policy of severe sentencing. In 1948 he argued strongly against the abolition of capital punishment, and played a major role in defeating the abolition clause in The Criminal Justice Bill. Ironically, a decisive swing in opinion favouring abolition followed the outcome of the trial of Bentley and Craig in which Goddard played such a decisive part.

On the eve of the trial both the accused teenagers were advised by their counsel to wear new clothes when they appeared at the Old Bailey. Observing Craig's style of dress while in Brixton Prison – 'brothel creeper' shoes and a suede jacket with bright blue trousers – Parris suggested he changed them for something quieter and more conservative. His father bought him a sports jacket and flannels for his appearance in court. Bentley's parents also bought their son new clothes, and in the top pocket of the suit was a sprig of white heather – a symbol of good luck.

Of the other principals in the case on the eve of trial, John Parris spent an instructive evening preparing his papers for court while Frank Cassels watched a performance of *Faust* on television. Christmas Humphreys was also engaged in intellectual pursuits. In his capacity as President of the London Buddhist Society, he entertained his fellow members with a lecture on the subject of 'The Strenuous Application of Buddhism in Daily Life'.

Tuesday, 9 December, dawned a grey day; it was foggy and damp in London. Derek Bentley had lain awake for most of the night in his cream-painted cell in the hospital wing at Brixton Prison. He half-dozed, listening to the distant sounds of the prison officer patrolling the perimeter wall accompanied by an Alsatian dog. As the cold morning light filtered through his barred window the prison slowly awoke. Shortly after 6 a.m. came the order to 'slop out' as his cell door was banged open. With the other inmates, he emptied his urine bucket into the communal sink and rinsed it out. A trustee handed out mops, buckets and disinfectant for cell-cleaning. This done, Bentley tidied up his bed, folding the grey blankets army-style in a sandwich at the bedhead with the pillow perched on top. Then he cleaned his teeth and waited for breakfast to arrive.

At around 6.30 a.m. the breakfast trolley rattled along the corridor and his tray was pushed through the hatch in his cell door. He and Craig were served first in order to give them an early start for their day in court. A security officer made his way from the prison reception building to the hospital wing, clutching day release forms for the two prisoners. The name cards in the metal holders on their cell doors were reversed to show the words 'At Court'.

The two youths were escorted to the reception unit, where they were given the clothes they were to wear in court. The garments had been placed in a large cardboard box, which had rather spoiled the neat creases. They dressed in a nearby cubicle, and Derek struggled into his loose-fitting trousers. He was not permitted to wear a belt, and in order to tighten the waist he rolled the waistband over on itself. This had the effect of hanging his trousers at half-mast, revealing squeaky new brown shoes which in the absence of laces flapped loosely on his feet. Craig, in well-fitting flannels and sports jacket, looked the better turned out of the two. Now that he was parted from his normally colourful clothes and 'brothel creepers' he looked less the American gangster and more the country squire.

Each youth was handcuffed to a prison warder and led to a green Morris van waiting in the courtyard to take them on the three-mile journey to the Old Bailey. Other participants in the unfolding drama arrived at Number Two Court, built on the site of the infamous Newgate Prison, by car and public transport. John Parris took a London omnibus, entering the Old Bailey with two bags heavily filled with papers in time to see the chauffeur-driven arrival of Craig's family. The *Sunday Pictorial* had bought the Craigs' story for a fee of £350 and was protecting its investment in style. The Rolls-Royce discharged Mr and Mrs Craig and their strikingly attractive daughter Lucy on the court steps, closely attended by Harry Procter and Madeline McLoughlin, reporters from the newspaper. Procter allowed the Press photographers gathered at the entrance to take 'one apiece, boys' before shepherding his charges into the building.

Like the thousands of people who travelled to the Old Bailey that day merely to satisfy their curiosity, the Bentley family journeyed by public transport. William and Lilian Bentley had been warned to stand by to give evidence for the defence if required. They were to spend the better part of three long days in a draughty corridor, not needed to appear in court and not able to bear facing their son at his time of ordeal. Members of the public thronged the entrance to the court, anxious to catch a glimpse of the principal participants or, better still, to gain a seat in the public gallery. Tickets for this were issued by the clerk of the courts and then sold on for a considerable amount by touts. Interest ran high at the prospect of two young thugs being dealt with by a judge known for his severity, and with the shadow of the ultimate penalty in the background. The case had been heralded by the newspapers as the 'most sensational murder trial of the twentieth century'. Of course, the same hackneyed description had been used countless times before and would be again, but no one cared.

Up in the counsels' robing room the atmosphere was as chilly as the weather outside. John Parris recalled the resentful welcome which the Old Bailey intimates extended to foreigners. His legal colleagues did not speak to him as he found a place on the table to deposit his wig box and papers. The Lord Chief Justice donned his splendid, ermine-trimmed robes and full-bottomed wig in his private chambers.

The court bustled with activity as people took their seats and clerks and solicitors arranged their books and papers, all helping to contribute to an atmosphere that became more charged by the minute. There was always something special about a murder trial when death was the supreme penalty. The prosecuting counsel, Christmas Humphreys, poker-faced and ascetic in appearance, took his seat alongside his junior Mr John Bass. They went into a huddle with Chief Inspector John Smith, the policeman in charge of the case. As defence counsel took their seats an usher placed a pointer against the blackboard in the well of the court on which was pinned a large diagram depicting the roof of Barlow & Parker's warehouse in Tamworth Road, Croydon. A hush settled on the court as at precisely 10.30 a.m. the Lord Chief Justice appeared from a door at the side of the Bench. The court rose as the scarlet-clad figure solemnly took his place in the judge's chair. Still wearing a plaster cast, Craig stood in the dock beside Bentley. The clerk of the court read out the charge: 'Christopher Craig, Derek William Bentley, you are charged that on the 2nd day of November last you murdered Sidney George Miles. Christopher Craig, are you guilty or not guilty?'

'Not Guilty,' answered Craig.

'Derek William Bentley, are you guilty or not guilty?'

'Not Guilty,' replied Bentley.

Bentley and Craig were also charged with the attempted murder of Detective Constable Fairfax, to which they pleaded not guilty.

Addressing the youth who was not long out of hospital, Lord Goddard said, 'Craig, you may sit down.' Dr Matheson had passed a note to the court clerk saying that Craig could stand when he was called in to plead but that he should be then allowed to sit. This privilege was not extended to Bentley, even though it was normal courtroom practice in a trial lasting more than a few minutes for the defendant to be seated.

A jury was empanelled of ten men and two women. John Parris immediately rose to challenge the selection, as was the defence's right, and the two women members were replaced by men. Parris later explained his reasons in his account of the trial. He was a shrewd practitioner working against the odds, and experience had taught him the importance of making an early impact on the jury and he took this opportunity to do so. It was also only human nature to believe that a woman might identify with the plight of the policeman's widow and take a less than dispassionate view of the affair. On the other hand, as Frank Cassels believed, the sympathies of any women on the jury might well have been in favour of the mothers of the two accused teenagers.

The tall figure of Christmas Humphreys rose to make his opening speech for the prosecution. At the age of fifty-one, and destined in a few short years to prosecute Ruth Ellis for murder, he was regarded as a formidable opponent in court. His observance of the Buddhist faith implied the acceptance of non-violence, and perhaps made it difficult for him to excuse aggressive criminal acts. In his later years, after he had become a judge, he asked himself in his autobiography the question, 'How far should one allow the fact that the prisoner is "abnormal" to influence the sentence?' He provided his own answer by posing another question, 'Is not any man who has become a confirmed and violent criminal "abnormal"?'

'May it please you, my Lord,' he began, and proceeded to unfold the prosecution's case against the two young men in the dock. His presentation was succinct; 'The case for the prosecution is this: that Craig deliberately and wilfully murdered that police constable and thereafter gloried in the murder; that Bentley incited Craig to begin the shooting and although technically under arrest at the actual time of the killing of Miles, was party to that murder and equally responsible under the law.'

Having been handed a ready-made headline, the *Evening Standard* reporter noted down the words 'Craig Trial Begins : He Gloried in Murder', which featured in heavy black type in the paper's lunchtime edition.

From these very first remarks, it became clear the prosecution conceded that Bentley was under arrest at the time the fatal shot was fired. It was equally clear that this was not seen as an obstacle to arguing the case for Bentley's guilt. Christmas Humphreys continued by retelling the story of the rooftop gun-battle and stated how all three police officers present heard Bentley say 'Let him have it, Chris'. 'That statement,' said counsel, in the submission of the prosecution, 'was a deliberate incitement to Craig to murder Sergeant Fairfax.' Bentley said it to a man whom he undoubtedly knew had a gun. That shot began a gun-fight in the course of which Miles was killed; that incitement, in the submission of the prosecution, covered the whole of the shooting thereafter and, he added, repeating his earlier admission,'even though at the time of the actual shot which killed PC Miles Bentley was in custody and under arrest'.

Referring to Bentley's statement, counsel quoted parts which he said were particularly pertinent to the case for the Crown. Bentley had said, 'I knew we were going to break into the place; I did not know what we were going to get – just anything that was going. I did not have a gun and I did not know Chris had one until he shot. I now know that the policeman in uniform that was shot is dead.' Commenting on this, Mr Humphreys remarked, 'May I say at once, of course, that this statement made by Bentley is in no sense any evidence against Craig; because their concerted action to break and enter these premises and steal what they could, and to resist their lawful apprehension by such violence as they might think necessary, was over, and the moment they are arrested, what they severally say is not evidence against each other.'

Whatever the legal basis may have been for this argument, it seems to contain a logical fallacy. John Parris found it hard to follow why, if the concerted action finished at the time of arrest – thereby making the statement of one participant inadmissible against the other – the arrest should not also logically conclude the responsibility of one for the acts of the other. David Yallop in his analysis of the proceedings encountered the same difficulty – he put it thus, 'we have the bizarre situation where what they *say* when they have been arrested is not evidence against the other, but what they *do* is'. The implication was that the prosecution held Bentley responsible for actions committed by Craig *after* the older youth had been put under arrest.

The waters were muddied further when counsel, referring to the time that Bentley was 'technically under arrest' on the rooftop, called the jury's attention to his shouted remark, 'Look out, Chris; they're taking me down.' He went on to ask the jury to consider whether this was a further invitation, a cry for help or a challenge. The use of the term 'technically under arrest' suggests something less than actual arrest. The prosecutor concluded his opening speech by summarizing the case for the Crown:

that Craig deliberately murdered PC Miles and, as I have said, thereafter gloried in the murder and only regretted that he had not shot more. Bentley incited Craig to begin the shooting, and although he was technically under arrest at the time of the actual murder of PC Miles, was nevertheless still mentally supporting Craig in all that

Craig continued to do; and in English law, and you may think in common sense, was in every sense party to that murder.

Then came the prosecution witnesses led by Police Constable Charles Beard, who gave evidence regarding the rooftop dimensions of Barlow & Parker's warehouse. He was followed by Chief Inspector Percy Law of Scotland Yard's photographic department. The evidence of these two witnesses was unexceptional, but the court stirred when Craig's father was called to the stand. The quiet bank official whose two sons had suddenly drawn his respectable life into the harsh spotlight of confrontation with the law was required to confirm Christopher's age. He verified that his son was born on 19 May 1936, thus making it clear that he was sixteen years old and too young to suffer the law's greatest penalty.

John Parris cross-examined Mr Craig, eliciting from him the information that Christopher was word-blind or dyslexic, and that the only reading matter with which he could cope was comics. Craig senior admitted his own interest in guns and marksmanship and said that he had taught his elder boys target-shooting with air-guns. Because Christopher was unable to read, he had developed a liking for the cinema and went to see films several times a week. Asked if his son had ever to his knowledge been a violent boy, he answered, 'Never; he was in fact quite the opposite.'

'Gentle?' suggested Parris.

'Very gentle,' was the reply. Mr Craig denied any knowledge of the cache of ammunition that his son had hidden in his house.

Mrs Edith Ware gave her testimony about the two intruders at the warehouse whom she had seen from her front bedroom window, and recalled that the police arrived about four minutes after she had raised the alarm. Then came Frederick Fairfax, newly promoted to Detective Sergeant, who relived the dramatic moments of the rooftop gun-battle. As he had done several times during the course of the first morning's proceedings, Lord Goddard interrupted counsel's examination of the witness. He asked Fairfax about the moment that PC McDonald joined him on the roof before the fatal shot was fired: 'Were either of you holding Bentley at this time?'

'We were both holding Bentley then,' replied Fairfax, thus making it perfectly clear that however 'technical' Bentley's arrest may have been he was nevertheless under restraint. This seemed to resolve the question of whether or not Bentley was under arrest at the time the fatal shot was fired although it did not absolve him from responsibility in the killing that followed.

John Parris questioned Fairfax about the number of shots fired, particularly his understanding that the Sergeant claimed the shot which killed his colleague was the third one fired. Fairfax had said the first shot was the one which had struck him, then there was another shot and the third one which killed PC Miles. Fairfax replied that there were 'somewhere like six or seven other shots' before the fatal shot was fired.

Parris took him to task: 'You had said not a word about these shots until a few moments ago, had you, officer?'

'No,' replied Fairfax, adding his contribution to the confusion which surrounded the total number of shots fired during the incident – confusion that was shared by Lord Goddard, and has never been entirely resolved.

Parris attempted clarification: 'So, if I am right in my addition, is this the story: two shots to start with, six or seven after that, the fatal one, and one later?'

'Yes,' answered Fairfax.

'That makes either ten or eleven shots in all that you say you heard?'

'Round about ten shots.'

'It was about that?'

'About ten shots, yes.'

It seemed that the endeavour to establish the precise number of shots fired was doomed to failure.

Frank Cassels now cross-examined Fairfax about the moments leading up to the shot which struck the officer, slightly wounding him, and the behaviour of Bentley at that time. Answering prosecuting counsel's questions, Fairfax had appeared to acknowledge that Bentley broke away from him when he was hit by Craig's bullet. Cassels probed further into this and established from the witness that Bentley had slipped from his grasp before the shot was fired.

At this point Lord Goddard intervened to confirm the answer from the witness's previous testimony: 'As we got to the bottom of the left-hand corner Bentley broke away and shouted, "Let him have it, Chris." There was a shot, a flash and I felt something strike me.' His Lordship was obviously keen to have it clear in the jury's mind that, having broken free from the policeman's grasp, Bentley shouted his alleged incitement to Craig.

Thus did the attempt by Cassels to exploit Fairfax's apparent equivocation on this point fail. Counsel also put it to the witness that Bentley did not utter a word before the shot was fired and did not say 'Let him have it, Chris' or any words to that effect.

'He did,' was Fairfax's emphatic reply.

After Fairfax had completed his evidence, the court rose for lunch. As Craig was being taken down by the warders, this youth, whose father had painted him as a gentle soul, burst out with reference to Fairfax, 'I ought to have killed that fucker as well.' It was fortunate for him that the remark was not heard by the jury for, as John Parris observed later in his autobiography, 'it was somewhat inconsistent with his defence'.

The morning's courtroom proceedings had gone unheard by Mr and Mrs Bentley, who had spent the entire time waiting outside. William Bentley believed he might be called to give evidence regarding Derek's overcoat. On the night of the break-in and shooting he had been wearing a light-coloured, camel-hair overcoat. According to the evidence given by Fairfax, after he had been struck by Craig's bullet he knocked Bentley down on the rain-soaked, tar-covered roof of the warehouse. Surprisingly, the overcoat bore not a single dirty mark, and Bentley senior thought this would tell in his son's favour by proving an inconsistency in the police officer's testimony. The poor man was due for a long wait as Frank Cassels, in full knowledge of this information, had determined not to call him as a witness, a fact of which he was unaware until the trial reached its conclusion.

Under English law, if defence counsel called any witness apart from the defendant, he would forfeit to the prosecution the privilege of having the last word to the jury. Having been denied an opening speech and the opportunity thereby of making an impression on the jury, the defence was forced into the dilemma of not being able to call the defence witnesses it might have chosen without jeopardizing this one remaining advantage. The jury would remain in ignorance of the defence case except through the medium of cross-examination until the entire prosecution case had been heard.

After the adjournment for lunch came Police Constable James McDonald, who was taken through his account of the incident that occurred on the night of 2 November. Early in his examination by John Bass, junior prosecuting counsel, he was asked if he had heard a shout as he was preparing to climb on the roof. 'I did,' he answered; 'I heard someone shout, 'Let him have it, Chris.'

Lord Goddard intervened to establish that at the time he heard this remark McDonald was still clinging to the drainpipe on the wall of the warehouse.

Bass continued his examination: 'I do not suppose you knew the voice at that time, did you?'

'I did not.'

'Have you heard the same voice since?'

'I could not say for certain.'

As he had done with the previous witness, John Parris attempted to extract from McDonald the precise number of shots that had been fired. 'Now, let us see what your recollection is like. How many shots do you say were fired before the fatal one?'

'Six.'

'Six,' repeated counsel.

'Yes,' confirmed the witness.

'Well, you were within hearing distance the whole time; is that right?'

'Yes; I think I was within hearing distance of all shots.'

'How many shots in all do you say there were?'

'Ten or eleven,' answered the policeman. As he did throughout the trial, Lord Goddard interjected with his comments. On a matter that was surely of the greatest significance the judge condoned inexactitude: 'I wonder how anybody could be expected to be accurate on a matter like this, on a night like this when these men are being fired at, in fear of their lives, and now they are being asked weeks afterwards to count how many shots were fired.'

Continuing his examination of the witness, Parris said, 'As his Lordship says, it is rather unnerving to hear shots on a rooftop?'

'It is, sir,' agreed Mc Donald. 'It rather disturbs one's recollection of what happened.'

'I do not know about that.'

Frank Cassels returned to the attack on the question of the remark allegedly made by Bentley while on the rooftop. Having confirmed that McDonald was descending the drainpipe after failing to scale the last six feet when he heard the alleged remark, 'Let him have it, Chris', counsel said: 'I am suggesting you never heard that remark used by Bentley, or used by anybody else?'

McDonald's answer, 'I could not say whether it was Bentley who used it or not' prompted a swift intervention from the judge.

'Well, did you hear the word, "Chris" used?'

'I did.'

'So far as you know, there were three people on the roof?'

'Yes.'

'There was Sergeant Fairfax and the two men?'

'Yes.'

'And you heard: "Let him have it, Chris"; is that right?'

'That is right, my Lord,' answered McDonald.

It seemed that while the judge was not interested in establishing how many shots had been fired, he was determined to make it clear to the jury that Bentley had made an apparently incriminating remark.

Next came Police Constable Norman Harrison, whose recollection of the position of the contestants on the rooftop was at variance with that of both Fairfax and McDonald. At the time that Craig fired at him Harrison maintained that the gunman was on the east side of the lift-head, whereas McDonald had stated he was on the other side. According to Fairfax, at the point when Bentley broke from his grasp and shouted, 'Let him have it, Chris', all three of them were positioned at the left-hand corner of the lift-head, which meant that Harrison's view from the sloping roof would have been completely obscured by the structure of the lift-head itself. Harrison insisted that they were positioned on the right-hand side of the lift-head and in clear view. When he cross-examined the witness, John Parris asked if PC McDonald's account of Craig's position at the crucial time was right or wrong, but before the officer could answer the judge weighed in once again. 'You need not tell us whether one man is right or wrong,' he told Harrison, 'you tell us what you remember and what you saw.'

When Police Constable Robert Jaggs appeared in the witness-box he was questioned by Christmas Humphreys about the number of times Craig's revolver misfired before the youth threw himself off the roof-top. 'Fairfax fired twice and Craig clicked two or three times?'

'Yes.'

'Was it two or three times, or once or twice?'

'Two or three times.'

Yet in his opening speech prosecuting counsel had said officers on the roof-top heard four clicks and then a shot before Craig dived off the roof. The contradictions in the evidence were never seriously challenged in court.

After the police came the medical witnesses; first Dr Nicholas Jaswon, the casualty officer on duty at Croydon General Hospital when Fairfax was brought in for treatment. He stated briefly that he had found a gunshot wound on the right side over the collarbone and confirmed that there was no fracture. The doctor agreed with John

Parris's description of the injury as a searing wound. He also agreed with counsel that the bullet's passage, up and over the shoulder, indicated that it came from a low level. Parris was attempting to show that the bullet was on a rising trajectory, having bounced off the roof in accordance with Craig's statement that he had not fired directly at any of the policemen. Lord Goddard intervened to say rather acidly, 'I do not know why the doctor has been brought from Manchester [where he was then working] to say that.' Addressing the witness, the judge asked, 'Well, are you competent to answer such a question?'

'No, I think not, really,' replied Dr Jaswon.

Parris pressed the witness: 'You prefer not?'

'I prefer not,' he answered.

A tetchy exchange followed between defence counsel and judge. Lord Goddard said, 'The doctor is here to give medical evidence, not to speculate on the flight of bullets.'

'I was asking whether what he found, the wound, is consistent with that theory,' countered Parris.

'That is a matter you can address the jury on,' declared the judge. 'It is not a matter for the doctor.'

'If your lordship will not allow me to ask the question, that is all,' concluded counsel.

But Goddard had not finished. Before telling the witness he was at liberty to go, he again said that he regretted he had been brought down from Manchester, saying, 'The wound you have given evidence about and the passing across the skin could have been perfectly well read [that is, from a statement]'.

Dr David Haler, who had carried out the post-mortem examination on the body of PC Miles, made a brief appearance in the witness-box. He confirmed that he had found the entry and exit wounds of a large-calibre bullet. There were no questions. Dr Douglas Freebody, the consultant orthopaedic surgeon at Croydon General Hospital who was called in to examine Craig three days after he had been admitted to hospital, was called next. John Parris asked him if, in view of the manner in which the youth had sustained his injuries, 'It is very probable that he was concussed at the time.'

The doctor agreed, 'It is possible.'

Parris's questioning on this point, and later on that of the drugs which Craig had been given while in hospital, was aimed at clarifying the youth's state of mind and the context in which various statements were taken at his bedside.

Croydon General Hospital's Medical Officer, Dr Gordon Hatfield, had kept a precise record of all the drugs administered to Craig. Soon after admission Craig was given two compound Codeine tablets to relieve pain. 'Do they have any effect upon the mental functions?' asked prosecuting counsel.

'No,' replied the doctor.

Subsequently the injured youth was given doses of the anaesthetic pentathol in order to set his broken wrist and, several hours afterwards, pethedine to relieve the pain. Christmas Humphreys, wishing to ensure that the defence gained no advantage from the suggestion that Craig's mental ability had been impaired either by being concussed or in a semi-drugged state, put questions directly to Dr Hatfield, 'Do you say, doctor, that none of these drugs, apart from pentathol – no other drugs he may have been given for other purposes from time to time – would affect the clarity of his mind to the extent that he did not understand what he was saying?'

'That is right.'

'After he had recovered from the anaesthetic, I mean?'

'Yes.'

'Was there any indication of any typical signs of any form of concussion?'

'No.'

In his cross-examination Parris decided to pursue the use of pentathol as a so-called 'truth drug' in the United States. He asked Dr Hatfield if 'It has the effect of removing inhibitions and making a person more talkative?'

The doctor replied cautiously that he did not know enough about that particular use of the drug. Nevertheless, Parris pressed on and the doctor agreed that, 'It is used for analysis and to make people talk to a certain extent, yes.'

'Makes them talk much more freely?'

'Yes.'

'Saying things, perhaps, that they would not normally say?'

'Yes.'

Before Dr Hatfield stood down, Christmas Humphreys asked him, 'Can you say if anything that Craig said could have been the result of confusion of mind caused by taking this pentathol?'

'Not after the period of time that I said – two hours,' answered the witness.

After the doctors came more police witnesses, first Detective Sergeant Stanley Shepherd, who had carried out the search at

Craig's home and later, with Detective Chief Inspector John Smith, had taken statements from both Craig and Bentley at Croydon Police Station. Prosecuting counsel asked who took down the statement. 'I wrote it down,' answered the witness.

'And is it as dictated by Bentley?'

'Yes.'

'Did he begin by signing the caution at the top of it?'

'Yes.'

'At the end is there the line: "This statement has been read to me and is true"?'

'Yes.'

'And is there then an attempt by Bentley to sign his signature?'

'Yes. He attempted to write his name, and he asked how to spell it, and eventually he wrote "Derek W. Bentley".' Detective Sergeant Shepherd then read out the statement, the penultimate paragraph of which contain the words, 'I did not have a gun and I did not know Chris had one until he shot.'

Frank Cassels cross-examined the policeman about the statement. 'First of all, it is right, is it not, that Bentley is illiterate? He cannot read and he cannot write?'

'So he says.'

'Well, can he write, do you think, from what he said, anything apart from his own signature?'

'He appeared to have difficulty in writing his name.'

'From the inquiries that have been made in the case, is it right that he is close to being a feeble-minded person? Do you know that?'

'No, I do not know that.'

Here was an ideal opportunity for defence counsel to pursue the question of Bentley's mental status. Shepherd and Smith had made many of the inquiries into Bentley's background and had knowledge of much of the information that had been passed on to the medical authorities at Brixton Prison. Thus, the denial of anything suggesting Bentley's feeble-minded state was less than convincing. But, apart from this brief reference, counsel chose not to take the question of Bentley's mental ability further. It seemed as if no one wanted to introduce any evidence that would favourably dispose the jury to anything less than total guilt.

The first day of the trial ended with a succession of police witnesses including the watchers at Craig's bedside after he had been admitted to hospital. They repeated the remarks made by the youth, whom it had already been established was neither concussed nor under the influence of drugs. Police Constable Vincent Denham conceded that at the time Craig made the remark with reference to the fatal shooting, 'That copper, I shot him in the head and he went down like a ton of bricks', the lad was not normal.

'In what way do you mean?' intervened Lord Goddard.

'Well, he was in great pain, my Lord.'

With the conclusion of the first day's proceedings, the participants dispersed. Craig's family were swept away in their Rolls-Royce for an evening meal provided courtesy of their newspaper guardians. They chatted and occasionally laughed, secure in the knowledge that, whatever the outcome of the trial, their boy could not be hanged. Bentley's parents and his sister Iris, all of whom had spent a bewildering day in the corridor outside Number Two Court, went home comforted by the belief that those responsible for Derek's defence were pursuing his best interests. 'We were never called,' said William Bentley; 'I have no comments to make on that. Counsel and solicitors must be left to conduct cases in their own way, guided by their knowledge of the law.' Their evening was spent mostly in silent contemplation of the awful fate that might confront Derek.

When he left the dock, following behind Craig, Derek Bentley – who had eagerly scanned the faces in court for his parents – called out to him, 'Chris, Chris, did you see me Mum an' Dad, Chris?' There was no reply for a youth who must have felt desperately alone. There is no record of any contact between Bentley and Craig while they were on remand during the trial. They were both A category prisoners and, as such, would have been confined in maximum security cells. On their return to Brixton Prison the prisoners were each fed a meal of fish and chips and escorted back to the hospital wing where they would be secured for the night.

Frank Cassels's failure to press the matter of Bentley's state of mind with Detective Sergeant Shepherd might have been redeemed when he had the chance to cross-question Detective Chief Inspector Smith the next day. 'You have made inquiries, no doubt, with regard to the accused Bentley?' he began.

'Yes,' replied the Chief Inspector.

'Do you agree with me that he is below average intelligence for his age?'

'Oh, yes,' said Smith.

'Well below it?'

'Below it, sir. I cannot say well below it.'

'So far as you can ascertain, is he capable of reading and writing anything else but his own name?'

'He can. His schoolmaster said that he could, but with difficulty.'

'With difficulty?'

'Yes.'

Here was a decisive moment in the trial; an opportunity for defence counsel to reduce the peril which Bentley faced. Cassels had among his papers all the material that John Stevens had gleaned about Bentley's life from his parents, doctors and teachers. Details of the youth's history of *petit mal*, his low IQ and his doctors' assessment that he had a mental age of eleven to twelve were known to him. This and much more was also known to the judge, who had all the reports on the two accused youths among his papers. Lord Goddard had already intervened many times during the trial and he would continue to do so. Yet on this matter he chose to remain silent. He did not prompt counsel, and Cassels chose the path of inertia. The judge's action in turning a blind eye to decency and fair-mindedness rank as moments of shame in the history of the courts.

The final witness for the prosecution was Lewis Nickolls, Director of the Metropolitan Police Laboratory, New Scotland Yard. Christmas Humphreys took him through the firearms evidence, and the witness confirmed that the piece of sawn-off barrel found in Craig's home had originally been part of the weapon used in the fatal shooting. Throughout this period of questioning, prosecuting counsel incorrectly referred to the weapon as a .45 revolver – the expert witness did not correct him. The judge asked if the undersized bullet that had struck Fairfax was capable of being fired by the weapon: 'Yes , my Lord.'

The prosecutor spoke of the cartridge-cases that had been filed down to fit the revolver: 'whoever loaded that revolver had to put in work on the cartridge cases before they would fit the revolver?'

'Yes.'

When John Parris began his cross-examination he showed that he had done his homework. 'Your description of this gun is wrong. It is not a .45 – a .455?' Nickolls acknowledged that the weapon was a .455 Eley Service revolver of the type that was standard issue in the First World War. Parris also made the point that some of the ammunition used was 'something of lower calibre than .455, was it not?'

'Yes, it was.'

'That, of course, would make a shot more inaccurate?'

'It would make it completely inaccurate.'
'It would make it completely inaccurate?'
'Yes.'

The difference between .45 and .455 calibre was a mere five-thousandths of an inch but Parris made it tell.

Christmas Humphreys was at pains to establish that even using undersized ammunition, the revolver would be reasonably accurate if fired at a human being at six feet. 'Yes,' answered Nickolls, 'I think if one aimed at the centre of a human being one could more or less guarantee to hit him at six feet.'

Once again Lord Goddard made his presence felt. He asked the witness, 'This revolver, if it is fired off, and even if it is fired indiscriminately, is quite capable of killing people?' Parris had already established from Nickolls, whom he suggested was 'not really a ballistics expert', that the revolver was inaccurate by as much as six feet at a range of thirty-nine feet. The miraculous shot which killed PC Miles was not pursued, and Nickolls declined to agree with Parris that Exhibit 8 was, 'in all probability, the fatal bullet'.

'I could find no evidence of blood on it whatsoever. Therefore, in all probability it is not the fatal bullet.'

Parris's examination had made it clear that Craig's revolver with its shortened barrel and use of an assortment of ill-fitting ammunition was wildly inaccurate. The expert witness's admission that if the gun were pointed directly at a person six feet away a shot could more or less be guaranteed to hit him should have made a telling impression on the jury. Perhaps realizing that his earlier intervention on this point might only have served to reinforce the impression of the weapon's inaccuracy, Lord Goddard decided to interrupt Christmas Humphrey's attempt to reconstruct the circumstances of the fatal shot. Counsel had established that of the six cartridges recovered from the cylinder of Craig's revolver, five were of .45 calibre and one was undersized. Strictly speaking, of course, as the weapon was a .455 all the cartridges were undersized. Building on this somewhat erroneous foundation, Humphreys asked if there was a reasonable chance of Craig hitting PC Miles as he emerged on to the roof at a distance of forty feet. 'If he fired at such people as are coming out of the staircase head, and fired more than once with the correct ammunition, was there a reasonable chance of his hitting them, or one of them, or some of them?'

Nickolls's reply to this amazingly loosely-framed question was equally vague. 'I think it would be an extremely dangerous thing to do,' he said.

Hardly were the words out of his mouth than the judge stepped in with a disastrous intervention. 'Mr Humphreys,' he said, 'this is a case in which an officer of justice was murdered, shot.'

'Yes, my Lord.'

'Very different considerations as you know, apply where an officer of justice in the course of his execution of his duty is killed.'

'Yes, my Lord,' said counsel, 'but, with great respect, I was following up with this witness what I imagine to be – I may be wrong – the opening of a certain line of defence.'

'Well, if that defence is run,' said Lord Goddard, 'I shall tell the jury it is no defence at all.'

Humphreys replied, 'If your Lordship pleases. My Lord, that is the case for the prosecution.'

The Lord Chief Justice's reference to the murder of the police officer was an extraordinary slip – after all, the purpose of the entire proceedings over which he presided was to permit the jury to decide whether the crime in question was murder. As John Parris wrote in his autobiography, it was 'scarcely the happiest note on which to call evidence for the defence. . . .' During the course of the prosecution's case Lord Goddard intervened with over fifty questions of his own, occasionally to elucidate a matter of evidence but usually to make a point detrimental to the defence.

6

'I'm not afraid to die because I am innocent'

William Bentley spoke of the trial as 'three days of agony'. He could not bring himself to watch his son's ordeal in court. With his wife and daughter Iris, he continued to sit in the corridor outside Number Two Court at the Old Bailey, leaving the building occasionally for a cigarette. 'I searched the faces of the lawyers for a hint as to how the trial was going,' he wrote later; 'they were like shut books.'

Christopher Craig, sixteen years old, dark-haired and stockily built, was called to give evidence. He moved slowly but purposefully to the witness-box and took the oath. No doubt the injuries he had sustained slowed his movements. Attired in his respectable sports jacket and flannels, he spoke in a quiet voice and cast a look towards his parents. 'Let him sit down,' commanded Lord Goddard. The belligerent youth who had flung defiant and obscene remarks at the police during the rooftop shooting had been transformed into a schoolboy speaking with such a soft voice that the judge had to ask him on several occasions to repeat his answers. Asked by John Parris about the outcome of his first encounter with the law in 1951, Craig said, 'I ran away.'

'What do you say?' asked Lord Goddard.

'I left home, sir.'

Defence counsel took him through his history of familiarity with weapons. 'When did you first start taking an interest in firearms?'

'When I was eleven. I liked them, though, when I was about seven.'

'What was the first weapon that you yourself fired?'

'A cap and ball pistol.'

'What age were you?'

'When I was eleven.'

'Between the age of eleven and your present age, how many weapons have you had?'

'Forty or fifty, sir.'

'Where did you get those from?'

'Swapped them with boys at school.'

'What?' interjected Lord Goddard.

'Swapped them and bought them off boys at school,' repeated Craig.

Continuing his examination, Parris asked, 'Why did you swap them or buy them off boys at school?'

'Because I liked them, sir.'

'You used to like them?'

'Yes.'

'Did you ever take any of those weapons to school with you?'

'Yes, I used to take all of them.'

Lord Goddard snapped, 'What?'

'I used to take all of them, sir.'

'What – forty or fifty do you mean?'

'Well, I had not got them at the same time, sir.'

At this point Parris had to ask Craig to speak up so that he could be heard, and, shortly afterwards the judge intervened to say testily, 'Let us get on to something that matters.'

Counsel drew from the youth that his interest in guns was such that he wanted to be a gunsmith, and that when he started work he nearly always had a gun with him. 'Why did you want to take a gun to work?'

'It just made me feel big,' answered Craig. The teenager confirmed that he was unable to read properly, and as a result people 'used to take the mickey out of me'. By way of compensation he went to the cinema three or four times a week to see mainly gangster films.

Having established that handling firearms and screen violence were part of Craig's everyday life, John Parris moved swiftly to the events that occurred on the roof of Barlow & Parker's warehouse. Referring to the plan of the rooftop and its various structures, Craig described the positions occupied by Bentley and himself at the point when Fairfax grabbed the older boy. 'Now, the officer has said,' began Parris, 'that some time at that stage of the proceedings Bentley said, "Let him have it, Chris." Did you hear any words like that?'

'No, sir.'

Craig gave his account of the various shots that he fired and, in answer to the Lord Chief Justice, said that he fired nine shots altogether.

'So you reloaded the revolver?'

'Yes.'

'Did you see the officer Miles come up on to the roof?' asked Parris.

'I did not see him come on the roof. The door flew open and I thought someone was rushing me, sir, saw someone was coming out, and I fired another one to frighten them away.'

'You fired another shot to frighten them away. Where did you fire that shot?'

'Towards this No. 30 house (No. 30 Tamworth Road, adjacent to the warehouse) over the roof.'

Lord Goddard queried, 'How did it come about that it hit PC Miles coming out of the door?'

'It might have ricocheted off. I do not know.'

'It might have ricocheted?' repeated the judge.

'Ricocheted or anything, sir.'

Parris resumed his examination with the question, 'Do you know how it came to hit him?'

'No.'

'Had you any intention at any time of killing any officer?'

'No.'

Turning to the taunts Craig made to the police officers on the roof, Parris asked him, 'Why did you say those?'

'Bluff, sir, so that they would not come at me.'

'It was all bluff?'

'Yes.'

'When you were standing up there with the gun in your hand, what did you think you were like?'

'In a film or something, sir.'

'Like the films?'

'Yes.'

'Had you any intention of hurting any officer at all?'

'No. I don't hurt people, sir.' Craig denied making the statements attributed to him while he was in hospital; 'I do not think I said them,' he answered in response to counsel's questions.

As John Parris noted subsequently, a great deal of Craig's cross-examination, which was conducted by Christmas Humphreys, was aimed less at discrediting him than at implicating Bentley. Prosecuting counsel launched straight into a series of questions about the relationship between the two youths. The questions had an aggressive edge: 'You had known him for some time; you went to school with him?'

'No.'

'You were never at school with him?'

'No.'

'How long have you known him?'

'About eight months.'

'You have been with him frequently?'

'No.' Craig held his own with his replies, and also fended off the inevitable queries put by Lord Goddard. When Humphreys suggested that he carried a gun with him when he went housebreaking, Craig corrected him, 'I do not housebreak.'

'What?' interjected the judge.

'I do not housebreak, sir,' the youth repeated.

'Well, shopbreak?' proposed his lordship.

'No sir,' came the reply.

'You were going to break into a shop this night?'

'Yes, sir, but I used to take it to work with me. I always carried it, sir.' This exchange between the sixteen-year-old defendant and the awe-inspiring figure of Lord Goddard gave the jury a brief insight into Craig's strength of character.

Having dealt with the gun, the Lord Chief Justice moved on to the knife. 'What did you take that knife for?'

'I always carried it, sir.'

'You always carried that knife?'

'Yes, sir.'

'What did you carry it for?'

'It is only a sheath knife, sir.'

Next came the knuckleduster, and questioning was resumed by Christmas Humphreys. 'Bentley was armed with a knuckleduster, which he says he got from you. Is that right?'

'Yes.'

'Where did you get the knuckleduster from?'

'I made it, sir'.

'Just look at it. You say you made that?'

'Yes.'

'Where?'

'At work.'

'When did you give it to him?'

'That night.'

Lord Goddard then waded in with a series of questions about the spike on the knuckleduster for which Craig had no real explanation. 'A dreadful weapon,' remarked the Lord Chief Justice.

Questioning now returned to the gun and again the prosecution was in effect led by the judge. 'Do you say Bentley did not know you had a gun?'

'No, sir.'

77

'Do you say you were out with Bentley that night to do this shopbreaking and you did not tell him you had got a gun?' Where he had repeated his answers before, Craig remained silent.

Christmas Humphreys resumed his cross-examination. 'You see, he has told the police, "I told the silly bugger not to use it", referring to you?'

'Yes.'

'Did he say that?'

'No.'

'He did not tell you not to use it?'

'No.'

'And again: "He has got a .45 and plenty of ammunition for it"?'

'I told him when I was on the roof.'

'You told him when you were on the roof that you had a gun?'

'Yes, sir, when I saw the police.'

'So before there was any shooting you told him in terms you had a gun?'

'Yes, sir.'

'And it was loaded?'

'Yes.'

'Was there any discussion about it being used?'

'No.' This exchange clearly implicated Bentley on the grounds that he knew, albeit at the eleventh hour, that Craig was armed, whereas he had claimed he was unaware of the fact until the shooting began.

Cross-examination next focused on the statements Craig was alleged to have made to various police officers after he was admitted to hospital. He said he did not remember saying that he had 'so much hate inside' for what had happened to his elder brother, and denied making a remark about his gun being 'on the wobble'.

He told Christmas Humphreys, 'That is ridiculous, sir. . . . If I did say it, sir, it shows that a person was not in his right mind.' He had already referred to being injected every twelve hours while he was in hospital. This ground had been well trodden during the first day of the trial, but Craig's mind was working overtime trying to find ways round the relentless questioning.

Christmas Humphreys now returned to events on the rooftop, teasing Craig with the question, 'You agree that you were both well armed, both of you?'

'I did not know what Bentley had got, sir, and he did not know what I had got,' replied the youth.

Claiming that he had wanted only to frighten away the police officers in order to avoid being arrested, Craig denied shooting Fairfax at a range of six feet, saying 'He was about twenty-seven feet away.' Counsel said that the officer had testified 'You deliberately shot me.'

'I did not, sir.'

'Having been incited to do so by Bentley saying, "Let him have it, Chris". Are you saying you did not hear that?'

Craig could have given a straightforward denial, but he framed his reply in a way that protected his companion, 'Bentley did not say it, sir.' The lad's adrenalin was flowing when Humphreys told him that three police officers at different positions on the roof heard the remark. 'I am saying I did not hear it, and if they heard it they must have better hearing than mine.'

The prosecutor moved on to the vexed question of the number of shots that had been fired. As the police officers involved, the prosecutor and the judge had arrived at different answers, perhaps the gunman himself would resolve the matter. Craig claimed to have fired nine shots in all. 'I had six in the gun and five in my top pocket clip.'

'What happened to the other two?'

'Two did not go off.'

'I beg your pardon,' said Humphreys, 'You mean you shot nine times but you had eleven bullets. Is that it?'

'Yes.' Craig denied firing directly at any of the officers, repeating as he had throughout that his intention had only been to frighten them off. Asked about the death of PC Miles, he said, 'I saw the door fly open. I thought someone was coming out, so I fired again to frighten them away.' Counsel put a barrage of questions to the witness about the circumstances of the policeman's death but Craig would not be shaken from his position that he had not deliberately fired at the officer.

Towards the end of his time in the witness box Craig's confidence turned to something like cockiness, especially in his replies to the Lord Chief Justice. When Lord Goddard referred to the moment when he had dived off the roof and sustained his injuries by asking: 'How do you know where you landed if you were unconscious?'

Craig answered, 'Because I am quite a good diver, and I have been off a lot of heights.'

Finally, Goddard asked him if he had felt any remorse about what had happened.

'Well, it is all I think about in prison, sir.'

'You may think about it. You were asked whether you ever expressed any regret to anybody?'

'Who is there to express it to, sir?' he returned. When re-examined by John Parris about his intentions on the night that he went out carrying his weapons he denied intending to use them, adding, 'I have never hurt anyone in my life, sir.' These were the last words that Craig would speak at his trial for murder. His fate now lay in others' hands.

When Derek Bentley entered the witness box it immediately became apparent that he was not the intellectual equal of Craig. His illiteracy prevented him from reading the oath, but with the clerk's assistance, he repeated the words. Frank Cassels led him gently into his examination with questions about his association with Craig but he stumbled into trouble when he was asked about the purpose of the bus journey into Croydon on the night of 2 November. Craig had admitted quite brazenly that they were bent on stealing from a butcher's shop; Bentley's misfortunes began when he contradicted his friend's honesty.

Lord Goddard led the assault. 'Where were you going?'

'Just to Croydon, sir.'

'Yes, but what for?'

'Just for the ride, sir, an ordinary ride.'

'Just for a ride?'

'I used to go down to Croydon a lot.'

'What did you jump on a bus for?'

'Well, if we go the other way there is nothing there; it is all quiet, so we went Croydon way, sir.'

'What were you going to do at Croydon?' pressed the Lord Chief Justice.

'Just walk around,' was the lame reply. In his simple-minded way Bentley probably thought that denying their journey had any purpose was smart. The effect in court was a feeling that the youth was not to be believed. Unfortunately for Bentley, he did nothing to dispel that impression while his immersion in lies did everything to reinforce it.

He denied that he and Craig had discussed any arrangement to commit a break-in. He tried to give the idea that he was window-shopping when he realized that Craig climbed over the iron fence at the warehouse.

'I see,' said Lord Goddard; 'Craig got over the fence without saying anything to you, did he?'

'Yes, sir.' Cassels asked him what he did next.

'I followed then, sir.'

'You followed him over the fence?'

'Yes.'

'Why was that?'

'I could not answer that,' said Bentley.

'What?' interjected Lord Goddard.

'I do not know, sir. I just went.'

'Well, you were going to break in, were you not?'

'I do not know why I went over the fence, though.'

'You do not know why you went over the fence?'

'No, sir.'

It was hardly believable; this backward lad carried no credibility in his replies, and he was slowly sinking in a sea of falsehood. His counsel would have done him a service by advising him at least to tell the truth. But even if Cassels had told him what to expect in court, it is difficult to imagine that a youth with an IQ of sixty-six would have fully comprehended such a briefing. Many mature adults would be overawed by court procedure; with his lack of intelligence and failure to exhibit bravado, Bentley was reduced to something approaching panic.

Cassels, as he was bound to do, launched into a creeping barrage of questions which mostly produced simple denials from the witness. 'Did you know that Craig had a loaded revolver?'

'No, sir.'

'Had you seen that revolver which is Exhibit No. 6?'

'No, sir.'

'Did you know at that time that he had a gun?'

'No, sir.'

'When Sergeant Fairfax took hold of you, did you make any effort to struggle?'

'No, sir.'

'Or any attempt to strike him?'

'No.'

'At the time when Sergeant Fairfax got hold of you, did you know that Craig was armed?'

'No, sir.'

'Did you say anything before any shot was fired?'

'No.'

'Did you break away from him once?'

'No, sir.'

'Did you say, "Let him have it, Chris"?'

'No, sir.'

'Up until the time a shot was fired did you know that Craig had a gun?'

'No, sir.' Bentley's examination had become a litany of denials. He steadfastly denied knowing that Craig had a gun, he denied making

81

or remembering any remarks on the rooftop and denied making any reference to a gun after he had been arrested.

Before his ordeal of cross-examination began, Bentley was asked by his counsel about one part of his statement where he had said, 'I didn't know he was going to use the gun.'

'I did not say that.'

'How did that come about?'

'I do not know.'

'Were you asked any questions about the gun?'

'I cannot remember.' The lad was hopelessly out of his depth; he lacked wit or guile and had no taste for defiance.

'Did you at any time tell Craig to use the gun or to use violence towards the police?' asked Cassels.

'No, sir.'

'Did you yourself at any time use any violence towards any of the police officers?'

'No, sir.

Cassels sat down, Parris declined to ask any questions, and the field was open for the prosecutor.

The deficiencies of the youth in the witness-box were unwittingly highlighted when Christmas Humphreys asked him to look at his statement. 'It is no good my looking at that, sir,' he said.

'He cannot read it,' explained the Lord Chief Justice. Counsel read out the lines to which he wished to draw attention; 'I knew we were going to break into the place. I did not know what we were going to get – just anything that was going.'

'That was an answer to a question,' explained Bentley.

'It was written down and read over to you?'

'Yes, sir.'

'And you signed that statement as true?'

'Yes.'

'Did you say it?'

'No, sir.'

'Then why did you sign the statement as true when it was read over to you?'

'Because I did not know what I was signing.'

Any vestige of credibility that Bentley may have had was quickly shredded when he was questioned about the weapons he was carrying. First the knife which he said had been given to him by one of his friends. 'Why were you carrying it on that night?'

'It was in a coat I do not usually wear, sir.'

'Why?'

'I do not know. I just left it in there, sir.'

'Left it in? It would tear the lining to bits, would it not?'

'It does not matter, because it is an old coat.' The jury were being asked to believe that he just put on an old coat when he went to the warehouse which just happened to have a knife in the pocket.

Then there was the knuckleduster. 'And on the way you were given the knuckleduster?'

'Yes, sir.'

'Why?'

'I do not know.'

'You do not know why he gave you the knuckleduster?'

'No, sir.'

'Then why did you take it?'

'Something I have never had, something I had given to me, and I just put it in my pocket.'

'When you got to this warehouse, are you saying you did not know you were going to break in?'

'No, sir.'

Christmas Humphreys elicited another denial when he returned to the alleged incitement of Craig by Bentley. 'So that all three officers who heard you say that are wrong, are they?'

'That is right,' replied Bentley. Asked why he did nothing to stop Craig shooting, he answered, 'That would have been stupid. His mind must have been disturbed. . . . If I had got in his way he might have shot me, sir.' This enabled the prosecutor to finish his cross-examination on the note that Bentley had only been interested in saving his own skin. As Humphreys resumed his seat, Frank Cassels rose to say, 'My lord, that is the case for Bentley.'

Pale and perspiring, Bentley stood down from his ordeal of questions and answers. He had destroyed his by then fragile position with transparent lies and denials. Reginald Paget, Member of Parliament for Northampton and a QC, wrote later in the book *Hanged and Innocent*, of which he was the leading author, 'It would not be correct to say that Bentley made a fool of himself in the witness box – God had already done that for Bentley.' As for Cassels's defence, the least that can be said is that he went through the motions. From the moment he had completed the examination of his own witness, he allowed the prosecutor and judge an uninterrupted barrage of questions. He did not step in to protect or to clarify – there was little passion, vigour or caring. To all intents and purposes Bentley was on his own.

Because of legal questions raised by Craig's defence, Lord Goddard asked the jury to retire early for lunch while he and counsel discussed them. John Parris had structured Craig's defence on the argument that the death of PC Miles was an accident and not a deliberate act. If this proposition went forward to the jury it would leave open the possibility of reducing the charge of murder to one of manslaughter. John Parris recounts in his autobiography how the Lord Chief Justice told him that the law for centuries had been that anyone who caused the death of an officer of justice by resisting arrest was guilty of murder, whether or not the act which resulted in death was committed with the intention of killing or causing grievous bodily harm. Defence counsel cited the case of *Rex v Appleby* (1940), which had some truly remarkable parallels with the case at issue although these were not mentioned. Parris went on to quote *Regina v Porter* (1873) in which a man died as the result of receiving a kick from a prisoner struggling to resist arrest. The jury was directed to consider whether the kick was delivered intentionally. If it was intended to cause grievous harm it amounted to murder; if it was administered during the course of resisting arrest, even if not intended to cause grievous harm, it was still murder. But if the kick was accidental, resulting from a wild struggle, the man would be guilty of manslaughter and not murder.

The Lord Chief Justice responded by asking Parris, 'How, with that statement of the law, can I give any direction to the jury but that this is plain murder?'

Counsel said, 'With respect, in my submission, it is clearly said there "if, in the course of the struggle, he accidentally causes an injury".'

'Causes an injury, yes; but your client admits he was firing a revolver for the purpose of frightening a policeman. That is not an accident.'

'He says he accidentally caused the injury,' persisted Parris, 'and in my submission that should go to the jury.' Christmas Humphreys was asked for his view, which was essentially that there was ample evidence to suggest that Craig was deliberately firing at the police.

John Parris was a fighter, and he stuck doggedly to his task. Lord Goddard was not inclined to give way, and other legal judgments were cited in the continued argument. The argument eventually hinged on Parris's point that it must be the injury which is accidental, not the act itself. 'I think that is a little too subtle for me,' said Lord Goddard. Nevertheless, he proposed that the jury should have the opportunity to consider whether the prisoner shot wilfully, intending to resist arrest, or whether the shooting was accidental. Thus a verdict of manslaughter was possible. There was no disagreement on the law as it applied to Bentley. The jury had to be satisfied that he was aware Craig was armed and that he intended with Craig to offer violent resistance. 'I do not think you quarrel with that, do you, Mr Cassels?'

'No, I do not, my Lord,' replied Bentley's defence counsel in his sole contribution to the proceedings.

The court reconvened after the lunch adjournment and all eyes were on Christmas Humphreys as he rose to make his closing speech for the prosecution. In order to pre-empt Parris's almost certain use of *Rex v Appleby* to argue that Craig was guilty only of manslaughter, the prosecutor cited the case himself. He first summarized the case for the Crown, which was that Bentley and Craig planned a crime of housebreaking which was their common purpose; they were both armed and had the common intent to resist arrest and to use such violence as they thought might be necessary.

Referring to the Criminal Appeal Reports for 1940 in respect of *Rex v Appleby*, he quoted, 'Where two persons engage in the commission of a crime with a common design of resisting by violence arrest by an officer of justice, they have a common design to do that which will amount to murder if the officer should be killed in consequence of resistance. If, therefore, an officer of justice is killed in such circumstances, both persons are guilty of murder.' He put it to the jury that the circumstances in which Craig shot PC Miles met the necessary criteria to make the act one of murder.

The prosecutor acknowledged inconsistencies in the evidence given by the police, 'some heard some phrase which others did not hear, and some remembered a particular phrase slightly differently.' He excused this on the grounds that the gun-fight took place in darkness, and that excitement was running high. As the Lord Chief Justice had done earlier in the proceedings, he used the circumstances of the event to condone inconsistency. The same flexibility was not extended to Craig's evidence: 'There is darkness, and he is shooting in different directions, and he is asking you to say that it was an accident, and by accident only, that he killed one officer and wounded another.'

When he came to the moment of the fatal shot Humphreys elected for an emotional statement. He quoted Craig, 'I saw the door fly open and thought someone was coming out, so I fired again to frighten.'

'To frighten!' exclaimed counsel, 'a boy of sixteen to frighten police officers when he knew the place was surrounded, who were closing in upon him! To frighten! Out of nine bullets that he fires he hits two human beings, and there is a not very wide miss of a third helpless target [PC Harrison] lying on the roof. That is his story. Do you believe it?'

In concluding that part of his speech devoted to Craig, Humphreys told the jury, 'I ask you to say it is beyond argument.' Then he turned to the case against Bentley, which he acknowledged was 'quite a different proposition'. He reminded the jury that although the two were charged together inasmuch as they shared a common purpose – as the result of which a police officer was killed – a separate verdict had to be found against each. Counsel said that he had put it forward in Bentley's favour that 'during the actual murder of PC Miles he was physically under arrest' but that Bentley had contradicted this in his evidence, saying he was not being held at the time.

Counsel told the jury it was quite clear that Bentley 'was in a common enterprise of crime with Craig'; he had admitted that he knew they were going to break into the warehouse. 'The all-important matter for you to consider,' emphasized Humphreys, 'is the evidence that he knew that Craig had upon him a loaded gun.' Then there was the deliberate incitement which began the shooting. 'Did he, or did he not, say right at the beginning of this incident to Craig while he is with Sergeant Fairfax, "Let him have it, Chris"?' Three police officers heard the remark. 'Therefore,' declared counsel, 'it was shouted.' 'If it was said, what does it mean but that he knew that Craig had a gun, and he was urging him to use it?'; the answer was the bullet which hit Fairfax.

Other remarks attributed to Bentley indicating that he had knowledge of Craig's possession of a loaded gun were exposed by Christmas Humphreys with damaging effect. 'Well, you have got all that evidence of all those officers and Craig's frank admission, against Bentley's bare denial that he did not know that Craig had a gun, and can you believe he did not know it when you have heard from Craig of his boasting and bragging of his great arsenal of guns. . . .' said counsel, 'and a friend he has known for years seems to be the only person who did not know it? Do you believe it?' he asked tellingly. The prosecutor's devastating final speech ended with the statement that Craig had confirmed he had told Bentley he was armed before any shots were fired. 'I repeat', he said, 'the evidence of all the officers and Craig against Bentley's bare word . . . I must ask you,' he told the jury, 'in accordance with the oath that you have taken, to return a

Family photograph of Derek in the garden of his home at Norbury. (*Popperfoto*)

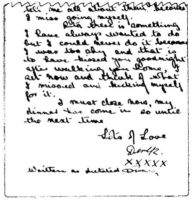

Portion of letter written to Rita on Derek's behalf by a prison officer.

Rita (standing, centre) with the actor Herbert Lom at the Astoria Cinema, Streatham.

Derek's mother arrives at the Old Bailey accompanied by Iris and Denis. (*The Press Association*)

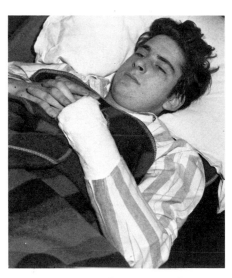

Christopher Craig leaves Croydon Magistrates' Court to a chorus of public abuse. (*The Press Association*)

Craig's family leaves the Old Bailey; his father and mother are on the right and his sister Lucy is standing on the left next to a newspaper representative. (*The Press Association*)

Police Patrol Car 7Z which
responded to Scotland
Yard's message about
'suspects on roof'.
(*Metropolitan Police*)

P.C. Miles, victim of the
rooftop shooting.
(*Popperfoto*)

Detective Sergeant Frederick Fairfax (left) and Detective Chief Inspector John Smith leaving the Old Bailey during the trial. (*The Press Association*)

And this deponent, FREDERICK FAIRFAX,

upon his oath saith:-

    I am a detective constable 'Z' Division, Metropolitan Police, stationed at Croydon.

    At about 9.25 p.m. on 2nd November, 1952, I went with P. c. Harrison and other officers in a police van to Messrs. Barlow & Parker's warehouse at Tamworth Road, Croydon.

    As a result of information given to me by another officer I climbed over an expanding metal gate which was across an entrance at the side of the premises.   I then climbed up a drainpipe at the western wall of the premises.   I think it was

other side we came face to face with Craig.   Craig was then on the westerly side of the stack.   Bentley then broke away from me and as he did so he shouted "Let him have it, Chris."   There was a loud report and a flash and something hit my shoulder which caused me to spin round and fall to the ground.   It was my right shoulder which was hit.   As I was getting up I saw one man moving away on my left and one on my right.   I rushed at the man on my right, who was Bentley and I closed with him and struck him with my fist, causing him to fall to the ground.   As he did so, there was a second report and flash and I dropped down and pulled Bentley in front of me as a shield.

    - 5 -

Section of the sworn deposition made by Detective Sergeant Fairfax.

Barlow & Parker's warehouse in Tamworth Road, Croydon, scene of the break-in and fatal shooting. (*The Press Association*)

The spiked knuckleduster made by Craig and given to Bentley. (*Syndication International*)

Craig's .455 revolver with its shortened barrel. (*Syndication International*)

Lord Chief Justice Goddard.
(*The Press Association*)

Christmas Humphreys,
Counsel for the Prosecution.
(*The Press Association*)

Frank Cassels, Bentley's
Defence Counsel.

People gather outside the Old Bailey waiting for admission to the trial. (*The Press Association*)

NOTIFICATION OF RESULT OF APPLICATION TO THE FULL COURT

REGINA v. **Derek William Bentley** (Appellant)

H.M. Prison **Wandsworth**

THIS IS TO GIVE YOU NOTICE that the Court of Criminal Appeal, as duly constituted for the hearing of Appeals under the Act, has this day considered the Application of the above-named Appellant for:-

(a) Extension of the time within which Notice of Appeal or application for leave to Appeal may be given;

(b) Leave to appeal against **conviction**

(c) Legal aid;

(d) Permission to be present during the proceedings in the Appeal;

(e) Bail;

(f) Leave to call further evidence -

and has determined the same, and has **refused the same**

Dated this **13th** day of **January** A.D.19**53**

A. HIGHMORE KING,
Registrar of the Court of Criminal Appeal

To Her Majesty's Principal Secretary of State
for the Home Department
To the Prison Commissioners
To the Governor of Her Majesty's Prison at **Wandsworth**
To the Clerk of **the Court**
To the above-named Appellant

DS 18750/1 511 ., 500 6/52 DL

Derek Bentley's Appeal is refused; portion of the notification sent to the Governor of Wandsworth Prison.

An angry crowd outside Wandsworth Prison pulls down the notice confirming that Derek Bentley has been executed. (*Popperfoto*) *Inset:* Albert Pierrepoint, Derek Bentley's executioner. (*The Press Association*)

verdict on this indictment of guilty of wilful murder against each of these two young men.'

John Parris rose to his feet to make the speech that the law allowed him in view of the fact that he called no other defence witnesses apart from the defendant himself. His monumental task was to plead Craig's case against a background of public hatred whipped up by the Press and the not inconsiderable prejudice demonstrated in court by prosecutor and judge. But Parris had Northern grit and he took up the challenge with determination. He reminded the jury that they were obliged to decide the case on the evidence, which meant that emotive remarks such as those made by the prosecution – 'Craig gloried in murder' – should be disregarded. He also urged them to dismiss prejudice. 'The tragedy of this trial,' he said, 'is that Christopher Craig has become a symbol of wayward youth; the nation's uneasiness and anxiety about the state of their youth has become focused on him.'

'How do the defence put their case?' asked Parris. 'We do not ask you to acquit him entirely, but we do ask you to say that he is not guilty of wilful murder with malice aforethought, which, in all conscience, is a serious enough crime.' He reasoned that to find the defendant guilty of murder the jury must be satisfied of two things; firstly that an act of his killed PC Miles and, secondly, that there was malice aforethought. Both of these had to be proved to the jury's satisfaction beyond reasonable doubt before a verdict of guilty of murder could be reached. That Craig's action had resulted in the death of a police officer was not disputed; what was at issue was whether or not Craig intended to kill him.

To support his argument that intent was lacking, Parris turned to *Rex v Appleby*, already cited by Christmas Humphreys to demonstrate Craig's guilt. To the ordinary men on the jury, the fact that two lawyers chose to argue starkly opposite points of view from the same case must have appeared farcical with a hint of Gilbert and Sullivan. Parris chose to ignore the emotive route. He might have pointed out that in 1940 two men named Appleby and Ostler attempted to break into a warehouse when they were surprised by the police. Appleby was not armed but Ostler had a gun and fired at one of the police officers after Appleby had shouted, 'Let him have it, he is all alone.' The wounded officer made a dying declaration to a colleague to the effect that Appleby uttered these words. There were extraordinary points of similarity between Appleby and Ostler and Craig and Bentley, but Parris adhered to the legal issues.

He argued that it was open to the jury to return a verdict of manslaughter in accordance with the ruling in *Rex v Appleby*, which stated that if in the course of a struggle an injury is caused accidentally, the outcome would be manslaughter. Counsel pointed out that the court then had not said it was the act which had to be accidental but that if any injury was caused accidentally it would be manslaughter. This was the subtle difference which had defeated the Lord Chief Justice during the earlier legal argument.

Parris painted a picture of Craig as a boy with an inferiority complex (due to his inability to read), who compensated for this by carrying guns with him. In this way he gained the admiration of his school-fellows, and in due course became receptive to the influence of American gangster films. Counsel read out the remarks alleged to have been made on the rooftop by Craig, and equated them with the language used in films. 'Here he is on the rooftop behaving like one of those men he has seen in films – in melodrama, play-acting – dramatizing his position. . . . He saw himself there as a brave crook surrounded by the police, whereas he was only a silly little misguided fool.'

Defence counsel then turned to a careful analysis of the evidence given by the police officers, pointing out the contradictions and inconsistencies. McDonald and Harrison were at odds in their description of where Craig was standing when he fired in Harrison's direction. Harrison thought he heard a bullet strike the chimney-stack behind him, yet there was no evidence of a bullet-mark on the brickwork. Nor was there any sign of a bullet-mark near the stairway door despite the statement from one of the officers that he heard a bullet strike close by. Parris swiftly moved on to the bullet which hit Fairfax, causing a superficial wound, and reminded the jury that Dr Jaswon had indicated the upward flight of the bullet. 'I invite you,' said Parris, 'to have a look at that jacket; I think it is Exhibit No. 17, and I hope you will have an opportunity of considering it.' Counsel proposed that although Fairfax claimed the shot struck him from a distance of six feet, the ragged nature of the tear in the jacket bore out Craig's contention that he fired at the ground and the bullet ricocheted up; he did not fire at the officer.

Coming to the shot that killed PC Miles, Parris said that, bearing in mind the condition of the revolver and ammunition, the jury might conclude it was 'a tragic, unfortunate, million-to-one shot, because Mr Nickolls told you that at that range of thirty-nine feet the weapon would be inaccurate by at least six feet.' He asked the jury if everything they had heard about the events of that night was not consistent with Craig's story that it was an unhappy, miserable, tragic accident that PC Miles was even injured. At this point the Lord Chief Justice intervened to tell Counsel that he believed it only right he should tell the jury that the defence of accident was not open to the defendant. 'My Lord,' said Parris, 'the Defence base it on the case of *Rex v Appleby*.'

'You have misread it,' retorted Lord Goddard.

Parris stood his ground, quoting the 1940 ruling, 'if in the course of a struggle, he accidentally caused an injury. . . .'

He was cut off by the judge; 'A man does not accidentally cause an injury if he shoots. The act has got to be accidental.'

'As I understand it,' replied counsel, 'it was the injury which has to be accidental.'

Concluding his speech, Parris said, 'Members of the jury, it is said on behalf of the Defence that this was an accident, a tragic accident, and not a deliberate act of murder. May I conclude with one final thing? If this boy had had the intention to murder police officers, as is suggested, why did he not kill Sergeant Fairfax when Sergeant Fairfax was within three feet of him, or six feet, on two occasions? I ask you if possible, members of the jury, to return in this case a verdict of manslaughter, which, in the submission of the defence, would be consistent with justice and law.' John Parris had made the most powerful defence he could with the materials at his disposal. It had been a fighting speech and one full of commitment and objectivity.

When Frank Cassels got to his feet to make his closing speech for Bentley there were in truth few options open to him at this late stage in the trial. His best hope lay in trying to put before the jury the mitigating circumstances of his client's involvement in the affair. First, he reminded members of the jury that they were bound to return a separate verdict on each of the accused. He also pointed out there was no suggestion that Bentley at any time had a gun and it was clear that the shot which killed PC Miles had been fired by Craig. If, therefore, the jury found that the killing was accidental and brought in a verdict of manslaughter against Craig, they could not then find Bentley guilty of murder.

There is no doubt, said counsel, that at some stage the two youths agreed to go into the warehouse for the purpose of theft; that amounted to common design to commit the offence of felony by warehouse-breaking. 'But before you can convict Bentley of the offence with which he is charged,' he went on, 'you have to be satisfied that at some time prior to the fatal shot being fired there was an agreement between the two of them – not necessarily so many words being spoken, but an implied agreement between the two of them that in order to commit this offence, or in order to prevent their arrest for the commission of this offence, violence should be used to resist arrest.' Applying this consideration to the facts of the case involved two questions; did Bentley know that Craig had a gun and, with that knowledge, did Bentley incite, counsel or inspire him to use it to resist arrest?

Once again the jury were taken through the events that occurred on the warehouse roof on 2 November. Counsel asked them to remember that at no time did Bentley offer violence towards any of the police officers, nor did he make any concerted effort to join Craig. That might be judged as unusual if he was indeed combining with Craig to resist arrest. Cassels pursued this, pointing out that Bentley had a wonderful opportunity during the confusion caused by the shooting to go to the assistance of his armed colleague or to take some violent action of his own. 'He did not do anything of the kind, members of the jury, and that is what you have to consider in this case, just as much as you have got to consider the various remarks ascribed to him either on the rooftop or subsequently when arrested.'

Regarding the shout attributed to Bentley and heard by all three police officers on the roof, 'Let him have it, Chris', Cassels said it was 'the all-important remark in this case'. 'I venture to suggest to you,' he continued, 'that if you are not satisfied that that remark was made by Bentley, it will go a long, long way in helping you to come to a decision as far as Bentley is concerned.' He omitted to mention that one of the officers, PC McDonald, even though pressed by the Lord Chief Justice, was unsure whether it was Bentley who said it or not.

Next, defence counsel drew the jury's attention to the fact that Bentley was armed to the extent that he was carrying a knuckleduster and a knife. Cassels rightly scorned the prosecutor's emotive description of the knife as a 'murderous dagger' when 'a small sheath knife' was a more accurate term. Nevertheless, these were weapons which a man disposed to violence might use. The prosecution contended that Bentley was at one with Craig in the agreement to use violence, yet there was not a single piece of evidence to show that he did so. The weapons he was carrying remained in his pockets. 'In my submission,' said Cassels, 'when you have formed in your mind a picture which indicates that a man has the opportunity to use violence if he so desires and he does not use violence, that is a matter you have to consider.'

Returning to the potentially incriminating remark, 'Let him have it, Chris', defence counsel asked the jury to consider what it meant. 'What is the correct interpretation we should put upon it?' He suggested that the prosecution's assertion that it amounted to incitement was not the only explanation. Could the remark not be linked to another comment, 'I told the silly bugger not to use it', meaning that far from urging his friend to use the gun, he was telling him not to do so. Then there was the phrase attributed to Bentley when he was taken off the roof, 'They're taking me down, Chris', which again had been interpreted as a plea from Bentley to his companion to fire on the police. Bentley might simply have been warning Craig (who was firing indiscriminately) that he might hit him when he was moved to the stairhead. He might indeed only have been concerned for his own skin 'and I suppose you would not hold that against him. . . .' Cassels told the jury.

Concerning the remarks made by Bentley after he had been taken off the roof and was being driven to Croydon Police Station, counsel drew attention to the fact that only two of the police officers present had been called to give evidence. 'We have heard from two of those officers,' he said. 'We have not heard from the third one who was there. You are, perhaps, entitled to wonder why.' This was a reference to PC Alderson, whose non-appearance as a material witness was never explained. It was a great pity that Alderson did not make a statement, because it leaves open the possibility that he might have had a different view from that of his colleagues.

Finally, Frank Cassels came to Bentley's statement and he asked the jury to remember that although the youth was nineteen years old, he could not read and was unable to write more than his own signature. Here was the defence's final opportunity, with the knowledge Cassels possessed, to give the jury a true picture of the mental status of his client. Among his documents were papers detailing Bentley's IQ, the EEG reports and the medical opinions indicating he had suffered from *petit mal* since childhood – everything the jury was entitled to know in order to reach a proper verdict. But the information, which would have put the defendant's pathetic performance in the witness-box into some kind of perspective, was not used. All that Cassels would do was to refer to Detective Chief Inspector Smith's statement that Bentley was below average intelligence and that he was unlikely to have dictated a statement to the police. He suggested the police might have done some 'jogging along' in order to take the statement.

In conclusion, defence counsel reminded the jury that they must make a decision based only on the evidence heard in court and not on any preconceived ideas or newspaper reports. 'Members of the jury,' he said, 'in my submission, considering fairly and squarely the whole of the evidence forming a picture in your own minds of what took place on that roof that night, it has not been proved with that satisfaction which you should have in a case such as this that Bentley is guilty, and I am asking you to say he is not guilty of murder.'

It was 3.25 p.m. when Cassels sat down and all that remained before the jury retired to consider their verdict was the Lord Chief Justice's summing-up. Earlier in the day, counsel had been advised that the judge intended the court should sit until a verdict had been reached, but, come the moment, he changed his mind. 'Gentlemen of the jury,' he said. 'I never like, in so serious a case as this to start a summing-up in the evening and then to resume it in the morning, so we will adjourn now until tomorrow morning at 10.30.' For whatever reason Lord Goddard made this decision, it was an action that helped no one, least of all the jury. The break in continuity was detrimental to their understanding of the contradictions and ambiguities in the evidence, which defence counsel had exposed. Frank Cassels had already observed that it was unlikely members of the jury could accurately transcribe evidence given half an hour previously. It was surely an exaggeration on the judge's part to describe 3.30 in the afternoon as 'in the evening'. In any case, as John Parris later pointed out, the court normally sat until after 4 p.m. so that there was a good chance that the judge could have completed his summing-up that day. In fact, he took only about forty-five minutes to deliver his speech the next morning.

Had the trial been completed on the second day – and it could well have been concluded by 5.30 – the jury would have been able to retire and begin their deliberations straight away instead of having to wait overnight for the completion of the trial. There are those who believed that had the jury retired at the end of the second day they would have reached a verdict of manslaughter on Craig and hence of not guilty for Bentley. But fate and the whim of the judge dictated a different course of events.

'On the third day,' wrote William Bentley in his book, *My Son's*

Execution, 'I was told that the Lord Chief Justice was about to begin his summing-up. Would I like to go into court?' He took his wife's hand and realized that she could not face the prospect. Arm in arm, they left the building, their dutiful daughter Iris following behind. 'It was a grey, wretched day,' wrote Bentley; 'the misery of life over-whelmed me.' He was still clutching his son's overcoat.

Inside Number Two Court, at 10.30 a.m., the Lord Chief Justice opened proceedings on an irritable note. 'Members of the jury and all persons within my court,' he began, 'I feel it is right for me to say that during the late afternoon when the jury were leaving this court with an usher, a member of the public approached a member of the jury and asked him what he thought of the case and what might be the verdict.' The juror in question had sought guidance and Lord God-dard now made it clear that this was a serious matter which was tantamount to contempt of court and was punishable with an imme-diate custodial sentence. Having made his point to a silent court, he said he would let the matter pass, warning that he would take action if such an incident occurred again. It was noted that one of the Press reporters who had been present throughout the case was absent from his place.

Having disposed of this matter, the Lord Chief Justice began his charge to the jury, telling them that it was a terrible case and one that should be approached 'in as calm a frame of mind as we can'. As he proceeded with his summing-up there were moments when his Lordship's own calmness of mind seemed to have deserted him. He dismissed the influence that films or comics might have on young people, making the point that Bentley and Craig were over fourteen years of age and responsible under law. 'It is surely idle to pretend,' he said, 'that a boy of sixteen does not know the wickedness of taking out a revolver of that description and a pocketful of ammunition and firing it when he is on an unlawful expedition and the police are approaching him.'

First he dealt with Craig, about whom he said it was not disputed that he fired the shot which killed PC Miles. 'You are asked to say that the killing was accidental, and that therefore the offence is reduced to manslaughter,' he told the jury, and instructed them in 'the considerations of law which apply'. He then dealt at length with the law governing murder of police officers, in the course of which he used as an illustration a ruling drawn up for the *Regina v Porter* case in 1873 by Mr Justice Brett, an eminent Victorian judge who later became Viscount Esher. The case as Lord Goddard described it involved the death of a police officer as the result of a kick. Mr Justice Brett told the jury that if the prisoner delivered the kick intending to cause grievous bodily harm and death resulted, he was guilty of murder. If the kick was inflicted without intending to cause grievous injury but in the course of resisting arrest, the result was still murder. But if the kick arose unintentionally in the course of a struggle, the outcome was manslaughter.

The Lord Chief Justice extrapolated from this case to that of Craig and Bentley, whom he said were bent on committing a felony so that their attempted arrest by police officers was lawful. '. . . therefore, if in the course of a lawful arrest the prisoner does an act which kills the police officer, that is murder, unless the act – that is, the firing of the pistol – was accidental . . . Now,' he asked, 'was it a wilful act which caused the injury?' The question was not whether the result was accidental in the sense that more harm was caused than was intended. 'A person who is doing such things as firing off a revolver at police officers cannot say: "Well, it was an accident that I killed him because I never intended to kill him." The answer is: "You were doing a deliberate act, a wilful act".' Lord Goddard's example was not as well chosen as he thought, for he was in error when he described the man killed by a kick as a police officer. The dead man was in fact a member of the public. It hardly made a great deal of difference to the jury, but they might reasonably have expected when being instructed on the law by the Lord Chief Justice of England that he would get his facts right.

Next, he turned to Craig's use of the revolver on the warehouse roof, reminding the jury that the youth fired, or attempted to fire, eleven times in all, necessitating reloading. 'If that is not a deliberate act, a deliberate firing, it is difficult to understand what would be.' Referring to the shots which injured Fairfax and killed Miles, the judge said, 'The aiming does not seem to have been bad, does it? – three shots, two police officers hit, one fortunately slightly, the other hit between the eyes, so that blood gushed out and he fell dead instantaneously.' Apart from the dramatic language, the Lord Chief Justice was again in error. Fairfax in his cross-examination had said the fatal shot was either the seventh or the eighth (in fact it was the fifth), but the judge seemed unclear about the sequence of shots and remained so throughout the entire trial. What is more, as his subsequent remarks proved, he didn't think it mattered! 'Before you can reduce this case to manslaughter,' he told the jury, they had to find 'that the shooting was accidental, not that the result of the shooting was accidental.'

Now Lord Goddard turned his attention to Bentley, reminding the jury that 'these two youths are tried together, and they are tried for the murder of the policeman'. He said it was unnecessary where two persons were engaged in a criminal act to show that 'the hand of both of them committed the act'. Using a simple illustration, he said that where two men were, for example, house-breaking it was common practice for one to keep watch while the other carried out the looting. The guilt of the watcher was no less than that of the looter – in the eyes of the law, both were equally guilty of the crime of house-breaking. Moreover, if one knew that the other was carrying a weapon and there was agreement to use violence to resist arrest which resulted in killing, both were guilty of murder. It was no answer for one to say, 'I did not think my companion would go as far as he did.'

'The first thing that you have got to consider,' the jury were told, 'is: did Bentley know that Craig was armed?' Lord Goddard asked, 'Is it not almost inconceivable that Craig would not have told him, and probably shown him the revolver which he had?' Then there was the knuckleduster, 'Have you ever seen a more horrible sort of weapon?' he exclaimed, brandishing the article and struggling to fit his hand into it. 'You can kill a person with this, of course . . . did you ever see a more shocking thing than that? . . . you can have it to see, if you like . . . it is a shocking weapon.' Lord Goddard's obsession with this 'shocking weapon', as he chose to call the knuckleduster, rather obscured the fact that while Bentley certainly had the article in his possession, he neither brandished it on the rooftop nor attempted to threaten with it.

The most serious piece of evidence against Bentley was his shout to Craig, 'Let him have it, Chris', if you believe it. 'Gentlemen,' Lord Goddard said, 'these words are sworn to by three police officers – Sergeant Fairfax, PC McDonald and PC Harrison; they all swear that they heard Bentley call that out, and that then the firing started.' Not for the first time, the Lord Chief Justice was in error, for McDonald had not said that he heard Bentley call out. Nevertheless, he pressed on, saying that if the remark were true it was 'the most deadly piece of evidence against him'.

Lord Goddard then moved on to the moment after Bentley was arrested and put into a car for the journey to Croydon Police Station. The youth had said, 'I knew he had a gun, but I did not think he would

95

use it.' This was sworn to by two police officers, said the judge, omitting any reference to the third officer who had been present but unaccountably not asked to give evidence. If he knew Craig had a gun and knew he was taking the gun for protection in their common unlawful enterprise, or to prevent arrest by violence, 'Bentley is as guilty as Craig; he is as guilty in law as Craig.' Again, the reference in Bentley's statement, 'I didn't know he was going to use the gun' indicated he knew his companion was armed. 'What had he got the gun for,' asked the judge, 'and what did Bentley think he had the gun for?'

And so the Lord Chief Justice came to the climax of his charge to the jury. In the case of Craig he said, 'I have pointed out to you the difficulties that there are in accepting manslaughter. Manslaughter can only be accepted here if you think that the whole thing was accidental. How it can be said to be accidental I confess seems to me to be extraordinarily difficult.' In the case of Bentley he said the defence was that he did not know Craig had a gun and a denial that he incited him to use it. Against that denial was the evidence of three police officers who have sworn that the words 'Let him have it, Chris' were used. Reminding them of their duties and obligations, Lord Goddard asked the members of the jury to consider their verdict.

Before they retired, one further piece of drama was to unfold in Number Two Court. John Parris invited Lord Goddard to correct a mis-statement of fact. He referred to the Lord Chief Justice's assertion that it was the third shot which had been the fatal one. Parris pointed out that Fairfax had said as much in his deposition but had corrected it under cross-examination, saying the shot that hit PC Miles had been preceded by six or seven others. The judge's reaction to this after searching his notes showed a characteristic disregard of the facts. 'It may not have been the third,' he said. 'It may have been the fourth, it may have been the fifth, it may have been the sixth. I do not know that it very much matters. . . .'

Having dismissed a point of accuracy as of no consequence, he turned to the jury and asked them to consider their verdict. Then he inspired one of the most controversial moments of the trial by asking the jury if they wished to take any of the exhibits with them into their room. The foreman of the jury answered, 'My lord, I would like to see Sergeant's Fairfax's coat and waistcoat.' The Lord Chief Justice's face coloured with fury and in a raised voice he said, 'Yes, you will remember, of course, gentlemen, you are not considering the wounding of Sergeant Fairfax. You are considering the murder of a policeman.' As he spoke, he raised his hand on which he had earlier placed the knuckleduster and smashed it down on to the bench.

In the official transcript of the trial proceedings, the word 'murder' does not appear and the sentence reads differently, mentioning 'the death of Police Constable Miles'. Fenton Bresler, in his 1977 biography of Lord Goddard, wrote of this incident, 'It would have been grievously improper if the presiding judge had referred to "the *murder* of a policeman" before the jury had brought in their verdict.' Bresler asked Christmas Humphreys some years after the trial if he recalled the judge's remarks on this occasion, but he said that he could not remember. In his book on the case David Yallop had mentioned the name of a young barrister, Anthony Samuelson, who was present at the trial and witnessed Lord Goddard's outburst. While researching his biography of the Lord Chief Justice, Fenton Bresler contacted Anthony Samuelson and asked him about the incident. Mr Samuelson said the incident was indelibly imprinted on his mind because he felt that, guilty or not, Bentley was not seen to be getting a fair trial. The barrister did not think it mattered too much whether the judge used the term 'murder' or 'death' in referring to the demise of PC Miles, but what upset him was the 'unjudicial and partisan manner in which Goddard said what he said and the fact that he said it not to the whole jury, but to less than half of them'. The passage of time and professional respect for an eminent figure of the Bench perhaps combined to dilute criticism of Lord Goddard. John Parris, however, was quite sure that his Lordship used the word murder.

Goddard's loss of control and reference at such a sensitive stage in the proceedings to the 'murder' of a policeman was unforgiveable, even though most of the jury had gone out. The time was 11.15 a.m.

7

'I've got nothing on my conscience'

While the jury were out, the Lord Chief Justice remained in court to hear another case. By a strange irony, the defendant was Norman Parsley, Christopher Craig's friend who had called with Frank Fazey at the Bentley home on 2 November and asked Derek to go out for a walk. The walk had turned into a nightmare for Bentley but Parsley, aged sixteen, had also trodden a path of violence with Craig. He was now on trial for the time he and Craig had threatened with a revolver the elderly couple who owned a greengrocer's shop, with the intention of committing robbery. Lord Goddard told the defendant that if he had been over twenty-one he would have been sent to prison for twelve years. 'I, and other judges,' he told him, 'will do our best to let young men know what will happen to them if they do this sort of thing.' He sentenced Parsley to four years' imprisonment; 'Take him down,' he ordered.

After the jury retired people rushed out of court and pushed past the Bentley family, whose vigil in the corridor was nearly over. 'We walked up and down,' said William Bentley, 'unable to control our nerves.'

The whole family was present when their solicitor asked Bentley if he would like to go into court to hear the verdict. 'I don't think the jury will be long,' he said.

Bentley consulted his wife, and she encouraged him to go in. 'I had to brace myself for the ordeal,' said Bentley, 'though inwardly I believed that Derek would be cleared of the charge of murder, of which I knew him to be innocent.'

Fortified by an early lunch, the jury told the court usher at 12.20 p.m. that they had reached a verdict. A bell rang throughout the court buildings, signalling to all present that it was time to draw near and give their attendance. The court was crowded, and an usher escorted William Bentley to a seat next to his son's counsel. His wife, together with Iris and Denis, had gone to a café to await the verdict. 'I prayed silently,' he said, 'saying the Lord's Prayer over and over again . . . there were moments of panic when I felt that I was going off my head . . . my wristwatch seemed to have stopped.' Time dragged by but by 12.30 everyone was seated. The judge took his chair, placing on the Bench his white gloves and a square of black silk. The defendants stood white-faced in the dock; a fly buzzed round in the still atmosphere and settled on Craig's jacket. William Bentley sat nervously clutching a damp handkerchief, waiting for the clerk of the court to speak. Walking up to face the foreman of the jury, the clerk asked, 'Members of the jury, are you agreed upon your verdict?'

The foreman replied in a firm voice, 'We are.'

'Do you find the prisoner Christopher Craig guilty or not guilty of murder?'

'Guilty.' There was a gasp of dismay from the public gallery; Mrs Craig seized her husband by the arm.

'Do you find the prisoner Derek William Bentley guilty or not guilty?'

'Guilty, with a recommendation to mercy.'

William Bentley's instinct was to rush out of court, but he was nudged back into his seat. The clerk continued, 'You find both prisoners guilty, and that is the verdict of you all?'

'It is,' replied the foreman.

The jury would have been well aware, as was the public generally at a time when capital punishment was the ultimate penalty, that they could make a recommendation to mercy. Although the judge could, if there were special circumstances, instruct the jury that they could make such a recommendation, in this case Lord Goddard had evidently decided not to do so. The recommendation was noted by the trial judge for later reference in the event that the Home Secretary might grant a reprieve. However, it could not affect the judge's sentencing.

The time-honoured formula was now played out. 'Christopher Craig', said the clerk, 'you stand convicted of murder; have you anything to say why sentence should not be passed according to law?' There was no reply. 'Derek William Bentley, you stand convicted of murder; have you anything to say why sentence should not be passed according to law?' There was no reply. A palpable silence descended on the court as the black silk square was placed on the head of the Lord Chief Justice. Bentley, still wearing an overcoat despite the warmth of the court-room, stood blinking in incomprehension at the ritual of which he had become the focus. He ached to be free of these events of which he understood so little; surely now they would let him go home and feed his rabbits?

'Derek William Bentley,' intoned the judge, 'you are nineteen years of age; it is my duty to pass upon you the only sentence which the law can pass for the crime of wilful murder. The sentence of the Court upon you is that you be taken from this place to a lawful prison, and thence to a place of execution, and there you suffer death by hanging, and that your body be buried within the precincts of the prison in which you shall have been last confined before your execution; and may the Lord have mercy upon your soul. Take him down.' Bentley stood ashen-faced, and stumbled slightly as he was ushered from the dock.

The black silk square was removed from the Lord Chief Justice's head, and he passed sentence on Craig. 'Christopher Craig, you are under eighteen, but in my judgement and evidently in the judgement of the jury you are the more guilty of the two. Your heart was filled with hate, and you murdered a policeman without thought of his wife, his family or himself; and never once have you expressed a word of sorrow for what you have done. I can only sentence you to be detained until Her Majesty's pleasure be known. I shall tell the Secretary of State when forwarding the recommendation of the jury in Bentley's case that in my opinion you are one of the most dangerous young criminals who has ever stood in that dock.

'While the jury were out considering their verdict in this case, I had to deal with another case in which you were concerned with another boy whom you led into it in holding up an elderly couple at the point of revolvers and stealing from them; and it is quite obvious that the people in this country will not be safe if you are out of prison. I shall recommend the time which I suggest to the Secretary of State that you shall be kept in confinement. The sentence upon you is that you be kept in strict custody until the pleasure of Her Majesty be known. Take him down.'

As the newspaper reporters made a rush for the telephones to inform their editors of the verdicts, Craig smiled in the direction of his parents and then disappeared down the steps to the cells below. The Lord Chief Justice now called forward to the Bench the three police officers who had featured in the rooftop shooting. Fairfax, McDonald and Harrison stood with their Chief Inspector, and the judge praised the men of 'Z' Division for their actions. 'They are all deserving of the highest commendation; but I have asked these three officers in particular to stand forward as they showed such commendable courage on that night ... the thanks of all law-abiding citizens ought to be tendered to you.' Their praise was richly deserved. They had shown great bravery and determination in carrying our their duty under the most hazardous conditions, particularly after one of their colleagues had been killed.

Craig's family left the Old Bailey as they had arrived – in a Rolls-Royce. They were entertained to dinner that evening by the newspaper which was looking after them. Photographs were taken and champagne was drunk. Later they were taken to a hotel at Shepperton where they provided details for an article to appear in the Sunday edition. William Bentley also left the court by the same means that he arrived – on foot. He stumbled out into the grey light of a November afternoon, 'sobbing inwardly' as he put it later, to meet his wife and children who were still waiting in the café. He braced himself, taking consolation from the jury's recommendation to mercy.

Lilian Bentley with Iris and Denis were sitting at a table with empty cups in front of them. 'Well, Will?' asked Mrs Bentley.

'They've found him guilty, but it will be all right. The jury have recommended him to mercy.'

She broke into tears, and Iris sobbed with her; Denis huddled up to his mother. 'Is it bad, Dad?' asked the ten-year-old.

'Not so bad, son. It might be worse,' replied his father.

The forlorn family collected themselves together and called a taxi to take them home. The bold headline in the *London Evening Standard* said it all, 'Craig To Be Held – Bentley To Hang'.

The *Sunday Express* in its editorial of 14 December reconstructed 'the crime that has stunned the nation'. Describing the nineteen minutes that led to murder, the article mentioned that guns were issued to six police marksmen. David Yallop took this up in his researches on the case and suggested that PC Miles might not have been shot by Craig at all but by a bullet from another gun. By the time that PC Miles was poised to burst through the door on to the warehouse roof, six armed policemen were in positions overlooking the scene. They gained access to their vantage points by going through houses and gardens in Tamworth Road.

There is no doubt that Craig fired four shots and only four shots before the fatal bullet hit PC Miles. Yet in his evidence at the Old Bailey, Sergeant Fairfax said there were eight or nine shots before the fatal one, and PC McDonald said there were at least six. The extra shots were not fired by Craig, so they must have been discharged from the only other guns trained on the roof – those in the hands of the police. The likelihood of Craig striking PC Miles at a distance of thirty-nine feet with a clean hit from his shortened .455 with its undersized bullets was a 'million to one' event. Whereas a police .32 using ammunition of the correct calibre might be expected to cause precisely the type of wound that killed poor Miles. It is not inconceivable that the policeman's death was an accident and that it was not Craig who pulled the trigger. The fatal bullet was never found, and no official account was ever given regarding the issue of guns to the police that night or, more importantly, a record of the shots fired.

This line of speculation has remained largely unchallenged but our recent research, which included an interview with PC Stuart Lowe, who was present at the time and witnessed Craig jump from the roof, has confirmed that no firearms reached the police officers on the rooftop until after Miles was shot. It seems that the press speculation was completely inaccurate. Two handguns only were issued from the gun cabinet at Croydon Police Station; if more firearms had been required Scotland Yard would have been asked to provide them.

In addition to the police marksmen on the scene that fateful night it has also been suggested that there was a third teenager initially involved in the break-in. John Parris in his book *Most of My Murders* said that five youths had in fact set out for the warehouse. Two thought better of it and turned back after they were thwarted in their original intention of breaking into the butcher's shop for which Bentley had the keys. Consequently, when Mrs Ware looked out of her front-room window opposite Barlow & Parker's warehouse she saw, not Bentley and Craig, but Bentley and the third youth; by that time Craig had already gained access to the premises.

According to Parris's account, the third youth escaped from the rooftop while Craig was occupying the attention of the police after Bentley had been arrested. He climbed on to the sloping roof at the rear of the warehouse and from there dropped to the ground and made off home without being seen. Mysteriously, the *Star* in its report on the shooting incident published on 3 November, carried a Stop Press item saying that 'Police are looking for a third youth believed to be on the roof of Messrs Barlow & Parker's premises when PC Miles was shot.' It is not known where that information originated, but Parris speculated about a police source. Significantly, Bentley's statement contains a denial: 'There was nobody else there at the time.' Why would he have included such a statement unless he had been asked a specific question by the police officers who took his statement?

Parris, whose account was published eight years after Bentley and Craig's trial, said: 'It would be unfair at present to disclose the name of the third youth . . . or to give other details from which he could be identified.' He also claimed that the two youths who had opted out of the original gang of five had been disturbed at the outcome of the rooftop foray and debated whether or not to go to the police. They apparently sought counsel from a school-teacher whom they respected and he advised them that no good purpose would be served by going to the police.

The purpose this information might have served would have been to put an entirely different perspective on Bentley's alleged remark, 'Let him have it, Chris.' As the Lord Chief Justice had been at pains to point out, with one police officer (Fairfax) and two intruders on the roof, the only person who would logically have made such a remark was Bentley. Acceptance of that logic was a major factor in the jury's mind when they found him guilty. If there really was a third youth on the roof at the critical time it was possible that he, and not Bentley, shouted those words to Craig which proved so damaging.

Parris said that Bentley took with him to the scaffold the secret that, had it been disclosed before he appeared at the Old Bailey, might have saved him. 'What he was too stupid to realise was that by covering up in this fashion for the third man, he was convicting himself.' Two hours before his life ended, Derek dictated a letter to his parents in which he included this sentence: 'I tell you what Mum the truth of this story has got to come out some day, and as I said in the visiting box that one day a lot of people are going to get into trouble and I think you know who these people are.' If Bentley knew there was a third youth on the rooftop, he did not tell Frank Cassels and Parris believed he did not tell his parents until the eve of his execution. One other factor concerning Bentley's alleged incriminating remark is that, according to his father, he never addressed Craig as Chris but always as 'Kid' or 'Kiddo'. This was later confirmed by Mrs Craig, following a visit to her son in Wormword Scrubs prison and she told William Bentley that it was so.

Ultimately, this all proved academic. There was no substantiation for the suggestion that there was a third man on the roof and there seems little doubt that Bentley normally called his friend Chris. Doubtless, nicknames were used by the group of cinema-loving youths and 'Kiddo' may have been one of them. But at a moment of high drama Derek was far more likely to have used Craig's first name albeit in abbreviated form. In any case the argument was flawed because Bentley was consistently on record referring to Craig as Chris. Furthermore, it takes time and commitment to follow up new lines of investigation, and in that December the forces that shaped people's destinies were busy with other things. The human story the newspapers wanted their readers to see was not how an intellectually sub-normal youth had been convicted of a murder he did not commit but how the parents of the boy who fired on the police had failed in their responsibilities.

Under the heading 'My Failure', Niven Craig, Christopher's father, bared his anguished soul, blaming himself for being too indulgent with his son. 'I should have supervised his leisure,' he wrote, 'Fathers must realize that theirs is the responsibility of seeing to it that their children do something useful with their time.' He acknowledged that they were so consumed with grief over their eldest son and his criminal career that they forgot the youngest. As a result of those disastrous events on 2 November they had received shock after shock about Christopher and the life he was leading. His break-ins, his secret arsenal, his bitter resentment and lack of Christian belief. 'I want to plead with all parents,' Craig senior wrote, 'not to make the mistakes I have made and not to allow love for children to destroy the responsibility they have as parents.'

Distraught though they were, and tortured with thoughts of what might have been, Niven and Edith Craig had time for the widow of the policeman and also for those other parents in distress, the Bentleys. Edith Craig wrote to Mrs Miles a letter full of respect and decent values.

Dear Mrs Miles

I have taken my pen so many times to write to you and put it down again feeling that I did not dare intrude upon your grief. Yet as the days go by I feel I cannot remain silent.

Believe me when I say that when I was first told of this horrible tragedy, my thoughts flew first to you. What could I do? Nothing. What can I say? So little.

I speak for my family when I try to say we are so terribly sorry.

Long after the papers, the public and the world in general will have forgotten your husband and my boy, this unhappy family will still mourn your husband and grieve with you.

Yours very sincerely

Edith Craig

Catherine Elizabeth Miles had been married for nineteen years to 'Milo'. She was no stranger to anxiety over her husband's work. 'A policeman's wife lives in a world where trouble is expected,' she told a newspaper reporter; 'I have always been prepared. He has been in several rough houses you know but "Milo" could always look after himself.' Sadly, it was not her husband's arrival that was heralded by the noise of the front gate opening at 11.20 p.m. on 2 November, but an Inspector to tell her that 'Milo' was dead.

From the moment he stepped out of the dock at the Old Bailey, Derek Bentley was a condemned man. He was taken to Wandsworth Prison, where he was given a full medical examination before being put into one of the condemned cells. These cells were larger than the ordinary ones. Each was furnished with a bunk, which was bolted to the floor, a wooden table and three chairs and there were washing facilities which in a future age would come to be called en suite. On the bed was a set of prison clothes – 'greys', as they were known – which lacked any buttons.

The condemned prisoner was subject to a strict and unvarying regime. Every time he left his cell, for whatever purpose – to exercise or to see visitors – he was strip searched and given fresh clothes. Derek changed into his 'greys' and met the first shift of Capital Charge Warders who would guard and watch over him constantly. There were three shifts and the men were brought in from another prison. Theirs was an obviously distasteful task and at times a harrowing one for in human terms they would become very close to their prisoner, sharing in his most intimate feelings. Condemned prisoners were permitted no extra privileges other than a daily pint of beer, books and newspapers and unlimited writing materials. They were allowed a maximum of ten cigarettes a day or half an ounce of tobacco if they preferred 'roll ups'. Facilities for playing cards, chess and dominoes were available in the cell, and officers were encouraged to join the prisoner in these pursuits in order to keep him occupied and to while away the deadly hours.

It was routine practice for the Prison Governor, Medical Officer and Chief Officer to visit the condemned prisoner twice a day. The

Prison Chaplain, or minister of any chosen denomination he wished to see, had free access, as did his legal advisers and family. Other visitors were permitted at the discretion of the Prison Visiting Committee. Bentley had the same diet as the rest of the inmates with the exception that it was specially prepared by an officer in the kitchen. His food was cut into small pieces to guard against the possibility that he might choke while eating. It seemed important that the man under sentence of death should not be rendered dead by any means other than hanging.

Bentley spent his first night in Wandsworth with only his Capital Charge Warders for company. His parents were bowed down with distress in their home at Norbury. His mother and sister had been put to bed, and the family doctor prescribed sedatives for them. There were messages conveying sympathy from well-wishers, but there was neither sleep nor consolation for William Bentley. 'I stayed up all night trying to think things out,' he wrote later. He comforted himself with the thought that the jury's recommendation to mercy would save his son from hanging. He turned it over in his mind again and again; Derek had killed no one – how could he possibly be hanged? There would be an appeal and that way lay hope but the next step was to see Derek in prison.

When the Bentleys arrived at Wandsworth Prison the following day they were shown into the central visiting room, which was really two adjacent cells with a glass-panelled partition separating the inmate from his visitors. A metal grille in the wall beneath the glass panel carried the sounds of the conversation between the two halves of the room. 'There was no difficulty in hearing,' said William Bentley, 'though the talk sounded rather muted.' Derek looked cheerful enough, which heartened his parents, and after the initial greetings his first questions were about Mrs Miles. 'I want you to get in touch with her and tell her how sorry I am,' he told his father. He had heard that despite her grief Mrs Miles had expressed the opinion that Derek Bentley should not die. 'I'm not going to die, of course,' said Derek 'but I want you to thank her for what she said.' Later that day Mr and Mrs Bentley called on Mrs Miles at her home in Shirley, Surrey. She was still too distressed to receive them, but she was told that they had called to express their condolences and appreciation of her remarks about Derek.

As the hours ticked away in the condemned cell, so the administration of the nation's business inevitably ground on. Two days after the trial jury had reached their verdict, a buff envelope bearing the letters OHMS dropped through the letterbox of a house near Preston, Lancashire. The addressee was not at home, and the letter was put on the mantleshelf to await his return. Albert Pierrepoint, when he returned home at about 5.30 p.m., knew the nature of the contents before he opened the envelope. He had received many similar letters since his appointment in 1934 to the Home Office list of 'Persons reported to be competent to act in the capacity of Executioner or Assistant Executioner.' He made a note in his diary for 28 January 1953: 'Wandsworth. Single execution.' The letter from the Secretary of State requested his attendance on that date at HM Prison Wandsworth, and he was asked to present himself to the Governor on or before 4.00 p.m. on the previous day 'to make the necessary arrangements as required by your office'.

The newspapers continued to be filled with stories about Craig. The *Daily Mirror* carried a photograph on its front page of Craig's revolver with a finger on the trigger and the headline 'Craig Killed with this Gun – How many more are there in boys' hands?' Perhaps building on the sins of omission to which Craig's father had confessed, an article in the *Sunday Chronicle* suggested that parents be made responsible in law for crimes committed by their under age sons. This reversed the doctrine regarding 'the sins of the fathers', but it struck a popular chord at the time. This particular article concluded by asking if the law should not be changed so that Christopher Craig could be hanged. The desire for retribution was a strong theme in the press, and journalist Beverley Nichols suggested there were better uses for taxpayers' money than providing the likes of Craig with pain-killing drugs so that he could have his broken wrist set. He wondered if there were not times when 'inhumanity becomes almost an essential duty'. Although the comment was made in reference to Craig, it was to prove prophetic for Bentley.

While the press had been content to court Craig's parents and vilify their son as a thug and a brute, they mercifully left the Bentleys relatively unscathed at this stage. The *Sunday Dispatch* carried a front cover story headlined 'The Untold Story Behind Craig and Bentley'. This contained William Bentley's account of how he had gone to Croydon Police Station in October 1952, eight days before the fatal shooting, to seek advice about the dangerous influence young Craig exerted over Derek and other youths. Bentley had asked the police to warn Craig or to see the boy's parents and alert them. He spoke of his fears, sensing trouble in the future. The police declined to take any action on the grounds that Craig had not broken the law.

The advice went unheeded, and a week later PC Miles paid the price with his life. None of this emerged at the trial – poor William Bentley made no better an impression with the police than he had with the doctors.

As the grounds for Bentley's appeal were being discussed some of those present at the Old Bailey might have thought back to the conduct of the Lord Chief Justice. It was estimated that he inter-rupted the proceedings on some two hundred and fifty occasions, and the transcript made it clear that his interventions were heavily biased in favour of the prosecution. But what of his outburst right at the end of the trial when the foreman of the jury asked to see Sergeant Fairfax's waistcoat and he thundered, 'You are consider-ing the murder of a policeman?!

The official transcript of the trial says Goddard referred to the death of PC Miles but, as discussed earlier, others present were certain he said murder. David Yallop suggested that the judge altered the edited version of the trial in at least one respect. In the volume of *Notable British Trials* devoted to the Trial of Craig and Bentley and edited by H.Montgomery Hyde, the courtroom reference by Lord Goddard to *three* police officers who swore to hearing Bentley's remarks after he was arrested, was altered to *two*. It will be remembered that PC James Alderson who was present at the time with his colleagues, Sergeant Roberts and PC Stephens, was never required to make a statement. Page 204 in the trial volume contains the relevant part of the Lord Chief Justice's charge to the jury where the text reads 'sworn to by two officers', not three as it is reliably recorded he said in court.

These may seem footling matters in a great trial where many thousands of words are spoken, taken down and subsequently transcribed. But when a person's life is at stake every error, especially if it works against the accused, should be critically examined. There is no doubt that both the prosecution and trial judge were mistaken about several basic issues, such as the total numbers of shots fired and the number which preceded the fatal wounding of PC Miles. Even when he was picked up on this, Lord Goddard implied that the number didn't really matter.

Will Bentley Hang? was the question being aired in the newspapers as the nation made its preparations for Christmas. Derek thought he would be reprieved; after all, he had not pulled the trigger, and in simplistic terms that was how the public saw it. The Bentleys visited their son daily, the trips to Wandsworth Prison taking on an almost routine air. Their observation that he wore no tie or belt and that his shoes lacked laces made them realize that his life was controlled by others. Perhaps they did not dwell too much on the thought that he might take his own life.

Derek could hear the sounds of advancing Christmas drifting over the prison walls and into his cell. During the quiet of the long evenings the singing of carols from the surrounding streets mixed with the clatter of trains approaching Clapham Junction. He thought of the childish delight of approaching Christmas and of the stocking filled with presents that always appeared at the foot of his bed. This particular Christmas there would be more presents than ever before; from family and friends anxious to express a kind of solidarity and also from well wishers. But they were destined to remain unopened lying round the Christmas tree.

On Christmas Eve the Bentleys' prison visit had a festive air about it, the place was full of noise and laughter and the warders, in good-natured mood, chaffed Derek. Gesturing to the officers, Derek said, 'They've given me the best cell in the place – haven't you? Why, it's even got a bath in it, Dad.' Later that evening, as the church bells signalled the arrival of Christmas Day, the Bentley family gathered round their Christmas tree at home and prayed. The object of their love and hope lay curled up on his bed in the condemned cell, the grey prison blankets bunched up in his fists around his face. He sobbed quietly. It was a time when everyone wanted to be with their families, not least the officers watching over Bentley. One of the men walked over to the tearful youth to console him. He was beginning to know Derek for what he really was; a backward boy terrified by events which he could not understand. He sat beside him and spoke softly, reassuringly, trying to ease the burden of a tormented soul on this Christmas Day. 'Come on, Derek', he said, 'you'll be all right, mate. Nothing will happen to you. We all have our troubles, too right we do. Look, it's Christmas Day now. Let's have a smile, shall we? Otherwise you'll have me and my mate in tears.'

The lad responded, encouraged by the officer's warm-heartedness. Yes, I'll be all right, he thought, me Dad won't let me down, nor will Uncle Albert. Then he slept.

When they visited on Christmas Day Derek's mother and father took him a large basket of fruit in the belief that condemned prisoners were allowed to have food brought in from outside. To their dismay, the prison authorities told them their son would not be permitted to receive this gift and they took it home with them, where it remained untouched on the sideboard. After Christmas it was announced that the date for Bentley's Appeal had been arranged early in the New Year, on 12 January.

Walking down the Strand a few days before the appeal was due to be heard, Frank Cassels had a chance encounter with Lord Goddard. They spoke about the appeal, and Goddard said, 'Do go easy on me; after all, I am sure the Bench will not overturn my sentence. But the Home Secretary surely will.' The Lord Chief Justice seemed convinced that the youth would be reprieved from the moment he returned home after passing sentence of death. According to Fenton Bresler's biography, he told his housekeeper, 'Well, I had to sentence him to death. But don't worry, he won't be hanged.' Cassels, however, was not so optimistic. He felt that Bentley would hang.

8

'Dad, help me, please help me'

There was no appeal against conviction on behalf of Christopher Craig; he was destined for removal from Wormwood Scrubs to Wakefield Prison to serve out his sentence for ten and a half years. For Derek Bentley, there were two grounds for appeal. Firstly, that the Lord Chief Justice in his charge to the jury failed to put Bentley's defence adquately and, secondly, that the judge failed to ask the jury to consider the question of whether or not the common cause between Craig and Bentley ended at the point PC Miles was shot.

The burden of arguing these points before the three appeal judges fell to Frank Cassels, who in his chance encounter with Lord Goddard in the street had said he did not believe Bentley would be reprieved. Indeed, he believed then as he had from the outset that Bentley deserved to hang. With an unfortunate sense of timing, at least as far as Bentley was concerned, it was announced from St James's Palace on 6 January 1953 – just six days before the appeal was due to be heard – that the Queen had been graciously pleased to make awards to four of the police officers involved in the rooftop battle at Croydon. The citation in *The London Gazette* included a detailed account of the shooting incident which praised the heroism of the police under fire. Sergeant Fairfax was awarded the George Cross, Police Constables Harrison and Mc Donald each received the George Medal and Police Constable Jaggs was given the British Empire Medal. The four men were personally congratulated by Sir Harold Scott, Commissioner of Police of the Metropolis, who commented in his autobiography on Fairfax's matter-of-fact attitude, 'It was part of the day's work. He had done what had to be done.' These awards were extremely well deserved, and, in due course, PC Miles was posthumously awarded the King's Police Medal for Gallantry. It was only their timing that was insensitive when another man's life was at stake.

As they had done throughout the Old Bailey trial, members of the public queued in their hundreds for admission to the Court of Criminal Appeal in the Royal Courts of Justice in the Strand. The appeal was to be heard on 12 January before Mr Justice Croom-Johnson, Mr Justice Ormerod and Mr Justice Pearson but after a delay of several hours their Lordships let it be known that they were detained by another case which necessitated postponing Bentley's appeal to the following day.

On 13 January the crowds turned up at the entrance to the elaborate cathedral-like building which had been constructed in 1880 as a monument to the Victorians' sense of pride in the law. The hearing of *Regina v Derek William Bentley* was listed for Number One Court, a dismal wood-panelled, book-lined room with light-fittings suspended from a faded, dirty ceiling. The three judges, all of whom were junior to the Lord Chief Justice who had tried the case, entered the court from a side door and took their seats. As at the trial, Christmas Humphreys, assisted by John Bass, appeared as Counsel for the Crown.

Cassels began the proceedings with the words, 'If your lordships please', and gave a summary of the Old Bailey trial.

Mr Justice Croom-Johnson responded with, 'We have all read those papers. We are all fully aware of the circumstances of the case, and the point is a short one, is not it?' It was indeed – it concerned a man's life.

Counsel confirmed the brevity of the point and went straight to his first ground for appeal – namely, 'that the learned judge failed adequately to put the Appellant's defence before the jury'. He referred to the paragraph in the summing-up where Lord Goddard had said, 'In the case of Bentley, Bentley's defence is: "I didn't know he had a gun, and I deny that I have said Let him have it, Chris. I never knew he was going to shoot and I didn't think he would." ' 'That', said Cassels, 'was the only reference to the defence of this Appellant.'

Counsel acknowledged that even in a long case the judge is not required to go through the whole of the evidence given on behalf of the accused. Nevertheless, the defence should be adequately put, and if it was not, that amounted to misdirection. He went on to say that while Bentley's defence was partly as stated, there was a further aspect to the effect that he did not use the words attributed to him and that his behaviour according to witnesses was not consistent with that of a person who was acting in concert with Craig. His behaviour was that of a person taking a passive part in the battle and, from the time the second shot was fired, he was in the custody of the police officers on the roof. Referring to the remark allegedly made by Bentley when he was being driven away from the scene in a police car, Cassels said his version was completely different from that given by the two police officers (no mention was made of the third officer). Bentley claimed there was a conversation during which he was asked the name of his companion on the rooftop and the type of gun he was using. He never said that he knew Craig had a gun and did not think he would use it.

Mr Justice Croom-Johnson asked if all this had not been a matter for the jury to consider. Cassels agreed, but argued that it was the duty of the presiding judge where he referred to prosecution evidence on a specific point also to put the defence's denial so that the jury had both sides of the issue. 'In this particular case,' said counsel, 'the learned Lord Chief Justice put before the jury in his summing-up the version given by the two police officers of what took place in the car. . .there is no reference whatever in the summing-up of the Appellant's version. . . .'

Mr Justice Ormerod read out the judge's summary of the defendant's evidence which consisted of thirty-six words. 'Does that cover it?' he asked; 'I agree it is short.'

This was surely an understatement, but Cassels restricted himself to the reply: 'It is the shortest possible description. . .What I say is this: If the Chief Justice had gone into the prosecution's case in the same short way as he went into the Appellant's case, I should have no complaint.' He also pointed out that because the summing-up was not delivered until the third day, the defence evidence, which had been given some twenty-four hours earlier,was not fresh in the minds of the jury.

Frank Cassels dealt next with Bentley's evidence regarding the statement he made and the fact that he could neither read nor write except to sign his name with difficulty. He drew attention to the two phrases, 'I did not know he was going to use the gun' and 'I did not know Chris had one until he shot'. Counsel's point was that whereas the Lord Chief Justice had referred to the police officers' version of these parts of the statement and apparently put it to the jury that Bentley had indeed used these phrases, he did not direct their attention to Bentley's denial that he had spoken those words. Mr Justice Croom-Johnson responded by saying, 'Be it so; this is the sort of controversy that arises in a great number of cases.'

'I appreciate that,' said Cassels.

'What became of this statement; was it eventually handed to the jury?'

'I do not think they did have it when they considered their verdict, though it was in fact available,' answered Counsel. In fact, the jury's deliberations were conducted on the basis of memory, for it had not been deemed necessary to provide them with transcripts of the proceedings.

Cassels agreed with Croom-Johnson that it was a matter for the jury but pressed his contention that in a case where there was disagreement on the content of the defendant's statement, the defence view should be included in the summing-up as well as the prosecution's. 'You do not seem to leave much to the discretion of the judge, do you?' asked Croom-Johnson. 'Surely it is for the learned judge to decide what he is going to lay before the jury, and so long as it is done – I will use an expression of my own which you will not find in the books – fairly and squarely, that is sufficient.'

'I entirely agree,' said Cassels, 'but in my submission, the defence of this Appellant was not put fairly and squarely to the jury.' He added that while the prosecution case covered four or five pages of the summing-up transcript, the defence was constricted to one sentence.

Frank Cassels's second ground of appeal was that while he had no disagreement with the Lord Chief Justice over the law concerning persons acting together, he thought the jury in this particular case should have been asked to consider at what point Craig and Bentley's joint venture finished. The question of whether or not their common purpose ended at the time PC Miles was shot was not put to the jury by Lord Goddard. This argument related to the apparent anomaly that Bentley was regarded as still acting in concert with Craig even though at the time PC Miles was shot Bentley had been under arrest for fifteen minutes. Mr Justice Croom-Johnson said, 'That may be true . . . do not be lulled into a false sense of security . . . were they arming themselves, or was one of them arming himself, with the knowledge of the other, on the basis that they were to resist arrest if apprehended or interrupted in their joint adventure? If that is the right view, it may be the fact that one of them having been arrested does not prevent the matter still being one in which the joint adventure is not over.'

'With respect,' replied Cassels, 'that may well be right in this particular case. My complaint is that no suggestion of that sort was put before the jury during the course of the summing-up.'

'A judge in the course of summing-up a criminal trial cannot deal with every little point,' said Croom-Johnson; 'the judge must be allowed a little latitude, must not he?' Cassels said the point was made at an early stage in the trial that Bentley was under arrest at the time the fatal shot was fired. That was not put to the jury, and there was no way of knowing whether or not they gave it consideration. Mr Justice Ormerod pointed out that Bentley had denied this on oath, an assertion which Cassels corrected. 'He said on oath that he was not being held all the time.' The evidence was that he was held by Fairfax up to the moment that PC Miles was shot; he was then released when Fairfax went to the aid of his colleague. Cassels completed his submission on this note, saying that he was satisfied with the rest of the summing-up and had no disagreement with the way the Lord Chief Justice had put the law to the jury.

Christmas Humphreys now joined the debate, commenting on what he called 'the negative type of defence' put forward by Bentley, which was that the prosecution had not proved its case. That being so, he argued that the 'fact that the Chief Justice took only a few lines to say it is perfectly reasonable, in as much as he might have said: "Bentley's case is that it is not true".' As to the dispute over what was said by Bentley in the police car, Humphreys believed the Chief Justice had made the prosecution case quite clear to the jury, and had said that it was disputed. Prosecuting counsel then turned to the oft-quoted remark attributed to Bentley, "Let him have it, Chris", which he claimed was far more important than the later 'They're taking me down, Chris.' The jury had to consider, if he did make the first remark, whether it did not show, firstly, that he knew 'Chris' was armed and, secondly, was calling on him to use violence to prevent arrest. 'So the Chief Justice is saying,' contended Humphreys, 'the arrest point does not matter very much one way or the other, and is certainly not putting it against Bentley.'

Mr Justice Croom-Johnson asked, 'You mean by that, that whether he was under arrest, he was still acting in the joint enterprise?'

'That was the case for the Crown,' replied Humphreys, 'and is today.'

Responding to the matters raised by prosecuting counsel, Frank Cassels took his learned friend to task for saying that Bentley's alleged remark, 'They're taking me down, Chris', was followed by further shots. 'That was not the evidence', he declared emphatically, quoting Fairfax's replies to Humphreys's questions at the trial.

Mr Justice Croom-Johnson's lame reply was 'I do not know' and he appeared to endorse all the previous confusion about the number of shots by his next remark. 'I have been looking through this shorthand note to see if I can satisfy myself as to how many shots were fired and at whom and what; but after struggling for a long time, I am afraid I gave it up, and the Chief Justice in his summing-up points out that it is impossible for anybody to say with accuracy how many shots were fired or how many particular witnesses heard these shots that were fired.'

So, in a case of a fatal shooting, neither the trial judge nor the appeal judge knew how many shots had been fired – it was a struggle, and the effort to find out was abandoned! With this weak admission on the part of the appeal judge and Christmas Humphreys's apology over his earlier mistake, the appeal submissions were concluded.

The discussion which had taken place before the three appeal judges meant little to William Bentley. 'I could not understand what they were trying to get at,' he said. 'All I knew was that my son was innocent of killing. What I could not grasp were the strict rules of legal procedure. The whole affair was conducted like a game of chess. . .thrashing out matters that seemed to me to have no bearing on the issue at all.' In his bewilderment and feeling that the whole proceedings lacked any human understanding, despair crept back into his soul. He left the court and returned only to hear the judgment. 'This was torture,' he said, asking why the judges could not say whether the appeal had succeeded or failed at the outset without first delivering their arguments in full. His agitation was understandable, and he thought the lack of feeling for prisoners and their friends 'seemed barbarous'.

It took Mr Justice Croom-Johnson about ten minutes to read their Lordships' judgment. Ten long minutes before William Bentley's worst fears were confirmed – his son's appeal was dismissed. The judgment is given in full in the Appendices, but in essence the appeal judges believed there was overwhelming evidence on which the jury could consider the question of Bentley's joint enterprise with Craig. As to the suggestion that the trial judge failed adequately to direct the jury, Croom-Johnson said, 'I can see nothing wrong with it, and that is the opinion of the members of this Court. The matter was carefully put, adequately put and properly put by the Chief Justice, and it was then for the jury to decide Aye or No did they accept the prisoner's denials. . . .'

On the matter of whether or not Bentley was still responsible for Craig's action in shooting PC Miles under their joint enterprise, even though he was under arrest, the Court believed, 'that depends on what the jury thought was the joint enterprise'. It was possible to think the affair was over at that point if their common purpose was 'to go out and murder somebody'. But if their purpose was not merely a 'burglarious enterprise' but one in which they determined to resist arrest by arming themselves, the jury might take a different view. Croom-Johnson added, 'It is a little difficult for Mr Cassels because his own client was asked specifically at the hearing whether he was under arrest at the time when this shot which killed Miles was fired. He would not have it. He said he had not been arrested, that he was not under arrest, that the police officer had not detained him, and all the rest of it.' Concluding the judgment, Mr Justice Croom-Johnson spoke the words that vitiated all but extreme measures to save Derek Bentley: 'In our opinion this is nothing more than an ordinary appeal in a murder trial, an ordinary appeal which is, in our judgement, without foundation and which is accordingly dismissed.'

The whole affair had taken about an hour. 'We left the court stunned,' said William Bentley. 'We had gone there knowing our presence would lighten Derek's ordeal.' They had expected to share in a joyous family moment when Derek's conviction was quashed, but their hopes had turned to ashes with those final words of judgment. Seeking to lift his family to a new horizon of hope, William Bentley reminded them of the jury's recommendation to mercy. He told them there was not a case on record where the death sentence had been carried out when a jury had recommended mercy. On that mistaken belief they hung all their hopes.

Commenting on the grounds of Bentley's appeal, John Parris wrote later that the first point, Bentley's denials as against the assertions of the police officers, was 'a common complaint in the Court of Criminal Appeal and rarely succeeds'. On the second issue, that of whether the joint venture between Craig and Bentley ended when PC Miles was shot, he believed the Court of Criminal Appeal was right to reject it but did so for the wrong reasons. Mr Justice Croom-Johnson had said that the difficulty lay in Bentley's assertion that he was not under arrest at the time PC Miles was shot. Parris believed that: 'Almost every word of that part of the judgment of the Court of

117

Criminal Appeal is inaccurate.' The value of his criticism is borne out by reference to Bentley's evidence at the trial. In his evidence-in-chief, he was asked, 'What happened after you got behind the stack?'

He replied, 'Sergeant Fairfax came and took me. . . and walked me across the roof.'

'When Sergeant Fairfax came and took you, did he say anything?'

'He said, "I am a police officer. I've got the place surrounded".'

'When Sergeant Fairfax took hold of you, did you make any effort to struggle?'

'No, sir.'

Later in the proceedings Bentley was asked, 'From that time until you were taken downstairs by the police, did you remain behind the staircase head?'

'I did.'

'Were you being held all the time by police officers?'

'No, sir.'

'Was there anyone to prevent you, if you had wanted, joining Craig?'

'No.'

Prosecuting counsel (who had previously used the term 'technically under arrest') now used the word 'grabbed'. Referring to Sergeant Fairfax's action, he asked Bentley, 'Then he grabbed you?'

'Yes.'

'And you knew you were grabbed by a police officer when you were trying to commit a crime – arrested? You know what that means?'

'Yes.'

Christmas Humphreys went on to ask, 'According to you, when you were over by the staircase head, you were not being held by the police officer. Is that right?'

'That is right.'

'So that you were not under arrest at that time?'

'I was standing there, sir.'

'But you were not being held?'

'No.'

'You were quite free to run if you wanted to?'

'Yes.'

John Parris argued that despite the confusion of words used to describe Fairfax's action in regard to Bentley – that he 'grabbed' him, 'held' him or placed him 'technically under arrest' – it was plain to any reasonable person that Bentley believed he was under arrest even though he was not under physical restraint. He had consistently maintained this, and in Parris's view, Mr Justice Croom-Johnson's version of the evidence was not accurate. Consequently, the basis for rejecting the second ground of appeal was entirely wrong.

If the appeal judges were wrong on this score, they were also sadly adrift on another contentious matter that appeared from time to time throughout the whole case. This was the remark made by Bentley in the police car in which he was driven to Croydon Police Station. His remark was attested to by two of the three police officers present – Lord Goddard had claimed that all three had confirmed the remark, but later altered this to two. In his judgment, Mr Justice Croom-Johnson (who had admitted giving up the struggle to find out how many shots had been fired during the incident) made an extraordinary statement. After saying the Lord Chief Justice had carefully put the matter to the jury, he said it was for the jury to decide. 'Did they accept the prisoner's denials or did they accept the evidence of two witnesses who spoke affirmatively to statements made by the Appellant and, I think, another witness who was not able to give the main evidence, but did depose to hearing the words or similar words spoken by somebody.' The 'other witness' could only have been PC Alderson, who was not called to give evidence and from whom no deposition was ever produced. This remark from the appeal court judge had no substance in fact.

After Mr Justice Croom-Johnson had delivered the Appeal Court's judgment, the Registrar, Mr Highmore King, made his way to one of the offices in the Royal Courts of Justice. His task was to give substance to the judgment. Taking a form DS 18750/1 511, he put it in a typewriter and filled in certain details, crossing others out with a stroke of the pen. This was the Notification of Result of Application to the Full Court which was to be sent to the Governor of Her Majesty's Prison at Wandsworth. It read as follows:

In the Court of Criminal Appeal
Criminal Appeal Act, 1907

REGINA v. Derek William Bentley (Appellant)

H.M. Prison Wandsworth

THIS IS TO GIVE YOU NOTICE that the Court of Criminal Appeal, as duly constituted for the hearing of Appeals under the Act, has this day considered the Application of the above-named Appellant for leave to appeal against conviction and has determined the same, and has refused same.

Dated this 13th day of January AD 1953

A.Highmore King
Registrar of the Court of Criminal Appeal

With several key strokes on the typewriter and a few seconds to delete those parts of the form which did not apply, the Registrar sealed Bentley's fate. Later that day the Governor of Wandsworth Prison entered Bentley's cell. The youth, who was playing cards, rose to meet the Governor. 'Derek,' said Mr Lawton, 'I have to bring you this piece of paper and, under the circumstances, I feel I ought to read it to you.' He read out the result of the youth's appeal. Bentley was stunned to hear that his appeal had failed. 'I am terribly sorry, lad,' said the Governor.

A copy of this document was sent to the Bentleys not, as might have been imagined in light of its importance, by special messenger, but by regular Royal Mail delivery two days later. It arrived with the sacks of letters which were being delivered to 1 Fairview Road, Norbury, SW16. Letters arrived in their hundreds and then in their thousands from ordinary people in the British Isles, and also from abroad. There were cables and telegrams too, all offering sympathy and help, and the GPO installed a telephone in their home so that William and Lilian Bentley could respond to other well-wishers. The public, which had been inflamed at the news of a policeman's death, now turned its sympathy to the young man who was being made a scapegoat. Hope rested in the hands of the Home Secretary, Sir David Maxwell Fyfe, and the prerogative he had to recommend a reprieve.

William Bentley told his son that there was to be a public petition to support the jury's recommendation to mercy. 'Thousands of people were behind you,' he said. 'They're all on your side.' Petition forms were printed each with a space for a hundred signatures, and they were dispatched to helpers throughout the country. Completed forms were returned at speed with requests for more, and people also called at the house asking for forms. The newspapers' correspondence columns bulged with readers' letters arguing that Bentley should be reprieved. Public opinion was running in the condemned youth's favour at an estimated rate of eight to one. There were suggestions about holding 'Reprieve Bentley' marches in London and stickers bearing the protest 'Bentley Must Not Die' began appearing on car windscreens.

The Bentley family was living a busy life at the centre of a campaign that was growing in optimism. His parents visited Derek every day, helping him to keep his spirits up and taking encouragement from his cheery attitude. They spent many hours at the House of Commons talking to Members of Parliament and gaining their support, and there were daily meetings with their son's legal advisers. The feeling was, as William Bentley put it, that 'It is inconceivable that he should not be reprieved.' Back at Fairview Road the telephone never stopped ringing – five hundred calls a day at their peak – and two secretaries volunteered their services to deal with the deluge of letters, for which the GPO organized a special delivery service. The tone of the majority of these communications was that Derek Bentley should be reprieved.

No possible avenue was ignored. Lilian Bentley wrote to the Queen, as one mother to another, and received a courteous acknowledgement by return of post. Her husband wrote to the Home Secretary putting his own plea for mercy, and a telegram was sent to the Prime Minister, Sir Winston Churchill, who was returning to England from the United States on board the liner *Queen Mary*. Many thousands of ordinary men and women, convinced of the injustice of sending a feeble-minded youth to the scaffold, sent letters and telegrams to their MPs and to the Home Office direct.

What began as a groundswell became a tidal wave. Where William Bentley had hoped to secure a thousand signatures on his forms petitioning the Home Secretary to grant a reprieve, he eventually obtained a hundred thousand. On 23 January, William Bentley took his petition to the Home Office. He had forms containing 11,000 signatures in two parcels which he had been advised would be sufficient for the purpose. He arrived in a taxi, having been delayed by the arrival of a last-minute flood of petition forms, and was greeted by newspaper reporters before being ushered into a waiting-room. There a member of the Home Secretary's staff received the two parcels which represented the formidable expression of public opinion, together with Bentley's own letter. 'The secretary was courteous and sympathetic,' said Bentley; 'I thought he seemed distressed.'

Delivering the petition took a mere five minutes, and on leaving the Home Office Bentley read out to the newspaper reporters the contents of a personal letter of appeal to the public.

We appeal to everyone in this country to give careful consideration to the following vital facts in the case of the State versus my son, Derek Bentley.

1. Derek had not been previously engaged in any crime of violence; he was not a hardened criminal; his only previous offence was a minor one for which he had paid.

2. On the night of the crime he was not armed.

3. If he acted in concert with Craig in the dastardly murder of PC Miles, why did he not make use of the knuckleduster to avoid being taken into custody?

4. At the time the shot was fired he was held by Sergeant Fairfax.

5. He did not have any reason to hold a grudge against the police, as did Craig.

6. The words 'let him have it, Chris', if said, could have meant, 'let them have the gun'.

7. If he had not been taken into custody it is likely he might have deterred Craig from the act that has left my boy, and not Craig, in the shadow of the hangman's noose.

8. It had been argued by some that the law should be allowed to take its course in order to set an example to other wrong-doers, but in the name of British justice only why pick on my boy, who has been guilty of a technical offence?

Questioned by a reporter, Bentley urged the public to 'do everything in their power to stop the State taking the course it is now upon', adding; 'Remember, a boy's life is in the balance. No amount of legal arguments or books written afterwards will bring him back to life.' The assembled Pressmen thanked Bentley and a sympathetic member of the public who had been listening told him, 'I beg of you, don't place all your hopes on man's justice.' It was a sensitive yet realistic piece of advice for Bentley's statement had an air of desperation about it.

His words may have been born out of disappointment that another of the few remaining channels of hope had been blocked the previous day. On 22 January had come the news from the Attorney General, Sir Lionel Heald, that permission to grant a fiat to appeal to the House of Lords had been refused. A few days before, on 18 January, John Parris had given vent to a passionate outburst at a public meeting that was to cost him dearly. He was speaking at Bradford as prospective Labour candidate for the North Ward, and decided to address the subject of 'Crime and Punishment'. He suggested that the prevailing mood advocating the reintroduction of punishment by flogging was almost entirely due to Lord Goddard's pronouncements on the subject. Somewhat incautiously, he went on to rebuke the Lord

Chief Justice, saying that 'It is undesirable that anyone holding high judicial office places himself in a position where he must be criticized for political utterances.' He dismissed many of Lord Goddard's contributions to debate in the House of Lords as 'sensational and untrue nonsense, so much so, that many of the members of that House regard them with complete contempt'. All this was reported in detail in the *Yorkshire Post*, and as a result Parris was suspended from practising at the Bar for four months by the Masters of Gray's Inn.

Events moved relentlessly on towards the ominous date in Albert Pierrepoint's diary. As Derek Bentley sat in his cold cell at Wandsworth, waiting and hoping, letters and telegrams of help and support continued to pour into his parents' home. It seemed as if the whole nation was voicing its protest. A telephone caller told them that thirty of his colleagues in the Civil Service had written to the Home Office, adding to the chorus of appeals for a reprieve. On 24 January a telegram arrived at Fairview Road addressed to Mr Bentley; its urgent message from a Mrs Bartley who lived at Southend was 'See me at once.' Bentley felt that the commanding tone of the telegram should be answered, so he hired a car and was driven through wintry weather to the Essex town. He knocked at the door of a house in York Road, and quickly found himself in the presence of Mrs Sarah Bartley, who said she was the Home Secretary's sister.

They talked for an hour, and Mrs Bartley, a lady in her seventies, told Bentley that she had written to her brother asking him to spare his son's life. 'Have no fear, Mr Bentley, Derek will not die,' she told him. She apologized for making him drive all the way from London but explained that she was an invalid. She told him that night after night she had prayed, and after writing to her brother felt that she had to let Bentley know from her own lips what she had done. 'Behind justice there is always injustice,' she said. 'Your son does not deserve to die.' She reassured him again when he took his leave that Derek would not die; 'Go home and tell your wife; it will comfort her,' she said. The lady's motives were no doubt of the highest order, but she was not who she pretended to be. Nevertheless, her positive attitude was a reflection of the general feeling, although there were occasional cruel reversals. One afternoon a parcel arrived at the Bentley home containing a length of rope fashioned into a noose and a message reading, 'Your son needs this.' The effect on the Bentleys' taut emotions can only be imagined.

Also on 24 January, Dr Denis Hill – who had examined Derek Bentley at Maudsley Hospital before the trial – wrote to the Home

Secretary telling the Minister on whom all hopes for a reprieve depended that the subject under review was a youth diagnosed as epileptic. As the days came and went without any communication from the Home Office, the Bentleys gave up all pretence at sleep. 'We snatched odd hours of rest in armchairs in the sitting-room,' said William Bentley. Their attempts at sleep were usually punctuated by the telephone registering another call of sympathy and solidarity. He judged that some of the callers were 'apparently as sleepless as ourselves'. Meanwhile the boy in the condemned cell whiled away the hours, talking to his warders about his family; the parents he loved and his brother and sister and his animals. He showed courage at this testing time, and perhaps his mental backwardness gave him a little protection from the sheer awfulness of what lay ahead.

On Sunday 25 January the Bentleys remained at home, expecting every hour to receive news of the Home Secretary's decision. They listened to the church service on the radio and prayed together. There were callers, mostly strangers. A man who left some flowers for Mrs Bentley, and a bus driver who pledged to help him in any way he could. 'If anything happens to your son there'll be the biggest bloody row in this country for years,' he said. The day dragged by and the hours after midnight seemed endless as Bentley roamed the house restlessly. 'The silence of the world was terrible,' he recalled. In the early hours he made some tea and waited for another day to dawn.

Newspaper reporters from all round the world had been making their way to Fairview Road since the appeal had been turned down. At around midday one of the reporters rang the door bell and asked Mrs Bentley if it was correct that the Home Secretary had refused a reprieve. Verging on collapse, she called for her husband, to whom the newspaper man repeated his question. 'I've heard nothing,' said Bentley.

Embarrassed, the reporter said, 'Oh, I understand that the Home Secretary has refused to act. We got the news this morning. I'm sorry, Mr Bentley. I hope it isn't true.' He courteously raised his hat and departed, leaving the Bentleys in a state of shock and mental turmoil. Then it dawned on William Bentley that a letter might have arrived earlier that morning in the usual deluge of mail. The several hundred letters had been dumped in the bath as the only receptacle large enough to contain them before the daily routine of sorting them through. Bentley thought that the letter which they had all been waiting for would have been regarded as sufficiently important to merit delivery by messenger. 'I do not know what gave me that idea,' he wrote later. They rushed upstairs, and there, among all the letters from well-wishers and sympathizers was a buff envelope marked OHMS. With trembling fingers, Bentley tore it open:

> Home Office
> Whitehall
> 24 January 1953
>
> Sir
>
> I am directed by the Secretary of State to inform you that he has given careful consideration to the petition submitted by you on behalf of your son Derek Bentley, and I am to express to you his deep regret that after considering all the circumstances of the case he has failed to discover any sufficient ground to justify him in advising Her Majesty to interfere with the due course of the law.
>
> I am, Sir,
> Your obedient servant,
> F.A. Newsam

Despite the greatest campaign of public disquiet ever expressed by the people of Britain over the execution of a convicted person, the Home Secretary saw no grounds for granting a reprieve. And the manner of conveying the decision to the condemned youth's parents – a decision bearing on a person's life in an incident of national importance – by consigning the letter to the ordinary mail is unbelievable. Not only did it deprive the Bentleys of valuable time in which to consult their advisers but it also meant that they first learned of the fate of their son from a newspaper reporter. After reading out the contents of the letter to his wife and daughter, words failed William Bentley, 'I shall hear their screams as long as I live,' he wrote.

William Bentley's despair was tinged with anger that officialdom should have treated his family and him with such cold indifference. 'What crime had we committed that we should be put on the rack in this inhuman fashion?' he asked. Later in the day, they took a taxi to Wandsworth Prison to see their son. They stumbled along the corridor to the interview room, warmed by the kindly behaviour of prison officers, but each fearing that they would break down under the ordeal of facing Derek. Their lad had been informed of the Home Secretary's decision, but even though his pale face showed the strain he was under, enough courage shone through to strengthen his parents.

Conversation was difficult. 'The fight's not over yet, Derek. Never fear,' said his father.

The youth looked up and said, 'Dad, I'm not afraid to die because I am innocent. As long as you keep your chin up I'll keep mine up, whatever happens. Everybody knows I didn't kill Mr Miles, so I've nothing on my conscience.'

In a moment of tender intimacy,his mother reassured him that she knew he had done nothing wrong. 'And God knows it,' she told him.

His father assured him he would do everything in his power to work for a reprieve. 'People are working for you outside,' he said. 'Members of Parliament are going to speak about your case in the House of Commons.'

Parting was painful. The Bentleys returned home exhausted at about seven o'clock in the evening. Their hopes now rested with the prospects that pressure from Parliament might force a last-minute reprieve in the thirty-six hours that remained. At about nine o'clock a newspaper reporter called at the house with an important message. He explained that he had just left Mrs Craig, who wanted to see Mr and Mrs Bentley to give them some information which she thought would help their son. Understandably, they hesitated but decided to accept the invitation.

The relationship between their sons had ended on the rooftop and, even if the boys had wished it, there was no opportunity for them to communicate after they had been taken into custody. As for the parents, there was a social gulf dividing them and, apart from this one meeting of emotional unity, there would be no further contact between the two families.

The Bentleys sat awkwardly in their outdoor clothes in the Craigs' sitting-room while Edith Craig explained that she had evidence which might help if it was placed before the Home Secretary. She offered to accompany them and personally confirm the information, which was that her son Christopher had told her Derek never called him Chris but always 'Kid' or 'Kiddo'. She had learnt this during a visit to her son at Wormwood Scrubs, when he had also said that Derek never called out 'Let him have it, Chris'. Nor did he shout out to the police that Craig had a .45 Colt and plenty of ammunition: Craig said that he had shouted that himself.

The ice having been broken, members of both families talked for about an hour over a cup of tea. There was no doubt about Mrs Craig's sincerity and her willingness to help. The Bentleys thanked her for her support and they arranged to meet the next day in order to present the new information to the Home Office. 'My wife and I returned full of hope,' wrote William Bentley. They were buoyed up with the prospect that Christopher Craig's statement to his mother would weigh favourably with the Home Secretary. In addition there was a steadily growing mood of indignation in the country which had been expressed over the radio news, and opposition to the failure to grant a reprieve was mounting in Parliament. Surely, there was still hope. But it was another night with little sleep for William Bentley, his mind tormented by the recollection of his son's pale face and wavering lips when he had asked his father, 'Dad, help me, please help me.'

9

'See you tomorrow....'

A few minutes past seven o'clock on 26 January, Sydney Silverman, Labour Member of Parliament for the Lancashire constituency of Nelson and Colne and an ardent campaigner for the abolition of capital punishment, appeared at the Table Office in the House of Commons. His purpose was to present a Motion, supported by fifty Members of Parliament, to debate the Home Secretary's decision not to grant a reprieve. The Motion read:

> That this House respectfully dissents from the opinion of the Home Secretary that there were no sufficient reasons for advising the exercise of the Royal Clemency in the case of Derek Bentley; and urges him to reconsider the matter so as to give effect to the recommendation of the jury and to the expressed view of the Lord Chief Justice that Bentley's guilt was less than that of his co-defendant Christopher Craig.

Supporters of the Motion included a former Solicitor-General, Sir Lynn Ungoed-Thomas, and a former Under-Secretary of State for the Home Office. Silverman's Motion was accepted at the Table Office without question, and he remained in the Commons until about 8.30 p.m., when he returned home. Later that evening, at about 10.15 p.m., he received a telephone call telling him that the Speaker of the House of Commons, Mr William Morrison, had given instructions that his Motion would not appear on the Order Paper for the following day. This precipitated an extraordinary discussion in the House of Commons about the real debate that was not allowed to take place.

Monday morning started nervously for the Bentleys, who were due to meet Mrs Craig and go to the Home Office. Lilian Bentley was in a distraught state and remained in bed. Bentley himself said he could hardly drag one foot after the other. 'My speech was affected,' he said. 'My eyes seemed unable to focus properly; everything was a blur.' He telephoned a friend for assistance, and he went with his daughter to the Home Office where Mrs Craig was already waiting. They were received by Sir Frank Newsam, the Permanent Under-Secretary of State, who had signed the letter to Bentley telling him there would be no reprieve. Bentley was too disoriented to make the case to Sir Frank, and his friend Kenneth Johnson put the information forward on his behalf. A secretary was called to take down the details of the statement made by Christopher Craig, and these were confirmed by his mother. The statement was read back and Newsam assured Bentley that the submission would be placed before the Home Secretary within the hour. He also promised that a reply would be sent to him during the day.

Mrs Craig and Mr Johnson left, leaving Bentley and his daughter in private discussion with Sir Frank Newsam. As Bentley wrote later, 'This was my opportunity to bring to his notice matters which had not been brought up at the trial.' Unfortunately, the poor man was nearly at the end of his tether, and his rambling account of Derek's medical history made little impression. 'Sir Frank listened sympathetically,' he said, 'but made no comment.' In truth, William Bentley was probably not capable of putting a forcible enough case at this level anyway, but in his present mental state, it was expecting too much that he should use the hour spent with the Permanent Under-Secretary to its utmost advantage. It was a rare opportunity to have presented the full force of the argument that Derek was an epileptic, that several doctors had said so, and that he was by all current definitions mentally sub-normal. It was an opportunity wasted, and a tragic case of if only. . . . 'I left the Home Office, hardly knowing where I was,' said Bentley. People crowded round him shouting 'Good luck' and pressing on him offers of assistance. He told reporters about Mrs Craig's action in coming forward, and said he and his family thanked her from the bottom of their hearts.

From the Home Office, Bentley made his way to the House of Commons to meet Sydney Silverman. The MP told him that the Speaker had not allowed his Motion to go on the Order Paper, but that he intended to fight the ruling. Meanwhile Dr Denis Hill – who had not received a reply to his letter to the Home Secretary dated 24 January – telephoned the Home Office with a request to publish the electroencephalograph results he had obtained on Derek Bentley. As his findings had been obtained from examinations carried out under the auspices of the Home Office, the doctor was duty bound to seek permission before he could make them public. This was refused on the grounds that it was not in the public interest. He would have to wait another day before receiving an official reply to his letter.

As the House of Commons prepared for the debate at 3.00 p.m. instigated by Sydney Silverman, the avuncular but shadowy figure of Albert Pierrepoint was en route to London, destination Wandsworth Prison. In his leather case nestled two lengths of hempen rope, each six feet in length (one was a new rope, the other had already been tried and tested on the scaffold), together with the other paraphernalia of his grim trade. He was required to report to the Governor at 4.00 p.m. to make his preparations for the following day.

Before a packed House of Commons, Sydney Silverman requested the Speaker's indulgence to question the decision he had made not to allow his Motion to go forward. He explained that the Motion was not a frivolous one but was well considered and 'would be regarded in any quarter of the House as one which obviously ought to appear upon the Order Paper'. This circumlocutory language and the debate which followed resulted from the rules of procedure which prohibited Silverman from discussing the contents of the Motion; he was only allowed to question why it had not been put forward. The Motion as given to the Table Office had by this time attracted over two hundred signatures, but, adhering rigidly to procedure, the Speaker referred the Honourable Member to page 384 of Erskine May, the guide to parliamentary rules and precedents.

There followed an exchange on debating points and procedures. Sydney Silverman mentioned the only precedent he could find of the Speaker intervening to prevent a Motion appearing on the Order Paper, and that was where the express purpose was to cause annoyance to another Member. He quoted from Erskine May, which stated that a notice was 'wholly out of order' if it contained a reflection on a vote of the House or was 'obviously irregular or unbecoming'. He contended that his Motion reflected that 'a Minister's action in the advice which he tenders to the Crown is, like any other action he takes, action for which he is responsible to the House of Commons. There is not any doubt about that at all.' No one has ever doubted, he argued, 'that when a Minister presumes to offer advice to the Crown upon the exercise of the Royal Prerogative, he is responsible to the House for the advice he tenders.' He believed that the Prerogative of Mercy in Britain was not an arbitrary act, as it might be in a totalitarian state but was as much subject to the constitutional principles of a Parliamentary democracy as any other act by any other person.

'There is nothing, on the face of it, that is out of order at all,' declared Silverman in respect of the Motion. And he continued, 'This was the first occasion in the new reign of the young Queen of the exercise of the most responsible of all the Royal Prerogatives . . . Is it to be said,' he enquired 'that this House may have its way – that the Home Secretary shall be responsible to the House for the advice he has given, but only when it is too late to overtake it? Is the House to wait until Bentley is dead before it is entitled to say that he should not die?' It was an electrifying question to put before the consciences of the assembled MPs. Speaking in tones of quiet reasonableness, Silverman's passion began to rise as he declared, 'I venture to think that if it were possible to put such a matter to the vote today, there would be an overwhelming majority of this House who would think that the Home Secretary had decided wrongly. I have here more than two hundred telegrams, from all sorts of people all over the country – all of them except one telling me only that the Home Secretary would probably tell me to mind my own business.'

'Sir, I am minding my own business,' Silverman shouted. 'That is why I am raising the question with you. It is the business of all of us if this boy hangs when we think he ought not to hang.' He told the Speaker that he believed he had exceeded his authority in withholding the Motion. Speaker Morrison acknowledged the deep feeling that existed on the matter, and proceeded to state what he understood was the nature of his authority. He said a long line of his predecessors in the Office of Speaker had ruled that while a capital sentence was pending the matter should not be discussed in the House. Referring to Silverman's argument that the Home Secretary was in effect answerable to the House of Commons for his decisions, the Speaker said that when the matter concerned a capital sentence which has not been executed, 'there is the strongest possible precedent for saying that the House should not discuss it, either by Questions, on the Motion for the Adjournment of the House, or by any other means whatsoever. On that there is no doubt at all in my mind; it has been upheld by successive Speakers for a great number of years, and I have the precedents here, if the House would like me to refer to them.'

The Speaker went on to quote a recent ruling given in connection with a case in the Gold Coast. This was about as remote as it could possibly be from the concern over a nineteen-year-old youth at

Wandsworth, but William Morrison steadily ploughed on, quoting Mr Speaker Clifton Brown's ruling from the Official Report, 1st May 1947; Vol 436, c.2180–81, in which he concluded, 'I cannot alter the practice of the House . . .' 'Neither can I,' said Morrison in defence of his decision the previous evening not to allow the Motion to appear on the Order Paper.

Sydney Silverman countered with his view that 'Every citizen in this country is entitled to bring pressure to bear upon the Home Secretary. A lot of them have been doing it during these last few weeks, and I dare say a good many more have done so today . . . It surely makes a mockery of the rights of the House to say that honourable Members of this House alone shall not be able to combine to put upon the Order Paper an expression of their opinions.' He thought that the ruling quoted was so narrow and so doubtful that it would be quite wrong to extend it. 'I submit,' he said, 'that in matters of this kind, where deep feelings are involved, not merely in this House but throughout the country, and on which the whole administration of justice might be brought into contempt, this is not the occasion to narrow still further the rights of Members of the House of Commons.'

Reginald Paget, a barrister and Labour Member for Northampton, supported Silverman, arguing that the ruling quoted was based on a decision of the Executive and not a decision of the House of Commons. Then, emotively, he spoke of the condemnation which was made of the German nation when they stood aside from terrible wartime events. 'We are a sovereign assembly,' he declared. 'A three-quarter-witted boy of nineteen is to be hanged for a murder he did not commit, and which was committed fifteen minutes after he was arrested. Can we be made to keep silent when a thing as horrible and as shocking as this is to happen?'

Leslie Hale, the Labour MP for Oldham West, spoke next about the background to the ruling on the previously quoted Gold Coast precedent in 1947. Hale had played a part in that debate, and unrelated as it seemed to the matter in hand, he argued that the two cases were not strictly comparable. In a debating chamber where precedent ruled this was an important point to make, and he believed that none of the authorities offered a precedent for the present circumstances. He then launched into a detailed account of what had occurred the previous evening after his honourable friend had delivered his Motion to the Table Office. The paper had been so full with signatures that he had added his own name in one of the small spaces that remained. 'No suggestion was then made that it was out of order,' he said. Leslie Hale produced a loud reaction of 'Oh!' from the Government benches when he suggested that by taking a decision which amounted to an invasion of Members' privileges the Speaker placed himself in a position where it was possible to suggest that he was protecting a Minister or a Government. 'I submit,' he concluded, 'that the Motion should have been on the Order Paper today.'

The Speaker assured Members that he was trying neither to invade their privileges nor to protect Ministers. He said he must act in accordance with the rules of the House, and he contended that his ruling the previous evening did not preclude the House from 'taking cognizance of the matter'. To cries of 'Too late', he said, 'A motion can be put down on the subject when the sentence has been executed.' He maintained that the Motion put by the honourable Member, because it would be interposed before the execution, was ruled out of order by all the authorities of the House. The Speaker went on to mention the cases of Florence Maybrick in 1887 and Israel Lipski in 1889, he referred to the rulings of Speakers Lowther and Whitley in 1920 and 1922, quoting chapter and verse, to illustrate that the Motion under consideration was out of order.

Almost unbelievably, this debate about virtually nothing save the niceties of precedent and procedure went on and on. Mr Aneurin Bevan, Labour Member for Ebbw Vale, pointed out the obvious, that 'It may be to the rest of the country rather stupid that the House of Commons can only intervene when the step taken is irremediable.' He thought it was quite clear from the precedents that the Speaker was in a strong position and could not be assailed. 'But there is another issue', he said, which was the precedent or rule on which the Speaker relied in order to intervene and prevent a Motion going on the Order Paper merely because, in his view, it was out of order. This denied a Member the opportunity to justify in debate why he considered a particular Motion was in order. He believed this was a serious step which should not be blurred by the separate issue of whether the Royal pleasure had been exercised.

Sydney Silverman then moved a Motion for the Adjournment of the House under Standing Order Number Nine, 'To call attention to a definite matter of urgent public importance, namely, the decision of the Home Secretary not to advise Her Majesty to exercise the Royal Prerogative of Mercy in the case of Derek Bentley.' The Speaker ruled that he could not accept the Motion for the reasons already given, 'which are an unbroken line of cases'. Desmond Donnelly, another Labour MP, moved an Adjournment on a different issue, 'To call attention to a definite matter of urgent public importance, namely, the action of Mr Speaker in directing that the Motion submitted by the honourable Member for Nelson and Colne [Sydney Silverman] should not appear on the Order Paper today.' Again the Speaker refused to accept the Motion on the grounds 'that the action of Mr Speaker cannot be a cause for the adjournment of the House'.

Further discussion ensued on the point raised by Aneurin Bevan and the Speaker said that he was the 'guardian of the Order Paper' and if an item of projected business could not be taken in the form in which it was presented 'it is quite proper to direct its removal'. Bevan contested this, arguing that never in his experience in Parliament had the Speaker used his function as guardian of the Order Paper to remove a Motion merely on the grounds that he said it was out of order. Mr Speaker Morrison made it clear that in taking the action for which he was being challenged he had not received representation from any Minister, or indeed from anyone else. Aneurin Bevan said he had not wished to convey the impression that the Home Secretary had seen Mr Speaker, and on that note the debate petered out and the House moved on to the next item of business – the Argentine Meat Agreement. Sir David Maxwell Fyfe had sat silently on the Government front benches while the debate with its many references to his actions swirled round him. Neither he nor any other Government minister contributed while the Opposition members grappled with the Speaker over points of procedure.

The indefatigable Sydney Silverman, aided by Aneurin Bevan, gathered over two hundred MPs' signatures on a petition which a group of six Members presented to the Home Secretary:

> We, the undersigned members of the Commons House of Parliament, believing the advice tendered by you to Her Majesty the Queen in the case of Derek Bentley to be grievously mistaken and out of accord with the natural justice of the case, urge that even now you will advise Her Majesty to exercise the Royal Prerogative of Mercy so that sentence of death upon him be not executed.

Mr Silverman told William Bentley that the Motion to debate the Home Secretary's decision had been turned down by the Speaker on technical grounds. Bentley, with his customary humility, did not understand what the reasons were but he supposed they were 'all above board and legal', and he praised Silverman's fine sense of justice and nobility of character.

When they left Westminster, Bentley and his daughter ran into a large crowd outside chanting, 'Reprieve Bentley' and bearing banners proclaiming the same demand. Father and daughter wept as they returned home to tell Mrs Bentley what had happened and to prepare her for the worst. As their car turned into Fairview Road they saw groups of people gathered on the street. They sensed the sympathy of glum, tearful neighbours, and there was a shout of 'God Bless You' as they reached their house. Lilian Bentley listened to her husband's report of the day's events, and then quietly handed him a letter which had arrived about fifteen minutes earlier by special messenger. It was from the Home Office and was signed by Sir Frank Newsam. Its brief contents read:

> I am directed to inform you that the Secretary of State has given the fullest consideration to your representations, but very much regrets that he has been unable to find any grounds for modifying the decision previously communicated to you.

Each member of the family read the letter in silence – no one spoke. Bentley wrote later, 'Lilian left the room and returned dressed to go out. I phoned for the hire car and we left for Wandsworth. . . .'

Crowds gathered throughout London, gripped by a kind of numbing horror of what was about to be done in the name of justice. There were noisy protests, and police were called to control some of the more aggressive groups. The pavements outside some of the capital's Government offices were thronged by protesting members of the public spilling out on to the roads and holding up the flow of traffic. The atmosphere was charged with anger and indignation. Two men who remained impervious to this display of public feeling were Albert Pierrepoint and his assistant, who made their way by public transport to the Caledonian Road and thence to Wandsworth Prison.

At about five o'clock Derek Bentley left his condemned cell and was escorted by two warders to the exercise yard. This was in preparation for the ritual of which he was the subject. Unknown to him, he was under observation by a balding, chubby-faced man standing by an upper window. Albert Pierrepoint was assessing the youth's physical build in order to prepare the scaffold. He consulted the hangman's bible – the *Home Office Standard Table of Drops*. With the information he had about the prisoner's height, weight and age, and aided by his assessment of the youth's physique, he calculated the distance that he would have to drop Derek Bentley in order to break his neck cleanly. Particular attention was paid to the muscular strength of the neck, for as Pierrepoint recorded in his autobiography, 'A master executioner is alone responsible for every detail of his craft.' The heavier the man, the shorter the drop; the weaker his neck, the shorter the drop. According to the Home Office rule book, an 8 foot 6 drop was the maximum, 5 feet the minimum. These were among the factors in Pierrepoint's mind as he made his calculations using the official formula:

$$\frac{1,260 \text{ foot-pounds}}{\text{prisoner's weight in pounds}} = \text{recommended drop in feet}$$

The drop for Derek Bentley would be 7 feet and 3 inches.

While the condemned youth continued his exercise, Pierrepoint and his assistant proceeded to the execution shed, which was situated next to the condemned cell and separated by a movable metal partition. This was pushed back while the two men, aided by the prison engineer, put their preparations to the test. A sandbag was filled to the same weight as Bentley and placed on the doors of the drop set into the floor. Pierrepoint took one of the ropes from his case and shackled the eye-bolt at its end to the beam overhead. The rope's noose was fastened round the sandbag and the level pulled to release the drop. The doors opened and slammed down into the rubber-lined retaining clips and the sandbag descended into the pit below. It was the intention to leave the bag suspended overnight; it stretched the rope, thereby minimizing any whiplash during the execution or possible slippage of the noose. By the time Bentley was returned to his cell the partition had been repositioned and from the coat hook on his side of it hung a warder's coat and cap. Although he was unaware of it, Bentley had for several weeks been living a mere seven steps from the scaffold.

Their stealthy preparations completed, the hangman and his assistant retired to the accommodation set aside for them in the prison officers' quarters. It was part of their code to be unobtrusive; their training had taught them to be discreet at all times. Pierrepoint informed the Governor of the length of drop he proposed to make. All that remained for them to do was to get a sound night's sleep in readiness for the next morning's work.

Derek Bentley no doubt spent some of his time thinking about his own predicament, but he also thought of those he loved and cared for. He had a crush on an attractive seventeen-year-old girl, Rita Bradbury, who, like his sister, was an usherette at the Astoria Cinema in Streatham. She had written to him in prison and sent him a photograph. With her good looks and slim figure, Rita could have been a model, and Derek's letters to her contained wistful longings of what might have been. He wrote to her first on Christmas Eve, dictating his letter to Prison Officer D. Povey who took it down on lined sheets of prison notepaper.

Dearest Rita,

I was very pleased to receive your letter it cheered me up a lot because I knew it came from an attractive young lady. I hope you mean what you write about standing by me, that in itself will comfort and cheer me no end, but I don't always want to be your brother, I think you know what I mean by this. I didn't come to the Astoria so often for nothing, the only reason I came was to see you.

I am very disappointed that you cannot come to see me, but if at any time it is possible for you to come up I would be very grateful.

Remind me to Evelyn, Pam and the rest of the girls at the Astoria, I bet you will have a grand time at the party. I only wish I was there with you, but one of these days we will do the town, just you and I. That is of course if you hav'nt any followers and I hope with all my heart that you havn't, for reasons that you should know only too well.

It sounds as though I am being forward, but I always wanted to say nice things to you and now this is my chance in this letter. I think I'll start by saying you have lovely eyes and the most adorable mouth to say nothing of that nice little nose. I don't know what you are thinking now, seeing that I have never said those things to you before, but I now have a lot of time to think and most of my thoughts are of you. I bet you never thought a big lout like me would think this way, but I always have thought about you since the day I met you, this must seem strange that I have never said nothing before, but please believe me I really mean it.

I need a girl like you to make me pull myself together, now you'll think I am joking about this, but I mean what I'm saying. If I had had the strength before I would have told you all these things and I am sure it would have made a lot of difference to me, I don't know whether you think it would have made any difference but if you do please tell in your next letter which I hope you will write as soon as you receive this.

I know I am not much of a prize, but beauty is only skin deep. I don't know if you agree with this.

I don't know if you will show this letter to the girls at the Astoria, but I would prefer that you didn't because I would like this to be between ourselves I'm sure this would be best.

I'm glad you think my parents are nice because I owe them so much and think the world of them myself and having at least that much in common makes it a lot easier for me to say what I have said in this letter.

I hope your family are well and that they will have a very happy Xmas. Don't forget to pop round to my Mum on Xmas day as I think she would be happy to see you sitting in the chair that I usually sat in.

Have you been to any dances lately, when you write tell me all about them because I miss going myself.

Rita there is something I have always wanted to do but I could never do it because I was too shy and that is to have kissed you goodnight after walking you home, I sit now and think of what I missed and kicking myself for it.

I must close now, my dinner has come in so until the next time.

Lots of Love

Derek

XXXXX

Poor Derek would never again have the opportunity to give the girl of his dreams a goodnight kiss. His second letter, written to Rita nearly a month later on 21 January, was cooler than the first and there were no loving kisses when he signed it off. Obviously Rita had told him that she was friendly with another boy, and although her letters are not extant it is likely that, in the kindliest fashion, she had written him a 'Dear John' letter.

My Dear Rita,

Many thanks for your kind and thoughtful letter it was good of you to write and I do appreciate it very much. I thought the photo was very nice and it is indeed nice to have it and I do thank you very much for it. I was sorry to hear that you were ill and I hope you are now better and back at work.

It is good of you to go and see my Mum and Dad sometimes and they like it very much. I am glad you liked your Xmas presents but it was a pity I was not there to give them to you. There is lots I would like to say but I will wait until I can see you and we can have a long talk.

138

I was pleased to learn that the party was a big success at Hinds and that you all had a good time. Yes, I like your idea of having plenty to eat at Xmas there is nothing like it.

Do you still go dancing, if so and you see any of my old pals will you please give them my regards and I hope they are all well.

By the way Rita will you please write more about John as I may know him, at the moment I can't place him. I was indeed surprised to learn that you were going with him as I did not know anything about it. The fact that you are going with him has taken the wind out of my sails. I will leave it at that for the moment.

You will be pleased to know I am keeping well and time is going by nicely for me. I am doing as you told me.

Do please write soon again, I will be looking forward to hearing from you and a letter in here goes a long way to cheer one up.

Do all my pals still get in the 'Astoria' I expect they make plenty of noise on Sundays.

Well Rita I must now draw to a close and I do hope that this finds you very well as it leaves, and my feelings are still the same for you and I hope you will be able to return the feelings in the same effort.

Goodbye for now

Your sincerely

Derek

The reference in the first paragraph to Rita being ill, resulted from the excuse she had to make because the authorities would not allow her to visit Derek in prison.

Derek was cheerful when he saw his parents and sister for the last time. They realized it was in all probability the final parting; mercifully perhaps, their son did not. He teased his sister about her eye-shadow and the laughter which followed broke the tension. Bentley wrote later that God must have given his son great strength at that point, 'He was absolutely calm. He spoke naturally and without effort. He did not once mention what awaited him the next morning, if all failed.' His mother gave him a newspaper cutting containing a photograph of him with his dogs. Derek was pleased with this, and asked her to stroke his pets for him. He was also given a letter from a friend and a rosary – his father noticed that his hands were steady.

William Bentley, suffering from the burden of what in his heart he knew was his son's last remaining hours alive, tensely grated his teeth together. 'There's old Pop grinding his teeth again!' said Derek, joking about his father's nervous habit. After the allotted visit of twenty minutes, a warder gently touched Derek's arm to signify that time was up. He smiled at his parents and sister and said, 'Cheerio, Dad! Cheerio, Mum! Cheerio, Iris' and as he turned away, called out, 'See you tomorrow. . . .' Those were the last words he spoke to his family. William Bentley said he reeled unsteadily along the corridor after leaving the visiting room, unable to control his legs. His wife and daughter, immobilized with grief, had to be helped into the car that took them home.

When they reached Fairview Road they found that the crowd gathered in the street had grown in size but the mood was quieter. The arrival of the Bentley family was greeted with respectful silence. Lilian, incapable of any further activity, was put to bed and an obliging neighbour came in to look after her. William and Iris prepared to go out again, this time to the House of Commons to see how Sydney Silverman and his parliamentary deputation had fared. Before leaving the house they looked at the latest postal delivery, and among the letters was one from the actress Diana Dors and her husband expressing their sympathy. 'Even at this stage,' said Bentley, 'every message kept hope alive.'

Around 7.30 p.m., the Home Secretary received the deputation of MPs led by Mr Aneurin Bevan and supported by Sir Lynn Ungoed-Thomas, Reginald Paget and Sydney Silverman. There were crowds of people in Whitehall making their way to the House of Commons where William Bentley and his daughter waited for news. One group of indignant protesters tried to break through the police cordon around the residence of the Foreign Secretary, Sir Anthony Eden in order to deliver a petition. The protest was directed at him probably because he was such an eminent public figure. Silverman told Bentley that the Home Secretary had seemed impressed by the deputation's submission 'that even now you will advise Her Majesty to apply the Royal Prerogative of Mercy so that sentence of death upon him be not executed'. Reference was also made to the considerable public reaction which the affair had provoked; 'the failure of the Home Secretary to give effect to the jury's recommendation to mercy has thoroughly roused the people,' said the leader of the deputation.

Soon after 10.00 p.m., William Bentley saw Silverman when he returned from the Home Office. He read the result of the deputation's efforts in the grave expression on the MP's face. He took Bentley to one side and told him, 'The Home Secretary's decision stands. This is final and irrevocable.' Sensing the outcome, Iris rushed over to her father and collapsed in his arms. Bentley knew that was the end of the road – his son had barely eleven hours to live. The huge crowd outside the House of Commons were shouting, 'Bentley must not hang! Bentley must not hang!' as they made their way to the waiting car.

William and Iris Bentley drove home in silence. They had exhausted the reservoir of hope – there was nothing else to say. A large crowd assembled outside the Bentley home in Fairview Road parted quietly to create a path leading to the front door of No 1. Lilian Bentley was in the sitting-room, the floor littered with envelopes and telegrams. Her husband told her, 'It seems to be all over.' The family prayed together in the solitude of their home while thousands of members of the public noisily demonstrated their anger in central London. A protest leader telephoned Bentley and asked if he and his wife would lead two hundred people on a march to Buckingham Palace. Everything had been planned, including banners and placards and a wheel-chair for Mrs Bentley if she needed it. The Bentleys declined the offer, saying that they would do anything to save their son but would not sacrifice their dignity by taking part in a demonstration.

About 1 a.m. there was another telephone call, this time from the police. Some of the public protests were growing into ugly encounters, and it was thought that Mr Bentley might be willing to turn out and pacify them. Bentley left the house accompanied by his daughter Iris, who had been such a faithful supporter throughout the family's ordeal, and they were driven first to one crowd and then another. Bentley urged them not to create a disturbance and to disperse peacefully. 'My family and I thank you from the bottom of our hearts,' he told them. 'We shall always be grateful to you. But nothing more can be done. My son is now in God's hands.' Some demonstrators urged him vociferously to lead a march to Buckingham Palace, but, as before, he declined. Other protesters sang *Abide With Me* and Bentley, bowed with fatigue and tension, wept. He and Iris returned home at about 3 a.m., physically and emotionally spent.

During the evening Derek Bentley had a visit from the prison chaplain. They talked about family matters and Derek inevitably chatted about his pets. As dawn was beginning to break on the bitterly cold morning, Derek asked his warders if he could dictate a letter to his parents.

Dear Mum and Dad

I was glad to see you on my visit today but I was a little disappointed that Rita could not come. I got the rosary and the letter and I saw the photo of the dogs. Iris looked quite nice surrounded with all those animals. I couldn't keep the photo because it was a newspaper cutting.

I told you Mum it would be difficult to write this letter, I can't think of anything to say except that you have all been wonderful the way you have worked for me.

Thank Rita for writing to me, tell her I am thinking of her. Don't forget what I told you today. 'Always keep your chin up', and tell Pop not to grind his teeth. Oh! I mustn't forget to thank Lil and Bert [a female friend and his Uncle Albert] for writing and coming to see me. Give my love to them both and to everybody else that we know. Tell Ronnie [a close friend] to keep away from the boys and to stay on his own.

I hope Dad has some more televisions in, I forgot to ask him how things were on the visit. Dad and I used to have some fun on that one of Leslie's, he certainly had some spare parts for it.

Oh Dad! Don't let my cycle frames get rusty they might come in handy one day 'cause old Sally [one of the bicycles] has got a cracked frame and I want you to change it before something happens to you, and Dad, keep a strict eye on Denis if he does anything wrong, though I don't think he will but you never know how little things can get you into trouble, if he does, wallop him so that he won't be able to sit for three weeks. I am trying to give you good advice because of my experience.

I tell you what Mum, the truth of this story has got to come out one day, and as I said in the visiting box that one day a lot of people are going to get into trouble and I think you know who those people are. What do you think Mum? This letter may sound a bit solemn but I am still keeping my chin up as I want all the family to do.

Don't let anything happen to the cats and dogs and look after them as you always have.

I hope Laurie and Iris get married all right. I'd like to give them my blessing, it would be fun to have a brother-in-law like him, we could have some fun together. We could have gone round the club and drunk ourselves to a standstill on that great occasion of them getting married, tell him to lob out my flower, tell him to keep my mac clean and my ties. Laurie and I used to have some fun at the pond till four o'clock in the morning, by the cafe. I always caught Laurie to pay for the pies, he never caught me once.

That will be all for now. I will sign this myself.

Lots of love   Derek

It was a dignified letter touching on all those things in his short life that mattered to him and ending on a cheerful note about good times with friends. These last thoughts from their son would not be received by his parents until after he was dead.

At 6 a.m. on that cold January morning, as Londoners began to rub the sleep from their eyes, Prison Officer Albert Beckman left his home in Clapham and headed for Wandsworth Prison. His ten-minute walk to work took him past the Globe Garage in Northcote Road, now derelict but once a thriving business. For those who bothered to know, it was the place where in 1927 the infamous pair of criminals Browne and Kennedy plied their dishonest trade before murdering PC George Gutteridge in a lonely lane at Stapleford Abbots in Essex. Frederick Guy Browne was executed at Pentonville and William Henry Kennedy was hanged at Wandsworth where he occupied the condemned cell in which another man was now awaiting death. Beckman was a Capital Charge Warder, and his duty on this wintry morning was to assist in the grim task of preparing Derek William Bentley for his fate on the scaffold.

Beckman banged on the heavy wooden gate of the prison and, while he waited, exchanged a few words with the milkman. There were some people outside the prison huddled into little groups; muttering, expecting. The wicket gate opened and Beckman was admitted to begin his turn. He collected his keys, which he attached to his belt by a long chain, and made his way through the inner security doors, across the courtyard and into the main building, where his first stop would be for a welcoming cup of strong tea.

Inside the prison the Senior Officer gave the order to 'Unlock! Stay in your cells' in the daily regime which controlled the lives of over a thousand inmates. Half a landing at a time, the men emerged from their green-painted cells (measuring ten feet by seven) and carried their buckets to the slopping-out sinks. Teeth were cleaned and the prisoners were then 'banged-up' again until breakfast. But this was no ordinary day, for one of their number was to be hanged. A chilling tension gripped the prison and resentment was in the air; inmates and officers alike were edgy. Oscar Wilde, a prison inmate in another gaol in another time, captured the mood:

> At six o'clock we cleaned our cells,
>   At seven all was still,
> But the sough and swing of a mighty wing
>   The prison seemed to fill,

> For the Lord of Death with icy breath
>> Had entered in to kill.

Derek Bentley had snatched what fitful sleep he could from his final hours. He felt dizzy when he awoke at about quarter to seven and, stricken with panic, he gagged for breath. His warders stood him on a chair by the barred window of his cell so that he could breathe in the fresh morning air to clear his head. The scene before him through the barred window was no 'tent of blue' but a cold, grey day, the early light of which glistened on the wet cobblestones of the prison yard. Beyond the high wall and down towards Clapham, lights blinked in a hundred dwellings whose occupants were preparing for another day. The thoughts that occupied his mind at such a time can hardly be imagined, but it is likely he thought of his family. Perhaps, despite everything and against all the odds, he believed his Dad would yet arrive with that important piece of paper from the Home Office that meant he could go home.

Unknown to Derek, the execution shed next to his cell had been the scene of silent last-minute preparations. If he had heard any muffled sounds, he would not have realized their significance. Albert Pierrepoint, a master of his particular craft, was thorough in everything he did. The sandbag suspended from the beam the day before was removed and a length of twine held the noose at the correct height. The trap, a pair of wooden doors measuring 8 feet 6 inches by 2 feet 6, was closed and a letter 'T' marked in chalk across the divide; this was where the condemned man would be told to position his feet. Two stout wooden planks were placed across the trap upon which the warders would stand to assist him should he falter near the end:

> He did not pass in purple pomp.
>> Nor ride a moon-white steed.
> Three yards of cord and a sliding board
>> Are all the gallows' need:
> So with rope of shame the Herald came
>> To do the secret deed.

As the clock moved inexorably to 9 o'clock, a crowd approaching a thousand people gathered outside the prison. They were in a truculent mood as they edged near the entrance and scuffled with the police. There were fears that public anger was running at such a pitch that a serious riot might develop. Among the crowd was sixty-five year-old Mrs Violet Van der Elst, a veteran campaigner against capital punishment for nearly twenty years. Since 1935 she had protested at most of the judicial executions carried out in Britain.

In the house at 1 Fairview Road, Norbury, where so much of the nation's sympathy was directed, Derek Bentley's family sat numbly in their sitting-room. His mother was in a state of collapse, and his sister sat unmoving, her head in her hands; his brother sat on the rug in front of the fire and his father paced the house. 'I have no recollection that any of us spoke a single word,' said William Bentley afterwards, believing that providence had mercifully blotted out most of those awful waiting hours. At about 6.30 a.m. he went to the front door. The crowd which had been outside the house the night before had left. A few passers-by on their way to work looked in his direction and, knowing what they knew, passed quickly by. The postman called and, without a word, gave Bentley a bundle of letters. Bentley returned to the warmth of the sitting-room, switched on the radio and waited for the dreaded hour.

Derek Bentley's last visitor was the Rev. Ball, the Prison Chaplain. His task was to prepare the prisoner spiritually. They prayed together in the presence of Albert Beckman and his colleague, the two warders who had seen the youth through his final hour. Waiting outside the cell was the Prison Governor Mr Lawton, the Under-Sheriff of the County of Surrey, Mr C.R. Wigan, the Prison Medical Officer, Dr James Murdock, a hospital orderly and the prison engineer. At the stroke of nine, as the chimes of Big Ben sounded on the radio in the Bentley family home, the door to the condemned cell was opened. White-faced and trembling, Derek faced the groups of officials and Mr Lawton, addressing the Under-Sheriff, said, 'Your prisoner, sir.' The metal screen separating the cell from the execution shed was slid back. The youth was given a tumbler of brandy by the hospital orderly. He drank it quickly, and Pierrepoint and his assistant then pinioned his arms above the elbow and ushered him gently to the scaffold where he was positioned on the chalked mark.

The executioner took a white linen hood from his pocket and placed it over the lad's head while his assistant deftly placed a leg strap around Bentley's ankles so that he would drop cleanly through the trap. The noose was placed over his head and tightened – the fabric of the white hood puffed in and out as Bentley took his last frantic gulps of air. Pierrepoint ran a quick eye over

145

the preparations – everything was ready. He dismissed his assistant – released the cotter pin with his foot and pulled the lever. 'Cap, noose, dismiss assistant, pin, lever, drop'; he had done it a hundred times. The heavy doors fell open and Bentley dropped. The rope hung taut with his suspended weight and the piece of twine that had held the noose ready at head height spiralled feather-like down into the drop. It was all over in less than twenty seconds from the moment that Pierrepoint had entered the cell.

> And as one sees most fearful things
> In the crystal of a dream,
> We saw the greasy hempen rope
> Hooked to the blackened beams
> And heard the prayer the hangman's snare
> Strangled into a scream.

Outside the prison the crowd had fallen silent and the men removed their hats. Mrs Van der Elst urged them, 'Let us be with him at his time of need.' After a minute's silence, she led them in singing the hymn *Abide With Me*, followed by the Twenty-Third Psalm and *The Lord is My Shepherd*. In the Bentley home, the four remaining members of the family clung to each other as Big Ben completed its chimes. Shortly afterwards Lilian went upstairs where she lay on Derek's bed, her face buried in his pillow.

Derek Bentley's body swung silently in the pit below the drop where the prison doctor applied a stethoscope to his chest. Hanging produced mercifully quick unconsciousness but it took several seconds for the heart-beat to slow and stop. His body was left for an hour to ensure that all life was extinct before being taken down under Pierrepoint's supervision. The corpse was stripped and placed in a plain black coffin ready for post-mortem examination.

By convention, the pathologist who had been first called in to the case saw it through to its conclusion. Thus Dr David Haler, who had examined the body of PC Miles, was now asked to examine the body of the man whom the law had deemed responsible for the officer's death. He established that there was no injury to the head and the brain was perfectly normal. Cause of death was a fractured neck and crushing of the spinal cord consistent with the effects of judicial hanging. Asked by the Coroner if 'that means instantaneous unconsciousness and practically instantaneous death', the doctor answered 'Yes.' It did not matter that Bentley's body had stretched by four inches.

The crowd outside the prison remained orderly after singing hymns under Mrs Van der Elst's direction, but the peace was disturbed when a warder emerged from the gate with two notices pinned in a glass frame and prepared to hang them up. One of the notices announced that the judgment of death on Derek William Bentley had been executed; the other stated that he had been examined by the Prison Medical Officer and was dead. The crowd surged forward, straining against the police barrier, as the warder struggled to fix the notices on the hook in the door. No sooner had he succeeded than the police cordon broke under the strain and two men seized the frame holding the notices and smashed it against the prison door, showering those close by with glass. With the notice hanging askew on its hook, pandemonium broke loose as the police were booed and pelted with coins. Three men managed to gain access to the prison through the main gate, but a more concerted attempt to breach the prison was thwarted by the combined efforts of police and prison officers. Fighting lasted for a quarter of an hour before order finally prevailed. It had been an unprecedented, bitter protest at unbending officialdom. The newspapers reflected the country's sad mood – the *Daily Mirror*'s headline read: 200 MPs sign Plea "Don't Hang Him," while the *Daily Herald* was even more poignant, 'Bentley Dies. MPs' Last Bid Fails. Crowd Shouts "No"'.

In his autobiography Albert Pierrepoint made a matter-of-fact reference to the duty he performed on 28 January 1953. 'I had to hang Derek Bentley,' he wrote, 'the nineteen-year-old youth of retarded intelligence who had already been taken into custody by the police after a factory break-in when his companion in crime fired a revolver and killed a policeman. Because the killer was aged only sixteen he was not sentenced to death. Bentley was sentenced, and the execution carried out after widespread national protest.' Contrary to a number of accounts, Pierrepoint said he did not shake hands with the prisoner on the afternoon before his death, he did not make any notes about him, the prison governor did not have to urge him to get on with his task and Derek Bentley did not cry on the way to the scaffold. 'I cannot be provoked into giving the witnessed details which would disprove these tales,' wrote Pierrepoint, 'but I state unequivocally that they are false.'

Later that day Derek Bentley was buried alongside the southern wall of Wandsworth Prison on top of two other graves. On the wall above his head the familiar prison crowsfoot motif pointed down. His coffin was covered with white lime and damp soil.

> For where a grave had opened wide
>> There was no grave at all:
> Only a stretch of mud and sand
>> By the hideous prison-wall,
> And a little heap of burning lime
>> That the man should have his pall.

Derek's last letter to his parents arrived two days after his execution. 'Reading it, I felt that he was still alive,' wrote his father. Symbolically, the basket of fruit which he and his wife had not been allowed to leave with Derek at Christmas, and which had since lain mouldering on the sideboard, he now consigned to the dustbin. A letter was also delivered to Dr Denis Hill from the Home Office. Dated 27 January 1953, it read;

Dear Dr Hill

Thank you for your letter of the 24th January about Derek Bentley. I appreciate the terms in which you have written and quite recognize why you were anxious to bring this particular point to my notice.

I can, however, give you an assurance that full regard was paid to the medical side of this case and that all the relevant information was before the Home Secretary when he came to his decision.

F A Newsam

If the Home Office's contention that they possessed all the relevant information was open to serious challenge, their lack of humanity cannot be doubted. On the eve of her brother's execution, Iris Bentley had written a personal letter to the Home Secretary on two sheets of paper torn from an exercise book;

To Sir David Patrick Maxwell Fyffe [sic]

I plead with you as Derek Bentley's sister to reconsider your decision if you could have been able to see Derek yesterday I am sure those words he said to my Mother 'I am not afraid to die because I am innocent Mum' would have moved you as they did us. I ask are these the words of a boy who has a life on his conscience.

Please, I beseach [sic] you save my Brother's life. Time is short but we are hopeful

Miss Iris Bentley

This distraught young woman could no more understand the logic or justice of the decision to hang her brother in the face of all the indications for a reprieve than could the nation, which protested in its thousands.

> And thus we rust Life's iron chain
>   Degraded and alone:
> And some men curse, and some men weep
>   And some men make no moan:
> But God's eternal Laws are kind
>   And break the heart of stone.

Writing in *Picture Post*, Kenneth Allsop, the author and broadcaster, described the public mood after Bentley's execution as being similar to that which had prevailed at the time of Dunkirk and on the occasion of the King's death.

10

'The truth of this story....'

Why was Derek Bentley hanged? His case, as Reginald Paget wrote afterwards, 'assembled in the highest degree every ground upon which the prerogative of mercy has formerly been exercised'. H. Montgomery Hyde, the barrister and MP who edited the volume of the *Notable British Trial* series dedicated to the case, asked the same question. Of Bentley, he wrote:

> This unfortunate young man would appear to be the first individual in our legal history who has been hanged as an accomplice in a crime for which the principal in the first degree (Christopher Craig) could not be executed on grounds of age. In addition, though legally liable to suffer the death penalty, Bentley was still a youth in his teens. He was also a youth considerably below the average intelligence, and it was said (though not at his trial) that he had been subject to epileptic fits as well as having been reported mentally deficient at an Approved School and rejected on mental grounds for national service with the Army. There was, too, in the case of Bentley, the jury's recommendation to mercy, in which the trial judge apparently concurred. Why, then was he not reprieved?

The only person who could answer that question was the Home Secretary, and he was not obliged to give his reasons for declining to advise the Queen to grant the Royal Prerogative of Mercy. When the trial verdict was announced William Bentley had sought to bolster his family's sagging hopes by telling them that a jury's recommendation to mercy always resulted in a reprieve. Sadly, this was not the case. In the years 1900 to 1949, of the 360 persons convicted of murder in England and Wales and recommended to mercy by the jury, 112 failed to be granted reprieves and were duly hanged. The reprieve rate was 68 per cent for the men convicted and 98 per cent for the women.

The discretionary grounds available to the Home Secretary in Bentley's case were his youth, the fact that he was not the principal offender, his mental status and the doubts which existed regarding some of his alleged statements. Youth had always been regarded as an important ground for exercising the prerogative of mercy. Persons aged under eighteen could not be hanged, and those near to that age were normally reprieved unless there were exceptional circumstances. Derek Bentley was nineteen, and the only exceptional circumstance should have worked in his favour – namely, that he did not fire the fatal shot.

It had invariably been the practice that where the principal participant could not for any reason be executed – in this case, Christopher Craig, on account of his age – his associates were not made to suffer the supreme penalty. The defence of insanity was only permitted where a person was judged to be wholly lacking in responsibility for their acts on account of mental illness. In cases where mental illness constituted impaired responsibility, the convicted person was usually reprieved. Bentley was an epileptic who had also been assessed as mentally deficient at an Approved School and had been rejected for military service on mental grounds. Few, if any, individuals as close to the borderline as Bentley evidently was have been executed.

It seems inconceivable that with this known medical history, Bentley should have been found fit to plead at his trial, let alone fail to be granted a reprieve after being convicted.

Both the Report of the Commissioners of the Central Law in 1839 and the Report of the Royal Commissioners in 1878 recommended that the definition of murder should be amended to exclude cases where a person was held responsible for a death which was never intended or desired. In the event, the law was not altered because it was believed that the prerogative of mercy could be relied upon in such cases. Derek Bentley certainly fell into a category that deserved such protection.

The final ground on which the Home Secretary could exercise discretion was that of doubt, which, if it existed in the smallest degree, supposedly led to commutation of sentence. In Bentley's case, the evidence was shot through with doubt. For a start, there was – or should have been – doubt about his mental fitness; there was certainly doubt about his competence to make a statement. Most

151

importantly, the remark he allegedly made on the roof, 'Let him have it, Chris', was open to two completely different meanings.

According to Montgomery Hyde, the Home Secretary had before him all the evidence that had been available to the courts, in addition to the judge's notes, the transcript of the entire proceedings and reports from the Prison Medical Officer on Bentley's mental and physical condition, together with police reports and information on his family and social background. Sir David Maxwell Fyfe touched on the subject in his autobiography *Political Adventure* published in 1964 after he had been ennobled as Lord Kilmuir. He referred to the 'sombre responsibility' represented by exercising the Royal Prerogative of Mercy and wrote that it 'cannot be emphasised too strongly that he [the Home Secretary] is intervening in the due process of the law, to decide, in short, if those processes ought to be diverted'. He was concerned that his decision might bring the law into public contempt, a factor which he believed was of great (although not overriding) importance. In this he was correct, for his decision not to grant a reprieve so incensed the public and Parliament that the law was changed with the advent of the Homicide Act in 1957.

Maxwell Fyfe's description of his position as 'bleak, solitary, miserable' is one with which few would disagree. In truth, to have advised the Queen to exercise the Prerogative of Mercy on the basis of the facts before him would have been a humane decision for which the nation – as distinct from the Establishment – would have praised him. The unprecedented volume of public protest and the strength of opinion in Parliament must have told him that, and yet he still refused. 'After brooding unhappily over the problem for what seemed an interminably long period,' he wrote, 'I decided that Bentley's case did not warrant the recommendation for mercy.' His decision brought down on him 'a storm of vituperation without parallel' in his career. He mentioned receiving a few lunatic telephone calls and recalled the humorous aspects of a hostile crowd protesting outside the residence which he had long since vacated. After Bentley was executed, Maxwell Fyfe travelled to Wales, where he had political engagements to fulfil. A member of the public asked for the reason which determined his decision in the Bentley case. He replied that it was not the practice for the Home Secretary to give reasons behind the advice he tendered to the Sovereign regarding the Prerogative of Mercy.

In looking for reasons, commentators have been drawn to the conclusion that Bentley was hanged in order to set an example at a time of rising violence. Concern over juvenile crime was shared by public and Government alike. The tragic loss of a police officer in the course of his duty in an incident involving two teenagers proved a traumatic turning-point. Whereas initial public anger subsided when it seemed that a witless youth of nineteen would be hanged, the Establishment proved to be intransigent. As Reginald Paget put it, 'the fact that Craig could not be hanged made the authorities more determined to hang Bentley'. The idea being that this demonstration of resolve would deter others from embarking on a similar path.

David Yallop took a similar view, which was reflected in the title of his book *To Encourage the Others.* This echoed Voltaire's famous comment about the execution of a British admiral after he had failed to recapture the island of Minorca from the French. Admiral John Byng was court-martialled and shot at Portsmouth in 1757, an act which inspired Voltaire to say of Britain, 'in this country we find it pays to shoot an admiral from time to time to encourage the others'. The killing of police officers at any time is a serious enough crime, but when the nation's police force was below full strength, and against a background of rising crime, the death of PC Miles took on special significance. Moreover, the Home Secretary's natural sympathies resided with the police of whom he was the head, as his attendance at the funeral of Miles had shown. It is not difficult to believe that among all the pressures to which he was subjected there was a strong police lobby for him to stand firm. Maxwell Fyfe acknowledged this in his memoirs when he wrote about, 'the possible effects of my decision upon the police force, by whom the murder of a police officer is justly regarded as the most heinous of crimes'.

Thus to encourage the police and to discourage the lawless, a nineteen-year-old youth, despite his mental defectiveness, his subordination to a younger criminal, his lesser guilt, the jury's recommendation and all the other factors of which justice should have taken account, was hanged. An act which Reginald Paget described as 'itself wrong and unjust'.

Writing about the Bentley case in his book, *Reprieve,* Fenton Bresler commented: 'Maxwell Fyfe's decision that Derek Bentley should hang was so unpopular that it played a part four years later in bringing about the first step in the abolition of capital punishment in this country.' Bresler's view was that there was no doubt in law as it then stood that Bentley was guilty of murder. He thought it was put properly by Lord Goddard at the trial and, of course, it was subsequently upheld by the Court of Criminal Appeal. What remained to be asked was why Bentley did not receive the benefit of compassion and mercy that was provided for in the system.

In a dispassionate review of the case, Fenton Bresler referred to the 'Bentley Industry', which inspired many books and articles, including some that were exaggerated and sentimental. He believed that several of the grounds on which it was argued the Home Secretary should have granted a reprieve were rightly rejected. For example, he pointed out that too much was built on the notion that the refusal of a reprieve was the more regrettable because the trial judge agreed with the jury's recommendation of mercy. On the basis of Lord Goddard's only reference to the recommendation, when he was sentencing Craig, has been constructed the notion that Lord Goddard believed Bentley should not die. Criticism of Sir David Maxwell Fyfe for rejecting this consideration was consequently not valid.

Where the Home Secretary was in error was in not taking account of the injustice whereby a chance difference in age put the younger boy who fired the fatal shot beyond the reach of the ultimate penalty, but ensured that his accomplice was denied the same privilege. 'It is surely a denial of justice,' wrote Bresler, 'that merely by the fluke of the ages Bentley – who did not fire the gun – was hanged, while Craig – who carried and fired the gun – is now free.' That is why Derek Bentley's execution was a miscarriage of justice, the more so because after ten years in prison, at the age of twenty-six, Christopher Craig successfully rehabilitated himself to lead the life of a respectable citizen. Sadly, in all the circumstances, his weak-willed, less intelligent companion was not given the same opportunity. 'For Sir David Maxwell Fyfe to say that Bentley should forfeit his life is, to me at any rate,' wrote Bresler, 'a monstrous decision.'

Fenton Bresler expressed that opinion in 1965, and, eight years later, when he was researching his book on Lord Goddard and re-examining the Craig and Bentley case, sought an interview with the Dowager Countess de la Warr, Maxwell Fyfe's widow. She said that her husband had discussed the issue with her, although he never involved her in any of the decision-making. His reasoning, as she recalled it, was that if a young man of Bentley's age got off because he accompanied an even younger man who did not hang it might lead to similar incidents. He strongly believed that the police had to be protected and there was a danger of creating a loophole if all that a young person bent on a felony had to do to avoid the consequences was to take with him someone slightly younger who was armed. Lady de la Warr said that her husband's judgements were based on reason but she did not remember a time when considering a reprieve was as difficult as that in Bentley's case.

Even after he had been made an example to encourage the others, Derek Bentley's case was dogged by meanness. After he had been executed his father collected a parcel containing his clothes from Wandsworth Prison. When he opened it all he found were an overcoat, a pair of socks and a tie; the new suit and other articles bought for Derek to wear during his trial were missing. Mrs Bentley brooded on the matter for a few weeks and then told her husband that she thought she would like to have the rest of Derek's clothes. She explained, 'I am going to get them and keep them in his wardrobe.' When her husband called at the prison and requested the return of the clothes he was told that, according to the usual procedure, they had been burnt. Mrs Bentley was so upset by this that she spoke to her constituency MP, Victor Yates, who took the matter up with the Home Secretary. He received the following reply:

Dear Mr Yates

You wrote to me on 31st July about clothing belonging to Derek William Bentley which was not returned to his parents after his execution.

The clothing was burnt after Bentley's execution, in accordance with what was then the usual practice. This practice has now been discontinued, and the clothing of an executed prisoner will be returned on demand to next of kin.

David Maxwell Fyfe

Like any parents grieving over the loss of a son, the Bentleys wanted to visit his grave and lay a wreath on it. Derek Bentley's remains, of course, lay within the bleak precincts of Wandsworth Prison. William Bentley approached the Home Office with his request which was denied:

Sir

I am directed by the Secretary of State to refer to your interview at the Home Office on 20th December and to say that he has given careful consideration to your request to be allowed to visit your son's grave at Wandsworth Prison but regrets that he is unable to grant it.

Bentley sought the assistance of the Bishop of Croydon, who had

155

extended much thoughtful sympathy to the family during their time of trial, to see if he might persuade the Home Office to change its mind. But he too failed, writing to Bentley to tell him that the Home Secretary was 'afraid that the answer must still be the same'. The Bishop had some kind words for Mrs Bentley in her disappointment, reminding her that like many mothers of dead Servicemen deprived of the opportunity to visit the graves of their loved ones, she could at least pray for her son.

On every anniversary of Derek's execution, his parents visited Wandsworth Prison to stand outside its walls and place flowers against the main gate in an act of remembrance. Their son's bedroom at his home in Fairview Road was left as it was on the evening he last used it. A jacket and trilby hat lay on the bed with a pair of shoes on the floor. His childhood toys filled the wardrobe and an alarm clock stood on the dresser next to a handsome jug and basin. Downstairs in the sitting-room a photograph of Derek relaxed and smiling stood on the sideboard. This too became a shrine on the anniversary of his execution, when the photograph was surrounded with cards and flowers from friends and well-wishers. Placed poignantly beneath the photograph was a small figurine depicting the three wise monkeys – hearing no evil, seeing no evil and speaking no evil.

The Bentley family was reduced to a low state by Derek's execution. The refusal of the Home Office to grant their request to visit his last resting-place left a wound in his mother's heart that 'is kept open and will not be healed', wrote William Bentley, who was unable to work for six months after the tragedy. He then devoted his energies to clearing Derek's name. Attempts during Question Time at the House of Commons to draw from the Minister of Education the facts regarding Derek Bentley's schooling failed, as did Sydney Silverman's endeavours to debate the execution. Thus all efforts to make public the facts concerning Bentley's epilepsy and illiteracy were defeated by Government ministers and the circumstances of his execution could not be debated for procedural reasons.

In 1966, the Home Office finally gave permission for Derek Bentley's body to be removed from its grave in Wandsworth Prison and released to his family for reburial. He was laid to rest in Croydon Cemetery. William Bentley died in 1974 at the age of sixty-nine and his death was followed by reports of psychic phenomena in the Bentley home. His wife, so it was claimed in newspaper reports, had seen her dead son's spirit in her home, and there were other strange manifestations associated with Derek's room. Iris Bentley took up the fight for justice where her father left it, and in 1974 wrote to the Queen seeking a posthumous pardon for her brother. She received a reply stating that her request had been passed on to the Home Office. Still campaigning in 1988 at a time when Parliament was due to vote on the reintroduction of capital punishment, Miss Bentley warned that 'hanging is murder' and that it brought with it possibilities for irredeemable mistakes.

This was a view broadly echoed by John Parris, who had put up a gritty defence for Christopher Craig. He believed that capital punishment was immoral, and in his book *Most of My Murders* expressed 'grave doubts whether Bentley was in fact guilty, though on the evidence before the court such a verdict was inevitable'. Of course, there were issues affecting Bentley, as this book has tried to make clear, which although known were not put before the court. As Parris put it, 'to deprive a man of his life and then put it beyond the power of society to rectify any miscarriage of justice is surely wrong'. The 'Angry Young Man of the Law' as he had been called, practised for twelve years before being permanently disbarred in 1959 for being an active director of a trading company. The *Daily Mail* noted that, 'The master of the unexpected lived up to his reputation.'

Christmas Humphreys was appointed a judge in 1968 and wrote a number of books on Buddhism after he founded what is now the Buddhist Society in London in 1962. In his autobiography, published in 1978 and called *Both Sides of the Circle*, he devoted a short passage to the Craig and Bentley case. 'I have only two memories to add', he wrote, mentioning 'the apparent injustice' of hanging only the less guilty youth on account of his age and 'the sheer drama of murder being conclusively proved by the shouting of five words, "Let him have it, Chris".' He acknowledged, as he had done in his opening speech for the prosecution at the trial twenty-six years before, that 'the man who shouted was actually himself under arrest at the time'. Humphreys retired from the Bench in 1976 and died in 1983.

The other defence counsel in court at the Old Bailey in 1952, Frank Cassels, became a full-time judge with his appointment in 1954 as Deputy Chairman of London Sessions. He held that post until 1965, and did not go into print with his memoirs.

Lord Goddard belonged to that hardy breed of judges who are conspicuous for longevity. He retired from the Bench in 1958 at the age of eighty-one, when the Queen bestowed on her Lord Chief Justice the GCB. At the age of eighty-two he sat as a judge in the

Appeal Court and made regular appearances at the House of Lords. He died in 1971, and at his own request there was no memorial service, a practice which he had dismissed as 'exercises in hypocrisy'.

In 1959 Arthur Smith, who had started work in Goddard's chambers as a barrister's clerk in 1903, published a biography of the 'Chief'. He had consulted Goddard on the advisability of doing so and was told to please himself, although it was made clear that Goddard himself would have no part in it. In the chapter devoted to Craig and Bentley, Smith showed a degree more understanding of Bentley than had his master. 'His dim, extinguished expression, and his groping, monosyllabic answers to the questions put to him by counsel, gave the impression of someone on the borderline of feeble-mindedness.' Regarding the final outcome of the case, Smith noted that Goddard 'thought all along that Bentley must be reprieved. Day after day he confidently awaited the news of the Home Secretary's decision. And day after day passed, and the news still did not come.' The Chief was reported as being 'profoundly distressed' when Maxwell Fyfe declined to advise the exercise of the Royal Prerogative of Mercy.

A year earlier a biography of Lord Goddard written by Eric Grimshaw and Glyn Jones appraised the former Lord Chief Justice's career and cases. His biographers noted that Lord Goddard appeared to have no misgivings about the value of hanging. A few months after Derek Bentley was hanged the Lord Chief Justice spoke at a Mansion House banquet given by the Lord Mayor of London. Goddard said, 'There are signs, not great signs, but there are signs that the wave of violent crime is to some extent receding. I think I can say that I attribute that, at any rate to a great extent, to the firm attitude of the Home Secretary in refusing to interfere with the due course of justice in a recent case in which great pressure was brought to bear on him at the beginning of the year.' This could only have been a reference to Derek Bentley and, as Grimshaw and Jones pointed out, the crime rate in 1953 did indeed show a smaller increase than the previous year. But the trend has been an upward one ever since, and Lord Goddard was obliged to acknowledge this in 1957. His biographers asked whether 'a Bentley must be hanged once a year, if possible, in order that the rate of increase shall be kept down?' They concluded that there may be a good defence to be argued for hanging Bentley, 'Lord Goddard certainly thinks there is. One can only reply that this questionable execution seems less and less justified the more one studies it.'

Fenton Bresler, in the course of writing *Reprieve* and subsequently his biography of the Lord Chief Justice, was granted an interview by Lord Goddard, then aged eighty-four. His Lordship would not at that time (1962) allow any of his statements to be attributed to him by name. Bresler said that in the course of the interview, 'he expressed himself forcefully on the case of Derek Bentley'. Bresler kept his notes of that conversation and was able to draw on them when writing *Lord Goddard*. He was told, 'Although Craig's offence was the greater of the two, they are both equally guilty of murder and should equally have hanged.' He continued by saying with reference to the age difference between the convicted youths, 'Because they couldn't hang the one doesn't mean to say they shouldn't have hanged the other.'

In 1956, led by Sydney Silverman, the House of Commons on a free vote resolved 'That this house believes that the death penalty no longer accords with the needs or the true interests of a civilised society.' The then Home Secretary, Major Gwilym Lloyd George, reprieved all convicted murderers condemned to death during the thirteen months of parliamentary debate which ensued. In the event, Silverman won the day in the Commons but the House of Lords rejected the Bill. In 1957 the Government brought in the Homicide Act which for all its faults was a step in the right direction. The views of Lord Goddard and his supporters were beginning to wane.

Derek Bentley's execution, however justified by the law as it stood in 1953, served no purpose. It did not have the effect of deterring criminal violence, which was one of the arguments used for not granting a reprieve. It was an act of retribution, and as such was a miscarriage of justice. In his book of that title, C.G.L. Du Cann wrote:

> The sentence ignored the circumstances of Bentley's participation. When Police Constable Miles was shot and killed, Bentley was utterly passive, technically under arrest by Fairfax, his impulsive – and ambiguous – words (which he and Craig denied), 'Let him have it, Chris', might have been an incitement to shoot. But that, if it was uttered, was not uttered (at worst) to induce the later shot at Miles; the 'him' was Fairfax and the time was earlier.

Save for the omission of any reference to Bentley's inferior mental abilities, this summary of the case provides an excellent perspective for the whole affair.

Derek Bentley's execution was a miscarriage of justice, and

because of his family's grief and the nation's indignation, his life became an anvil on which was forged new, more humane laws. His death accelerated the pace of change that ushered in criminal-law reform in the shape of the Homicide Act. The reforms had about them the air of compromise, for the driving force of public opinion was still partially blocked by a reluctance to let go of capital punishment completely. The new Act categorized murder under two headings – those which attracted the death penalty (capital murders) and those which did not. Murder in the furtherance of theft and murder of a police officer executing his duty constituted capital murder. The concept of 'diminished responsibility' was introduced to allow a verdict of murder to be reduced to manslaughter where appropriate.

Even while Derek Bentley was sitting in the condemned cell at Wandsworth, confidently expecting news of the reprieve that never came, one of the major reforms was well under way. A Royal Commission set up under Sir Ernest Gowers had been working for four years inquiring into the question 'whether capital punishment for murder should be limited or modified and, if so, to what extent and by what means'. The Commission took evidence from over two hundred witnesses, including Albert Pierrepoint, the public executioner who hanged Bentley and many others. Pierrepoint repeated at length the evidence he gave to the Commission in his autobiography. What he had to say – and there was no one better qualified to say it – concerned the method of judicial execution used in Britain. His opinion as to the value of capital punishment was not sought by the Commission, but he gave it anyway in his book. Writing in 1974, he said, 'I now sincerely hope that no man is ever called upon to carry out another execution in my country. I have come to the conclusion that executions solve nothing, and are only an antiquated relic of a primitive desire for revenge which takes the easy way and hands over the responsibility for revenge to other people.'

The Royal Commission delivered its report in September 1953, too late for its recommendations to do anything but heighten the tragedy of Bentley's death. By a majority vote the Commission advised that the statutory age-limit for the death sentence be raised from eighteen to twenty-one years. It was also recommended that 'Any test of criminal responsibility must take account of the fact that, where a grave crime is committed by a person who is so grossly disordered mentally that he could properly be certified as insane, the presumption that the crime was wholly or largely caused by the insanity is, in ordinary circumstances, overwhelmingly strong, and there is an equally strong presumption in the grosser forms of mental deficiency and of certain epileptic conditions.' Further recommendations were made regarding the law covering insanity and mental disease, with the conclusion that 'The sentence of death ought not to be carried out on any person who is certifiable as a mental defective' and 'the mental state of every prisoner charged should be examined by two doctors, of whom one at least should be a psychiatrist who is not a member of the prison service and the other usually an experienced member of that service.' As David Yallop observed, if these recommendations had been published earlier they would have served to prevent the hanging of Derek Bentley.

The last executions in Britain were carried out in 1964, and capital punishment was abandoned altogether in 1969. With the other reforms came a fresh look at the law relating to mental illness through another Royal Commission which reported in 1957. The Commission's main conclusion was that the Mental Deficiency Act, which had been in force since 1913, was completely outdated. In its place, in 1959, came the Mental Health Act in which the section dealing with mentally disordered offenders required the evidence of two doctors, 'one of whom must be approved for the purpose'. Thus future offenders with the mental characteristics akin to Bentley's would not be damned by a single opinion.

Welcome though these changes in the law were in a civilized community, it cannot be claimed that Bentley's execution alone triggered them off. Nevertheless, his death and the circumstances surrounding it inspired a singular public reaction that changed the climate of opinion and opened the way for reform. The denial of a reprieve to Derek Bentley given all the circumstances could only illuminate those unyielding views that required an example to be made.

All criminal proceedings in the English courts are carried out in the Monarch's name, and it is a tradition that the Crown is the fountain of justice. One of the means by which the Crown can right a wrong is the Royal Pardon, usually exercised through the Home Secretary. A Royal or free pardon is not an especially rare phenomenon; a number are issued each year to rectify wrongful convictions. The effect of a pardon is not to quash a conviction in the manner of a successful decision at the Court of Appeal, but it is generally accepted as eliminating the conviction and its consequences.

It seems an anomaly that a person erroneously convicted of a criminal offence may finally be pardoned for an act that was never committed. Nevertheless, the pardon remains a formula by which a miscarriage of justice can be put right. It has the effect of nullifying an error of the courts, although it does not necessarily involve compensation and cannot be claimed as a right, being offered only as an act of Royal grace. There are good reasons, as this book has sought to demonstrate, why Derek Bentley should be granted, posthumously, the Queen's Pardon for the most powerful reason of all – to right a wrong. Such a gesture will give peace of mind to the surviving members of his family, especially his sister, who demonstrated such sterling human qualities, but it will also heal the conscience of a generation whose voice of indignation at the time went unheeded. Moreover, it will bind the victims of this tragedy together in natural justice. For all the grief suffered by Mrs Miles and her family at the loss of her husband, it is clear that neither by deed nor intent did Derek Bentley cause his death.

While there may be strong emotional reasons for advocating a pardon for Derek Bentley, there are also compelling legal arguments. The fact is that the law was broken several times both in spirit and in the letter in his progress to the gallows. Although he had the age and physical build of a nineteen-year-old, Bentley's mental age was indisputably that of an eleven- or twelve-year-old child. Various Acts of Parliament were in force in 1952 to protect young people, in particular the Children and Young Persons Act of 1933 and the Education Act of 1944. Section 52 of the Children and Young Persons Act stated that no child under the age of fourteen could be imprisoned and no young person (unless unruly) could be sentenced to penal servitude or imprisonment. Nor could sentence of death be pronounced or recorded against a person under the age of eighteen. This was the provision which spared Christopher Craig.

The 1944 Education Act stated that, 'A child is a child till sixteen, if he or she is blind, deaf, defective or epileptic.' A child was defined under the 1933 Act as 'a person under fourteen' and a young person as 'a person who has attained the age of fourteen years and is under seventeen'. The violation of Bentley's legal rights began in 1948 when, as a fifteen-year-old, he was arraigned before the magistrates at Croydon Juvenile Court on a charge of theft. He was remanded for reports (which it has since been confirmed have been destroyed) and subsequently sent to Kingswood Approved School for three years. A youth of his age, with his poor school record and assessment as unsuitable for normal education, should never have been subjected to the Approved School system but should have been referred to a school for educationally sub-normal children. The magistrates were clearly in breach of their responsibilities by not complying with the laws as they then stood to protect the interests of young people.

The tragedy of errors which engulfed Bentley stretched further back to the time when the education system had a duty towards him. When he was nearly fifteen, he still could not write his name, and was almost illiterate.

According to his teachers in the summer of 1947 when he theoretically attended Norbury Manor School, he was a dull-witted, uninteresting boy, who, if he attended 'once a week we were lucky'. In their efforts to correct matters, the magistrates placed an attendance order on this illiterate boy with a background of epilepsy and chronic truancy, compelling him to attend a school which was further from his home. Not only was this decision lacking in common sense but it was also unlawful. Under the Education Act of 1944, responsibility for the medical examination and assessment of children unsuitable for normal education lay with the Local Education Authority. The system clearly defaulted in Bentley's case and it appeared that he was written off by those who had both the moral duty and the legal responsibility to protect his interests.

When Bentley appeared with Craig before the Croydon Magistrates on the most serious charge of all in 1952 it was known from his medical records that he was epileptic and educationally sub-normal with an IQ of sixty-six – equivalent to that of a child of eleven or twelve years. Once again the magistrates failed to take proper cognizance of the legislation that should have been applied and instead committed him for trial. The double standards practised during the Bentley case were nowhere better exemplified than in the attitude of Lord Goddard. As holder of England's highest criminal legal office, save the Lord Chancellor, he was very familiar with the laws that had been enacted to protect as well as those intended to punish. Derek Bentley was a person who needed the protection of the law, yet Lord Goddard with all that he knew about the youth from the various reports on him as well as from the previous omissions allowed a mentally deficient youth to stand trial for his life.

In 1956, ruling in a case where a mentally deficient girl was detained in an institution, Lord Goddard ordered her release on the grounds that, under the 1913 Act, it was not enough merely to have two medical certificates; it was also necessary to call witnesses to give evidence on the person's state of mind. The provisions of the Mental Deficiency Act were no different in Derek Bentley's time, yet Lord Goddard failed to correct the errors made by two sets of magistrates and indeed compounded them by his silence. As Lord Chief Justice he had the obligation and the power to apply the law correctly but neglected to do so. Bentley was the victim of wrongfully applied justice at several stages in his life and suffered the ultimate miscarriage of justice when his life was taken from him by judicial execution.

Derek Bentley's execution neither encouraged nor discouraged the others – it merely saddened. The dull-witted youth's unfitness to stand trial, the incomplete defence put forward on his behalf and the discrepancies about what happened on that Croydon rooftop on a wet November night in 1952 were serious enough matters. But the monumental failure to grant a reprieve from execution in the face of the nation's demand for fair-minded justice is a matter for shame. Rarely in the history of this United Kingdom has there been such a display of public feeling against an execution. Speaking of his dead son, William Bentley wrote, 'For me he was not an example' and he went on to say that, 'he was a martyr and he deserves to be honoured as such.'

It would be wrong to think of Derek Bentley as a martyr. He is more a symbol of an error of judgement committed in the name of a society emerging from an age of outmoded legal concepts and verging on the edge of great reforms. Many of those reforms came and their humane provisions were welcomed. The focus that Bentley's case provided helped to turn people's minds towards a more civilized sense of justice. The least that the present generation can do is to support a claim on his behalf for a pardon. Perhaps then the bottle of unopened champagne, bought in the expectation of celebrating Derek's appeal against sentence and kept by his sister, could at last be opened. Not for a martyr but in modest celebration of society's acknowledgement that a great wrong has at least been recognized.

> For oak and elm have pleasant leaves
>   That in the spring-time shoot:
> But grim to see is the gallows tree,
>   With its adder-bitten root,
> And, green or dry, a man must die
>   Before it bears its fruit!

APPENDIX I

Firearms Evidence

In order to appreciate the full importance of the firearms evidence it is necessary to discuss some of the principles involved. Forensic ballistics, or simply firearms examination, became an exact science between the two World Wars, and owed much to the invention of the comparison microscope.

The working principles of firearms examination are based on the functional design of modern weapons and their ammunition. When a gun-barrel is machined in the factory spiralled grooves are cut on the inside throughout its length to produce a finish known as rifling. This is the basis of the modern 'rifle', and the technique is also used in the manufacture of revolvers and pistols. The effect of rifling is to spin the bullet when it is fired and passes down the barrel, giving it greater accuracy in reaching its target and better penetration when it strikes.

The number of grooves in the rifling, their pitch and direction of twist, vary from one weapon to another depending on the gun-maker's design. Thus particular makes of gun possess known rifling characteristics. The raised surfaces spaced between the rifled grooves are called lands, and it is the measurement of diameter between opposing lands which determines the calibre of a weapon. Correctly specified bullets are slightly wider than the official calibre of the gun that is to fire them. This ensures that they fit closely in the barrel, so that when they are fired, they will leave the weapon with their designed velocity.

When the soft metal bullet is forced down the rifled barrel it expands into the grooves during its passage, sealing the barrel behind it and thereby making full use of the propellant gases discharged from the cartridge. During this process the bullet is marked by the lands and grooves in a way that is unmistakably characteristic of the firing weapon. This phenomenon, as unique as a fingerprint, lies at the heart of firearms examination.

What makes the process so individual, and has made firearms

examination an exact science, is the principle that every gun-barrel is individually machined. The marks made by machining during manufacture are impressed on every bullet fired, and by that means a bullet can be traced to the weapon that fired it. Guns also leave similar indelible marks on the cartridge-cases ejected from the breech after their bullets have been fired. Thus even after they have separated, both bullet and cartridge case can be traced to the gun in which they were used.

This is where the comparison microscope represented such a breakthrough when it was first used in the 1920s. The instrument is essentially an optical device which allows two different articles to be viewed together in the same field of vision. While it had been understood for a considerable time that every weapon left its own individual marks on the bullets it fired, it had not hitherto been possible to make effective use of this knowledge in criminal cases. The advent of the comparison microscope made it possible for the markings on a bullet fired at a crime scene to be compared directly under magnification with markings made on a bullet test-fired from a suspect weapon. If the sets of markings matched it was evident that the suspect weapon was also the weapon used to commit the criminal offence. Since 1927, when firearms evidence played such an important role in the Gutteridge Case[1], the comparison microscope has been a standard tool in the hands of the firearms examiner.

An important distinguishing feature between handguns is the method of loading, and of dealing with spent cartridge-cases. In the revolver, on the principle of the Western six-shooter, the cartridges are loaded individually into a six-chambered cylinder which revolves to bring each round successively into alignment with the barrel. Once the bullet is fired the empty cartridge-case remains in the cylinder. After firing a full cylinder of six rounds the firer has to eject the empty shell-cases and reload with fresh ammunition.

In a pistol the ammunition is loaded into a magazine which fits into the handle, and the act of pulling the trigger fires each bullet and automatically ejects the empty cartridge-case. The significance of this is that spent casings from automatic pistols are usually left at the scene of the crime.

Guns are designed to perform specified tasks; when they are in good working order and using correct ammunition they will function

[1] Police Constable George Gutteridge was shot dead in an Essex country lane on 26 September 1927. Two men, Frederick Guy Browne and William Kennedy, were tried, convicted and eventually executed for the murder.

in a characteristic way. This was certainly not the case with the firearm used by Christopher Craig, which was far from being an orthodox weapon. The Colt .45 was produced in large numbers in the late 1890s, and the revolver was used in both World Wars. The standard army calibre was .455 in., with a muzzle velocity of 600 fps (feet per second). Using ammunition with a bullet weighing 230 grains, this produced a stopping power about six times greater than the force required to knock down a standing man. The correct ammunition for the service revolver was slightly larger than that for .45 calibre – 11.55 mm as against 11.43 mm.

Striking velocities (fps) of the .455 Revolver at different distances

Distance from muzzle	0 yd	5 yd	10 yd	15 yd	20 yd
FPS	600	596	593	590	287

Craig's gun was a .455 Colt of First World War vintage. He had sawn two inches off the barrel, apparently to make the gun easier to carry in his pocket. He also used a variety of ammunition, which he collected from the army firing range at Caterham in Surrey. Some of it had to be filed down to fit the gun. The hoard of ammunition found at his home included over a hundred rounds of mixed rifle and revolver rounds in six different calibres.

It was acknowledged that Craig's revolver was an inaccurate weapon by virtue of having lost some of its rifling in the piece of barrel that had been sawn off. The lad himself recognized this, when he commented to PC Brown that had he not shortened the barrel he might have killed more policemen.

Lewis Nickolls accepted that the gun would have been inaccurate by as much as six feet at a range of thirty-nine feet. Because of the shortened barrel, the weapon's performance would have been substantially impaired, not just in its accuracy but also in its ability to deliver a bullet to its target with penetrative force. This was amply borne out by the shot that hit Fairfax. Fired at a distance of six feet, according to the policeman, the bullet tore a ragged hole in his jacket in the region of the collarbone without breaking the bone or penetrating the flesh, and came to rest inside his clothing. Although the shot knocked the officer down, it did not incapacitate him, as his subsequent courageous actions were to show.

A shot at this close range fired from a .455 revolver with an intact barrel and using correct ammunition would probably have broken any bone it contacted and lodged in the wound. If the bullet had encountered a fleshy part of the shoulder the likelihood is that it would have passed clean through.

It is interesting to compare the outcome of the shot which hit Fairfax with the circumstances of the bullet which killed Miles. Covering a distance of about thirty-nine feet, the bullet struck the latter officer in the front of the head on the inner side of the left eyebrow, passed through the brain and out of the head, making an exit hole slightly to the right at the back of the skull. The wound was described by the pathologist as being 'a typical wound of entry of a large-calibre bullet'.

Not only was the bullet travelling with sufficient velocity to pass clean through the man's head but it had energy left to continue its flight into oblivion. A search of the rooftop and of the ground surrounding the crime scene failed to retrieve the fatal projectile.

Comparing the circumstances of the two incidents, an objective observer might be forgiven for thinking that two different weapons had been used. Indeed, it was alleged later that two guns had been used – a hypothesis made possible by inconsistencies in the statements made by the police and by gaps in the firearms evidence. David Yallop, writing about the case in his book *To Encourage The Others*, published in 1971, contended that PC Miles was shot dead not by Craig but by an armed police officer on the roof. There were reports at the time of the shooting, including one from E. V. Tullett, a reliable Fleet Street crime reporter for the *Sunday Express*, claiming that guns had been issued to six police marksmen.

In support of his thesis, Mr Yallop referred to the pathologist's report on PC Miles in which the entry wound was described as being typical of a large-calibre bullet. Dr Haler subsequently expanded on this remark in an interview with David Yallop. He said that he had formed the opinion that the wound could have been caused by a bullet with a calibre between .32 and .38. It follows that a .38 bullet fired from Craig's .455 Colt would have had little more power than a pea-shooter. Indeed, Mr Yallop's information from a ballistics expert was that it would not be possible to fire such a bullet from a .455 revolver. Dr Haler, asked about the likely distance the bullet would have travelled after exiting from the dead policeman's head, suggested it might have gone another fifty yards.

Despite the fact that the fatal bullet was never found, leaving open the sort of speculation mentioned, it was nevertheless feasible to pinpoint the cartridge-case from which it was fired, and by that means at least to identify its calibre. That this investigation was either not carried out at the time by the firearms examiner or was excluded from the presentation of evidence at the trial was, to put it mildly, poor procedure.

The firearms evidence collected by the police and examined by Lewis Nickolls may be summarized as follows.

Exhibit No.	Description	Where found
5	Spent bullet of an old-fashioned type, undersized for a .455 revolver. Its appearance was consistent with having been fired from the revolver (Exhibit 6)	Waistband of PC Fairfax's trousers
6	.455 Colt revolver with a normal trigger pull of $14\frac{1}{2}$ pounds; the barrel had six grooves with a left-hand twist	Greenhouse at Tamworth Road
7	Piece of a gun barrel which matched Exhibit 6	Craig's home
8	A spent bullet of.45 calibre, weighing 230 grains. It had been fired from a weapon with similar grooving to Exhibit 6. This bullet was too distorted to allow exact comparison	Inside doorway leading to warehouse roof
9	A spent .32 automatic casing, described as a Spring cartridge case. Similar to the type of ammunition used in police hand guns	Outside doorway leading to warehouse roof
10	A spent .45 bullet similar to Exhibit 6 but too damaged to show rifling marks	On eastern corner of warehouse roof
11	A string holding four spent cartridges and two unfired rounds which had been struck by the firing pin but had not discharged. The unfired rounds were .45, 230 grain ammunition of the same type as Exhibit 8	In the revolver found in the greenhouse by Detective Inspector Smith
12	Three spent cartridges filed at base to fit a .455 weapon. Described as ammunition of Italian origin and of First World War One vintage	Warehouse roof near lift-head

What was missing from this catalogue, of course, was the bullet that had killed PC Miles. Thus there was no incontrovertible proof that a shot fired by Craig had killed the officer.

Within hours of the shooting, Craig confirmed to Detective Sergeant Shepherd that his revolver was fully loaded at the outset. 'I had six in the gun,' he said, adding that they were 'Tommy-gun bullets'. The Thompson sub-machine gun and its association with cinema gangsters would doubtless have appealed to young Craig. The weapon used .45, 230 grain bullets, and some of Craig's ammunition was indeed of that type.

Seven shots were the total fired by Craig during the rooftop battle, and these are accounted for by the police statements. To these must be added three misfires, one separating the last two live shots, and two right at the end of the incident – ten trigger pulls in all. That seven bullets were fired from the revolver is confirmed by the firearms evidence; *three* spent cartridges, filed down to fit a .455, were found on the roof by the lift-head, and in the cylinder of Craig's revolver were *four* spent cartridges. In addition, the cylinder contained *two* rounds that had misfired and *one* spent round that had been struck twice by the firing pin, once discharging a bullet and again as a misfire on an empty cartridge-case, thereby accounting for ten trigger pulls.

The sequence of shots was as follows:

1. The bullet which hit Fairfax (F1)
2. Second shot aimed at Fairfax but which missed (F2)
3. First shot aimed at Harrison but which missed (H1)
4. Second shot aimed at Harrison but which missed (H2)
5. The bullet that killed Miles (M)
6. Shot aimed in the direction of the stairhead (SH)
7. First misfire (MF1)
8. Single shot (SS)
9. Second misfire (MF2)
10. Third misfire on an already spent cartridge (MF3)

Of the seven bullets fired from the weapon, only three were recovered (Exhibits 5, 8 and 10), including the projectile which hit Fairfax, but four were missing, including the fatal bullet. Exhibits 8 and 10 found on the roof were badly misshapen, indicating that they had probably struck some part of the building. Exhibit 5, the bullet which struck Fairfax, was presumably in better shape, as it retained sufficient rifling characteristics to enable it to be matched to Craig's revolver.

In order to ascertain the calibre of the bullet which killed Miles by identifying the cartridge of which it had once been an integral part, it is necessary to consider the question of reloading. At some point Craig ejected three spent cartridges from his revolver. This raises a number of intriguing questions, chief of which are, why were only three cases ejected and at what point in the incident on the roof did the reloading take place?

Obviously, there was an opportunity to reload after all six rounds in the revolver's cylinder had been fired. But why eject only three of the spent cartridges? It might be supposed, preparing for a lengthy shootout, that Craig used the first lull in the hectic activity on the rooftop to reload. Perhaps, therefore, having fired three shots, he ejected those empty cartridge-cases and replaced them with three new rounds. This seems unlikely, because it would put the reloading operation between the two shots fired in quick succession at Harrison.

If Craig wanted partially to reload, a good time to do it was between shots four and five, when there was a brief interlude. This was after Harrison withdrew from his exposed position on the sloping roof and before Miles burst out on to the roof by way of the stairhead door. But, having fired four shots, why eject only three of the spent cartridge cases? A possible explanation is that in the excitement of the moment, and bearing in mind that some of his ammunition had been doctored to fit the weapon, he was only able easily to eject three of the four spent cartridges – but which three?

Assuming that Craig did reload after firing four shots, it is possible to pinpoint the cartridge-case which expelled the bullet that killed Miles; it would have been one of those remaining in the cylinder of the weapon when it was retrieved. It is also possible to identify the places in the shooting sequence represented by the three spent cartridges which Craig ejected from the gun on to the warehouse roof and which became Exhibit 12.

To begin to find answers to these questions it is necessary to work back from the known configuration of rounds in Craig's revolver at the completion of the shooting incident. This is confirmed by Detective Inspector Smith's statement in which he noted that the cylinder of the revolver contained four spent cartridges and two misfired rounds in the order shown in Fig. 1.

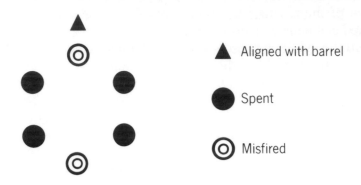

Fig. 1.

Any answers to questions concerning reloading must conform to this final pattern. It has already been suggested that Craig reloaded his revolver during the lull in activity after he had fired at Harrison and before Miles appeared on the rooftop. This seems to be the most likely point to reload, when both the gunman and his police adversaries were taking stock. The firing sequence can thus be divided into two phases:

PHASE ONE
1.	The bullet which hit Fairfax	(F1)
2.	Second shot at Fairfax	(F2)
3.	First shot at Harrison	(H1)
4.	Second shot at Harrison	(H2)

PHASE TWO
5.	Shot that killed Miles	(M)
6.	Shot in direction of stairhead	(SH)
7.	First misfire	(MF1)
8.	Single shot	(SS)
9.	Second misfire	(MF2)
10.	Third misfire	(MF3)

The two phases were separated by the reloading when Craig found that he could only eject three of the four spent cartridges. It is suggested that the three cartridges ejected from the gun were F1, F2, and H2, leaving H1 remaining as a spent casing in the weapon's cylinder. Three new rounds were pushed into the empty chambers alongside the two live shells remaining from the original six. It should be borne in mind that Craig was fascinated with guns and more than capable of mastering an unorthodox situation which might have panicked someone less adept. Before closing the gun he would have adjusted the cylinder and cocked the weapon to make sure the spent round was to the right of the barrel, thus allowing him, as he hoped, to fire all the remaining bullets without interruption. As events turned out, he ran into difficulty because two of these rounds misfired.

After reloading, the state of the gun was as shown in Fig. 2.

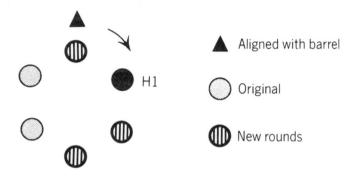

Fig. 2.

When the gun was cocked the cylinder moved round clockwise one position to align with the barrel the round that killed Miles. The details of Phase Two of the shooting are given in Fig. 3.

This explanation of the second phase of the shooting conforms to the final configuration of cartridges found in the gun (Fig. 1). It clearly identifies the cartridge which fired the fatal shot and shows that the third misfire in the sequence was the already spent cartridge (H1) which was the one not ejected by Craig when he reloaded. Cartridge-case MF2 (H1), which ended up as part of Exhibit 11, should have shown evidence on its base of being struck twice by the revolver's firing pin. This account of the reloading and subsequent firing sequence unites the total number of trigger pulls with the ejected cartridges found at the scene and the four spent and two misfired rounds that remained in the revolver at the end.

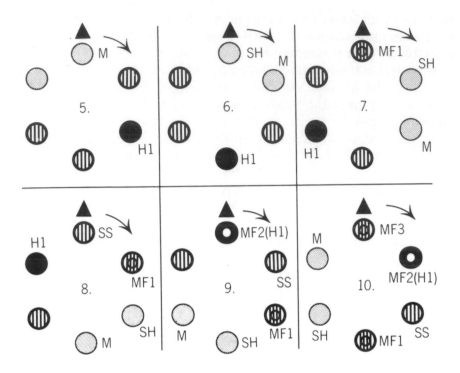

Fig. 3.

David Yallop contended that at the conclusion of the rooftop drama Craig attempted to take his own life. He allegedly put the gun to his head twice, and on both occasions the weapon misfired. On the face of it, this is not confirmed by the state of the cartridges in the revolver when it was finally retrieved, for its cylinder did not contain two consecutively misfired shells. That the gun appeared to misfire twice at the end was borne out by PC Robert Jaggs, who was on the roof at the time. Describing the final moments, the policeman said, 'There was another shot fired and I then heard the gun click a time or two as though empty.' This is now explained by the likelihood that when Craig pulled the trigger for the last time the hammer came down on an empty shell (H1). At that point he knew he had exhausted his ammunition and he leapt off the roof.

This attempt to extrapolate from the known firearms evidence, by reconstructing the reloading operation and identifying the cartridge which fired the fatal bullet, solves some questions, but raises others. All are ones which should have been answered at the time. The bullet which struck Fairfax and was retrieved in such good condition could have been matched to the cartridge which fired it. This linking of evidence appears not to have been carried out, and a further example of poor procedure lay in the failure to identify each of the casings left in the revolver (Exhibit 11) with their final position in the cylinder. The balance of probability is that the bullet which killed Miles ended up in the ten o'clock position in the gun's cylinder as shown in Fig. 4.

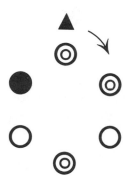

Fig. 4.

The two misfires (live rounds struck by the firing pin but not discharged) were described by Detective Inspector Smith as .45 ammunition, which meant they were smaller than the .455 calibre of the revolver. Neither Smith nor Lewis Nickolls gave the specification of the four spent cartridges. Nickolls stated that the bullet which struck Fairfax (Exhibit 5) and one of the misshapen bullets (Exhibit 10) had been derived from cartridges similar to one case in Exhibit 11 and to all three cases in Exhibit 12 – that is, undersized for Craig's revolver. If the fatal bullet was indeed similar to the one which, happily, struck Fairfax so ineffectively, it makes the killing of PC Miles a remarkable, one-in-a-million ballistics event. A summary of the firearms evidence is given over the page.

To put the shot that hit Fairfax into perspective, it should be said that the officer's estimate of the distance, six feet, was probably exaggeratedly close. The distortion of distance is understandable in the drama of the moment, and the real range was probably greater. If Craig's account of the distance between him and Fairfax is to be believed, the range was nearer thirty feet. The lad claimed that he fired not directly at the policeman but at the ground in front of him. Whatever his intention, it is clear that the bullet which struck Fairfax had not ricocheted from the ground, for it was in perfect

Shot No.		Target	Exhibit No.
1	F1	Fairfax (wounded)	5 (bullet)
2	F2	Fairfax (missed)	12 (ejected case)
3	H1	Harrison (missed)	12 (ejected case)
4	H2	Harrison (missed)	12 (ejected case)
5	M	Miles (fatal)	11 (case left in revolver)
6	SH	Stairhead	11 (case left in revolver)
7	MF1	Misfire	11 (case left in revolver)
8	SS	Single shot	11 (case left in revolver)
9	MF2	Misfire	11 (case left in revolver)
10	MF3	Misfire	11 (case left in revolver)

condition when recovered. The distance was probably greater than Fairfax's estimate, and he was saved from serious injury or death by the idiosyncratic behaviour of Craig's revolver and ammunition.

An interesting discussion point regarding David Yallop's theory is the reference made by Dr Haler in his official report to the large-calibre bullet which killed PC Miles. This contrasts strangely with his opinion reported later that the calibre of the bullet was between .32 and .38. Comparison of the different calibres is easier when they are converted to metric units:

Inch		*mm*
.32	=	8.13
.38	=	9.65
.45	=	11.43
.455	=	11.55

It can be seen quite readily that there is a difference in calibre of over 3 mm between .32 and .455 bullets. This difference makes it difficult to reconcile the doctor's two statements; a .455 bullet is of large calibre, whereas a .32 is not. In any case, it is unwise to assume too much about the likely calibre of the bullet by examining the entry wound it caused. Dr Abdullah Fatteh, an expert on gunshot wounds, noted in his book *Medicolegal Investigation of Gunshot Wounds*, published in 1976, that 'one must give a guarded opinion about the calibre of the bullet from the examination of the wound'. He pointed out that the diameter of the wound may be smaller, greater or equal to the diameter of the bullet, depending on whether or not the bullet struck its target cleanly. A tumbling or yawing bullet, for example, could be expected to inflict a wound greater in size than its calibre.

Conversely, a clean hit may leave an appreciably smaller entry wound than the calibre of the bullet, due to the natural elasticity of the skin.

APPENDIX II

Dr Matheson's Report on Derek Bentley

8664.BENTLEY, Derek William, aged 19 years.   HM PRISON,
Central Criminal Court,   Brixton
Murder.
No.27 in the Calendar.

At the request of the Director of Public Prosecutions I have to report as follows on the mental condition of the above-named. He was received into custody at this Prison on 3.11.52. I examined and interviewed him immediately on reception. He was placed under close mental observation in the Prison Hospital where he has remained since.

I have had further interviews with him. He has been seen daily by myself or a colleague. I have read the daily reports of the Hospital Officers who have had him in their care. I have interviewed his father. I have read and studied the following reports.

1) A report from the Warden of Kingswood Training School, where he was from 27.10.1948 to 28.7.1950.

2) A report dated 16.11.49 of an Electroencephalographic examination which was carried out at the Burden Neurological Institute, Stapleton, Bristol, by A.L. Winter, Assistant Electroencephalographer.

3) A report by Dr James A. Munroe, Physician in Psychological Medicine, Guy's Hospital, where the prisoner was a patient when a baby, from 30.6.33 to 10.7.33 and where he was examined on two later occasions, viz. 20.6.49 and 9.8.49.

4) A report from Mr C.F. Towes, Welfare Officer for Home Office Schools, who had the duty of supervising the prisoner after he was released on licence from the Kingswood Training School on 28.7.50. During this period of supervision, Mr Towes made 31 visits to the prisoner's home. On 16 of these visits he had interviews with the prisoner himself.

5) A copy of a letter sent by the Ministry of Labour and National Service to the prisoner's father on 19.11.52.
6) A report of the result of an Electroencephalographic examination carried out at the Maudsley Hospital on 27.11.52 by Dr Denis Hill.
7) The police report and depositions.

Family History (informants – the prisoner, his father, Mr Bentley, and the police report).
His father and mother are alive. The prisoner is the third eldest of a family of five. The younger brother died as an infant and was a Mongol, this is a form of feeble-mindedness accompanied by characteristic physical abnormalities.

The father informs me that he knows of no morbid mental history on his side of the family. The police state that on the mother's side there is a history that a cousin of his mother's suffered from epilepsy. This history, taken in conjunction with the birth of a Mongol to the prisoner's mother, suggests that the stock on the mother's side is not good.

Personal History (informants – the prisoner, his father, Mr Bentley, the police, and the medical authorities, Guy's Hospital).
Within 24 hours of being born the prisoner was admitted to Guy's Hospital suffering from pneumonia. As a result of treatment he recovered and was discharged after 10 days. He was a difficult child to rear on account of his bad temper.

School
At the age of 3 he started attending a Nursery School. He afterwards attended the Secondary Modern School at Norbury. After 7 months at this school he was transferred to another school by order of the Local Authority as he was a source of trouble to both teachers and other pupils. His attendance record was bad and the school could not get co-operation from his parents. He stayed at this school for just over a year and then returned to the Norbury Secondary School. There he stayed until March 1948 when he left having reached the Inferior Top Class. The Headmaster there found him backward and workshy but he did not consider him to be feeble-minded. At that time he was very slow in learning to read and write. While at school he took no interest in games.

As a result of a finding of Guilty at a Croydon Juvenile Court in September, 1948, he was committed to Kingswood Training School,

Bristol; while there his IQ was estimated to be at 66 and that he had a reading age of $4\frac{1}{2}$ years. There, too, he was found to be lazy and indifferent to training and it was found that he showed no interest in learning but was content to drift along doing as little as possible.

During a period of home leave in 1949 he attended, on two occasions, Guy's Hospital. He had been sent to the Out-Patient Department for investigation of his complaint of constant headaches. Dr Munroe considered that he might be feeble-minded but that he did not co-operate well in the examination. He recommended that he be returned to the Approved School for further training. He was taken back to the Kingswood Training School and in November of that year (1949) he was examined by the Burden Neurological Institute. The result of an Electroencephalographic examination suggested very strongly that he suffered from 'petit mal', a form of epilepsy.

On release from the school on licence in July 1950 he came under the care of Mr C.F. Towes, Welfare Officer for Home Office Schools. Mr Towes visited his home 31 times and on 16 of these visits interviewed the prisoner himself. Mr Towes reports that he formed the impression that the parents were over-indulgent to the prisoner and he, Mr Towes, found it difficult to get full co-operation from the parents and from the prisoner.

He did not work from the time of his release from the School until 1951. During this period his father says he was trying to get him employment with the Electricity Authorities, with whom he, the father, worked. During this period of unemployment the prisoner spent a good deal of his time at home repairing radio sets, etc. During this period too he had trouble with his ears.

In March 1951 he got employment with a firm of furniture removers. He remained there for a year; this is the longest period he has been in one job. When he left this employment in March 1952, the reason given was that he was finding the work too heavy for him. Just before he left this employment he was examined on behalf of the Ministry of Labour and National Insurance. The Medical Board who examined him placed him in Grade Four as they had before them a report from the family doctor that he suffered from 'petit mal'.

From March to May 1952 he was unemployed and the Welfare Officer reports that his attitude became more uncooperative than ever.

In May of this year he started work with the Croydon Corporation Cleansing Department. He appeared to be making an effort to do his best and to improve in his conduct. But this effort was not maintained

180

and after a month's employment as a dustman, at a wage of £6 15s 0d a week, he was considered so unsatisfactory that he was re-employed as a road sweeper at a lower wage of £4 7s 0d a week. He was no more successful at this than his previous employment and in July 1952 he was dismissed. Since then he has been unemployed.

Medical History

As already noted, as a baby he suffered from pneumonia. His father tells me that while still an infant he had several falls on his head, but says they were never very serious.

Between the ages of 3 and 5 (his father cannot be sure of the exact age) he had a fit. From the description the father gave to me it would seem that this could have been a major epileptic fit. His father said he had 4 similar fits, the last one being when he was aged about 8 years. Since the cessation of the fits the prisoner states he has often suffered from headaches.

During the early part of the air attacks on London the houses in which the family were living were damaged and on one occasion, the father says, the prisoner was buried by debris.

At puberty he suffered a good deal from acne and boils in his ears.

Sex and Habits

No history of marked perverse sexual habits has been elicited. He has associated with girl friends but denies ever having had sexual intercourse. His usual associates were boys of a younger age than himself.

He says he always has been a heavy smoker, and that from time to time he has taken alcohol, sometimes beer, sometimes spirits.

Present Condition

Physical examination on the day of his admission (3.11.52) showed no evidence of old or recent disease.

His ears were dry and showed no infection. He is of asthenic build, i.e. he is loosely built and his body muscles are poorly developed.

At interviews he has been rational and has shown no evidence of insanity.

His account of the alleged offence corresponds with the statement he made to the police.

At all times he said that he did not know that his co-defendant was armed.

At interviews he gives the impression of a youth of low intelligence.

He is careless in his attitude and although expressing great concern at the position in which he now finds himself, he does not, in my opinion, show any real appreciation of the peril in which he stands. His attitude is, that he has always hitherto got out of serious trouble and that, on this occasion he will again be successful.

Mental tests which involve educational training show him to be just above the level of a feeble-minded person.

He is illiterate and cannot read or write.

Tests which do not involve a scholastic knowledge give him a mental age of between 11 and 12 years.

In view of his past history which, in my opinion, indicates that he has been allowed to grow up without any discipline or educational training, his present low intelligence is an educational defect rather than an innate defect. The social incapacity and failure which his history reveals is also, I think, the result of the absence of any discipline or training. It should be pointed out, however, that when he was at the Kingswood Training School, efforts were made to discipline and train him but the Warden states that he was always being encouraged by his father not to co-operate but continually to make complaints.

At no time while he has been under observation at this Prison has he shown any evidence of epilepsy, either of grand mal or major epilepsy, or petit mal; nor has he shown any signs of having any minor epileptic manifestation. His conduct, while under observation in the Ward, has been that of an undisciplined young boy.

On account of his inability to read properly, he spends a good deal of his time looking at 'comics' and picture papers. He tries to mix with the other inmates of the Ward but, as a rule, they do not like his company on account of his arrogant, boastful conversation.

The result of the Electroencephalographic examination at the Maudsley Hospital was compatible with and suggestive of a diagnosis of Epilepsy. No focal abnormality occurred to suggest acquired brain damage.

Summary
The picture he now presents is of an immature youth who has never been subjected to any discipline and has been allowed most of his life to have his own way, whether good or bad.

Although there is a history suggestive of epilepsy which is supported by the Electroencephalographic findings, I have failed from my personal observations to find any evidence of epilepsy. If he did, in fact, suffer from epilepsy, I am of the opinion that, at the time of the alleged offence, he was not suffering from any form of epilepsy.

His conduct before, during and after the alleged offence was always purposive.

I have been unable to find any genuine loss of memory or degree of mental confusion which occur during an epileptic manifestation.

I do not consider that he is a feeble-minded person under the Mental Deficiency Acts.

I am of the opinion that he is:

1) Sane;
2) Fit to plead to the indictment;
3) Fit to stand his trial.

J.C.M. Matheson.
Principal Medical Officer.

APPENDIX III

The Lord Chief Justice's Summing-up and Charge to the Jury at the Trial of Craig and Bentley

The Lord Chief Justice: Now, members of the jury, in many respects this is a very terrible case, and it is one, therefore, that it is desirable you and I should approach in as calm a frame of mind as we can.

Here are two lads, one of sixteen and one of nineteen, admittedly out on a shopbreaking expedition at night, armed with a Service revolver, a dreadful weapon in the shape of a knuckleduster, and two knives which may or may not be described as daggers – one of them I should think certainly could be – and the result is that a young policeman is shot dead while in the execution of his duty. You may think it was almost a miracle that others were not shot too. One of them, we know, Sgt Fairfax, was wounded, but fortunately only slightly.

Now let us put out of our minds in this case any question of films or comics, or literature of that sort. These things are always prayed in aid nowadays when young persons are in the dock, but they have really very little to do with the case. These two young men, or boys, whatever you like to call them, are both of an age which makes them responsible to the law – they are over fourteen – and it is surely idle to pretend in these days that a boy of sixteen does not know the wickedness of taking out a revolver of that description and a pocketful of ammunition and firing it when he is on an unlawful expedition and the police are approaching him. You will remember that so far as Craig is concerned, by his own words he supplied a motive for what he was doing, for he said that he hated the police because they had got his brother twelve years – which seems to show that his brother was convicted for a very serious offence to receive a sentence of that length.

Now there are one or two preliminaries to which I call your attention, though it is hardly necessary. The first one is hardly

184

necessary, because you know as well as I do that in all criminal cases it is for the prosecution to prove their case, and it is said correctly that it is not for the prisoners to prove their innocence. In this case the prosecution have given abundant evidence for a case calling for an answer, and although the prisoners do not have to prove their innocence, when once a case is established against them they can give evidence, and they can call witnesses, and then you have to take their evidence as part of the sum of the case. The effect of a prisoner's evidence may be to satisfy you that he is innocent, it may be it causes you to have such doubt that you feel the case is not proved, and it may, and very often does, have a third effect: it may strengthen the evidence for the prosecution.

The second thing that I have to remind you of is that you have to consider the case of both of these youths separately. Different considerations will apply, and do apply, in the case of Bentley and the case of Craig. I say different considerations apply – you have to apply different tests. Then, of course, as you have been properly warned, any question of fact in the case is entirely one for you, not for me. I have to direct you as to the law, and you will have to consider the facts and apply the facts in accordance with the law as I tell it to you.

Now let us take first of all the case of Craig: it is not disputed, and could not be disputed, that he fired the shot which killed that Police Constable. You are asked to say that the killing was accidental, and that therefore the offence is reduced to manslaughter. Gentlemen of the jury, it is the prerogative of the jury in any case where the charge is of murder to find a verdict of manslaughter, but they can only do it if the evidence satisfies them that the case is properly reducible to one of manslaughter – that is, not with regard to any consequence that may happen, but simply whether the facts show that the case ought to be regarded as one of manslaughter and not of murder; but when I have explained to you the considerations of law which apply in this case, it may be – and, indeed I think it is – probable that you will see that there is no room for manslaughter in this case. However, it is a matter for you.

Now, the law of this country with regard to murder is this: if a person does an act towards another wilfully – that is to say, intentionally – which a reasonable person would know may cause death or grievous bodily harm, and death results, that is murder, and you can see, if you think of it for a minute, that that is merely a matter of common sense. If I were to whip out a revolver and point it at you and shoot one of you gentlemen, and it killed you, it would be no

185

answer for me to say 'Oh, I did not mean to kill him; I only meant to wound him.' The fact is, I am doing a dangerous thing with a dangerous weapon. The same with a revolver or a dagger: if I am doing an act which I know may cause grievous bodily harm, though I may not intend to do more than grievous bodily harm, and death results, that is murder. If in an ordinary case – I say 'ordinary case', a case in which no police officer was concerned – you thought a prisoner only meant to fire wildly, and was not aiming at anybody, but simply letting off a revolver in a grossly negligent way, so negligent that it deserved punishment, and death resulted, that would only be manslaughter, but you would have to consider all the facts before you could come to that conclusion, as to whether he was merely firing wildly or whether he was firing with a deadly intent.

But, gentlemen, there is another and further consideration in this case to which I want to direct your particular attention: Miles, the dead man, was a police officer, and the law for centuries – in fact, ever since there has been law in this country – has given special protection to police officers while in the execution of their duty, or perhaps it is more accurate to say that in the case of the killing of a peace officer – I use the expression 'peace officer' which is the old expression in English law for the modern police constable; he is in exactly the same position as the old parish constables were before there was any regular police force, and who were the only peace officers in the country – in the case of a peace officer who is killed, the law does not give the accused the same defences as in the case of other persons; it takes one away, and I am going to direct you that this is the law: 'If a police officer has arrested, or is endeavouring to arrest (and that includes coming on the scene for the purpose of arresting) a person, and the arrest, if effected, would be lawful, and that person, for the purpose of escaping, or preventing or hindering the arrest, does a wilful – that is to say, an intentional – act which causes the death of the officer, he is guilty of murder, whether or not he intended to kill or do grievous bodily harm.'

Now, will you bear that in mind – and I will read it to you again: 'If a police officer has arrested, or is endeavouring to arrest (which includes coming on to the scene for the purpose of arresting) a person, and the arrest, if effected, would be lawful, and that person, for the purpose of escaping, or preventing or hindering the arrest, does a wilful act which causes the death of the officer, he is guilty of murder, whether or not he intended to kill or do grievous bodily harm.'

In that case the only possible way of reducing the crime to manslaughter is to show that the act was accidental, and not wilful – the act.

Now I cannot do better to illustrate this than to read to you a few lines from a direction given by one of the greatest Judges of Victorian times – Mr Justice Brett, who was afterwards Lord Esher – to a jury in a case where a police officer was killed by a kick – not a kick on the head. A kick in the ordinary way would not be grievous bodily harm; it might hurt, it might wound, but it would not be grievous bodily harm. A kick is not like a blow with a fist, is not anything approaching the use of a deadly weapon; but unhappily, the kick, though it was not intended to kill, did kill a police officer, and this was the direction that the jury were given: 'If the prisoner kicked the man intending to inflict grievous bodily harm, and death ensued from it, he was guilty of murder. That is what I told you first. If the prisoner inflicted the kick in resistance to his lawful arrest, even though he did not intend to inflict grievous injury, he was equally guilty of murder, but if in the course of a struggle he kicked the man not intending to kick him, then he was only guilty of manslaughter. Now, you see, there you get the difference – the deliberate kick. Though it was not intended to do grievous bodily harm, if it was a deliberate kick and caused the death of a police officer, that was murder. If it was not a deliberate kick, but it merely so happened that the prisoner's knee or foot came into contact with the police officer's body owing to a struggle, then it was an unintentional act, and that would only be manslaughter.'

Now, there is no question here but that the arrest, or the attempted arrest, by the police officer or the police officers who were there was lawful. These two young men were engaged in intending to carry out a felony – that is to say, warehouse-breaking – and it was not only a lawful arrest; it was an arrest which the police officers were bound to make if they could; so it was a lawful arrest, and, therefore, if in the course of a lawful arrest the prisoner does an act which kills the police officer, that is murder, unless the act – that is, the firing of the pistol – was accidental.

Now, was it a wilful act which caused the injury? As I told you, the question is not whether the result was accidental in the sense that more harm was caused than was intended. A person who is doing such things as firing off revolvers at police officers cannot say: 'Well, it was accidental that I killed him, because I never intended to kill him.' The answer is: 'You were doing a deliberate act, a wilful act.'

Now that I have explained the law to you, it may be that you will have some difficulty, as I do not hesitate to say I have, in understanding what defence there can be in the case of the prisoner Craig. There he was on this roof, armed, his revolver was loaded, when he took it there he had spare ammunition from which at some time he reloaded it, and you heard, too, that some of this ammunition had been specially filed down to fit the revolver. There he was on the roof with a loaded revolver, firing off shots until his revolver was empty, and then he reloaded the revolver and continued to fire, because, as you know, the revolver contains six chambers and he fired altogether nine shots, and two, I think, that were found that had not detonated; so in all he tried to fire eleven. If that is not a deliberate act, a deliberate firing, it is difficult to understand what would be. But you will remember, and you will bear in mind, that we are only concerned with the death of Police Constable Miles on this indictment, and Police Constable Miles, you will remember, was killed by the third shot which this youth fired. You will bear in mind Detective Sergeant's Fairfax's evidence. He told you of the firing. The first shot was when he first got on to the roof and had arrested, or had attempted to arrest, Bentley, and it was the first shot that hit Sgt Fairfax.

Let me help you to come to a conclusion whether this man was deliberately firing at the officers. The very first shot that he fired hit a police officer, fortunately doing him very little harm. The second shot that was fired, according to Sgt Fairfax's evidence, was when Bentley was on the ground, because you will remember that what the police officer said was that the first shot caused him to spin round and fall to the ground, and he brought Bentley to the ground. Sgt Fairfax got up, and while Bentley was on the ground he was trying to pull Bentley up, or get him as a shield, when the prisoner fired a second time. Then other police officers were heard, because the prisoner himself told you he heard police officers coming up the stairs, and then the third shot was fired in the direction of the stairs, and Police Constable Miles fell dead. The aiming does not seem to have been bad, does it – three shots, two police officers hit, one fortunately slightly, the other hit between the eyes, so that blood gushed out and he fell dead instantaneously.

Then you know that Police Constable McDonald appeared. He had appeared, I should have said, before Police Constable Miles came up the stairs. We will leave Sgt McDonald out for the moment. That was not the only shooting. The next shooting that was spoken to was spoken to by another very gallant officer, Police Constable Harrison, who was working his way on his back along that sloping roof towards the prisoner, and if you accept Police Constable Harrison's evidence – it is a matter for you, but if you accept it – the prisoner fired at least twice in his direction, one of which shots he thinks he heard strike the brickwork. Still, he fired at him.

Now I think the only other thing I need remind you about is what Craig said, according to the evidence of the police officers. You will remember that Sgt Fairfax, having dragged the dead body of Police Constable Miles into the doorway, went downstairs, and by this time reinforcements had arrived and brought a revolver or an automatic for the police, and when Sgt Fairfax at once went back to the roof armed with the automatic he called out to Craig that he had a pistol, and thereupon, according to Sgt Fairfax's evidence, if you believe it, the prisoner said: 'Come on, you coppers! Let's have it out!' Police Constable Jaggs told you that he shouted 'Come on, you brave coppers! Think of your wives!' and to Police Constable Harrison he said: 'I'm Craig. You've just given my brother twelve years. Come on, you coppers! I'm only sixteen.' You may wonder why he said: 'I'm only sixteen.' Possibly you may know that the law does not allow a capital sentence to be passed on a boy of sixteen. Was it a boast? – 'Aha! Come on! I've got a gun. I can't be hanged.' You will think of that.

I do not think it is necessary to go through all that he said in hospital. Enough he said on the roof, in all conscience, if you believe it, to show that that boy, inspired, apparently, by a deadly hatred for the police, was meaning, so you are asked to find and to assume – to infer, I mean – that he meant to kill the police if he could and he did kill one.

Now, gentlemen of the jury, think of those facts together. Is it possible – if it is, you will always find a merciful verdict if you can – to say that that shooting was accidental? I have told you that you have got to find, before you can reduce this case to manslaughter, that the shooting was accidental, not that the result of the shooting was accidental – quite a different matter.

Well, now I turn to Bentley. Members of the jury, these two youths are tried together, and they are both tried for the murder of the policeman. It is quite unnecessary, where two or more persons are engaged together in an unlawful criminal act, to show that the hand of both of them committed the act. The simplest illustration I could give you – after all, this is only a matter of common sense – is this: If two men go out housebreaking, it is a very common thing for one of

189

them to break into a house and the other to stand outside and keep watch, but they are both taking part in the unlawful enterprise, and therefore they are both of them guilty, so if one stands outside so that the other may hand out the loot to him, he is not guilty merely of receiving stolen property; he is guilty of breaking in, because he is a party to the breaking in; and where two people are engaged on a felonious enterprise – and warehouse-breaking is a felony – and one knows that the other is carrying a weapon, and there is agreement to use such violence as may be necessary to avoid arrest, and this leads to the killing of a person or results in the killing of a person, both are guilty of murder, and it is no answer for one to say 'I did not think my companion would go as far as he did'.

Now you can only judge whether there is an agreement to use such violence as may be necessary by looking at what happened and all the circumstances of the case, but I do remind you that it is no excuse and no defence to say 'I knew he was carrying a loaded revolver' – if you find he was – 'that he was carrying a loaded revolver, or a revolver, but I didn't think he would use it.' If one is carrying a revolver and the other knows that he intends to use some degree of violence, it is no answer, if that violence results in death, to say 'Well, I didn't think he would go as far as that.' What you have to consider is: Is there evidence from which you can properly infer that these two youths went out with a common purpose not merely to warehouse-break but to resist apprehension, even by violence if necessary? That is all. It is, as I repeat, no answer, if you come to that conclusion, for one to say: 'Yes, but I didn't think he would go as far as he did.'

Now let us see what the evidence is with regard to Bentley. The first thing that you have to consider is: Did Bentley know that Craig was armed? Now, you know, because I sit on the Bench and you sit in the jury-box it is not necessary that we leave our common sense at home. The great virtue of trial by jury is that jurymen can exercise the common sense of ordinary people. Can you suppose for a moment, especially when you have heard Craig say that why he carried a revolver was for the purpose of boasting and making himself a big man, that he would not have told his pals he was out with that he had got a revolver? Is it not almost inconceivable that Craig would not have told him, and probably shown him the revolver which he had? That is quite apart from what Bentley said afterwards. I should think you would come to the conclusion that the first thing, almost, Craig would tell him, if they were going off on a shop-breaking expedition, was: 'It's all right. I've got a revolver with me.'

190

Then see what Bentley had on him. Where is that knuckleduster? Apparently it was given to him by Craig, but Bentley was armed with this knuckleduster. Have you ever seen a more horrible sort of weapon? You know, this is to hit a person in the face with who comes at you. You grasp it *here*, your fingers go through – I cannot quite get mine through, I think – and you have got a dreadful heavy steel bar to strike anybody with; and you can kill a person with this, of course. Then did you ever see a more shocking thing than *that*? You have got a spike with which you can jab anybody who comes at you; if the blow with the steel is not enough, you have got this spike at the side to jab. You can have it to see, if you like, when you go to your room. It is a shocking weapon. Here was Craig armed with a revolver and that sheath knife. Hand me that sheath knife – the big one. One wonders, really, what parents can be about in these days, allowing a boy of 16 – they say perhaps, they do not know, but why do not they know? – to have a weapon like this which he takes about with him? It is not a new one, you can see; it is pretty well worn. That was the thing that Craig was taking about. Where is the other knife? Here is Bentley with a smaller knife, but you can feel it is sharp and pointed. What is he carrying that with him for in his coat, not even with a sheath on it?

Can you believe it for a moment although Bentley had said he did not know Craig had the gun? You are not bound to believe Bentley if you think the inference and common sense of the matter is over-whelming that he must have known that he had it. Now, of course, the most serious piece of evidence against Bentley is that he called out, if you believe the evidence, to Craig 'Let him have it, Chris!', and then the firing began, and the very first shot struck Sgt Fairfax. Gentle-men, those words are sworn to by three police officers – Sgt Fairfax, Police Constable McDonald, and Police Constable Harrison; they all swear that they heard Bentley call that out, and that then the firing started. There is one thing I am sure I can say with the assent of all you twelve gentlemen, that the police officers that night, and those three officers in particular, showed the highest gallantry and resolu-tion; they were conspicuously brave. Are you going to say they are conspicuous liars? – because if their evidence is untrue that Bentley called out 'Let him have it, Chris!', those three officers are doing their best to swear away the life of that boy. If it is true, it is, of course, the most deadly piece of evidence against him. Do you believe that those three officers have come into the box and sworn what is deliberately untrue – those three officers who on that night showed a devotion to duty for which they are entitled to the thanks of the community?

Now the other statement on the roof, the other exclamation of Bentley on the roof, is nothing like so important. He shouted out 'They're taking me down, Chris'. Whether that was an invitation to Craig to go on shooting or whether it was an invitation to Craig to stop shooting lest his (the previous Bentley's) body should suffer, is a matter which really does not matter: by that time Police Constable Miles was dead. What does matter is whether Bentley shouted in the first instance 'Let him have it, Chris!' – 'Let him have it, Chris!' – because if he did, then you can consider whether that does not show, firstly, that he knew that 'Chris' had the revolver, and, secondly, was calling upon 'Chris' to use violence to prevent arrest.

Then in the car first of all he said 'I knew he had a gun' – that is sworn to by three officers – 'I knew he had a gun, but I did not think he'd use it.' As I have told you, if he knew he had a gun, and knew he was taking the gun for protection in their common unlawful enterprise, or to prevent arrest by violence, Bentley is as guilty as Craig; he is as guilty in law as Craig.

Then in his statement he said: 'I didn't know he was going to use the gun.' Again, if he said that, it shows that he knew it. If he knew that he had the gun, can you believe he did not know he had ammunition? Why did he have ammunition? Why did he have the gun? Why did he have the ammunition? You will remember that at one stage the officers said that Craig on the roof told them he had a .45 and lots of ammunition. I think they said something about 'blowing your head off' – 'He'll blow your head off'. Then later in his statement he said he did not know 'Chris' had a gun till he shot. That, of course, is quite inconsistent with what he said earlier in his statement. You can have the statement when you go to your room, if you like. He did say 'I didn't know he was going to use the gun', and then he said afterwards 'I didn't know Chris had one until he shot.' It does not seem very consistent, but, as I say, the real thing is, is it not, as a matter of common sense, can you believe for a moment that if Bentley had gone on that expedition with this boastful young ruffian who said he carried a gun for the purpose of making himself out bigger than he was, he would not have told Bentley he had the gun? What had he got the gun for, and what did Bentley think he had the gun for?

Members of the jury, that is the whole case. The prisoner's defence, as I told you, is, Craig asks you to reduce the offence to manslaughter. I have pointed out to you the difficulties that there are in accepting manslaughter. Manslaughter can only be accepted here if you think that the whole thing was accidental. How it can be said to be accidental I confess seems to me to be extraordinarily difficult. In the case of Bentley, Bentley's defence is: 'I didn't know he had a gun, and I deny that I said "Let him have it, Chris". I never knew he was going to shoot, and I didn't think he would'. Against that denial (which, of course, is the denial of a man in grievous peril) you will consider the evidence of the three police officers who have sworn to you positively that those words were said.

Gentlemen of the jury, I started by saying this was a terrible case. It is dreadful to think that two lads, one, at any rate, coming, and I daresay the other, from decent homes, should with arms of this sort go out in these days to carry out unlawful enterprises like warehouse-breaking and finish by shooting policemen. You have a duty to the prisoners. You will remember, I know, and realise, I know that you owe a duty to the community, and if young people, but not so young – they are responsible in law – commit crimes of this sort, it is right, quite independent of any question of punishment, that they should be convicted, and if you find good ground for convicting them, it is your duty to do it if you are satisfied with the evidence for the prosecution.

I have reminded you of what the defence is, and I think I have sufficiently reminded you of what the prosecution's case is, and with those words I will ask you to go to the serious and solemn duty that you have of considering your verdict.

APPENDIX IV

Judgment Delivered at the Court of Criminal Appeal
Regina v Derek William Bentley

Mr Justice Croom-Johnson: In this case the Appellant appeals against a verdict of murder substantially on the ground that he was not engaged in a joint enterprise with a boy of 16, the murder having been committed of a police officer by the boy of 16 firing shots from a Colt pistol, as it is called, and the question which was involved was whether the two people were engaged on a joint enterprise which took them up to the roof of a building at Croydon where they were in process of being apprehended by a number of police officers who had been appraised of the adventure which they were upon so far as their presence on the roof was concerned. The question was the familiar question which arises in a great number of criminal cases: Two people go out on a joint adventure and one stands by. As a matter of law each of them is responsible for the consequences of the particular crime and is liable to be punished as such, but if death results it has to be shown that the man who did not commit the murder, fired the shot, aimed the blow or all the other variations of that sort of thing, knew or is judged by the jury to have known that his companion in the adventure was armed. It must not be taken that I am purporting to give an exhaustive account of all the circumstances in which one of two joint criminals may be liable for the consequences of the acts of the other, but that was the sort of case which was presented here and there was a good deal of evidence which was called about it. In the end the jury found that this Appellant was guilty of murder, a verdict which could only be returned on the facts of this case if the jury were satisfied within the principles of our criminal jurisprudence that this prisoner knew that the other man was armed and knew what was the adventure they were upon.

There was overwhelming evidence fit to be considered by the jury and upon which the jury could come to the conclusion that the prisoner, the Appellant, knew all about what the other individual was ready to do. I will not reiterate the statements which have been referred to this morning, it being remembered that an appeal in such circumstances is not a retrial of the whole case; it is an appeal on matters of law to see whether the trial has been properly conducted in the sense that the case has been properly and adequately presented to the jury. It is on that aspect of the matter that we have listened to a careful and concise argument by Mr Cassels with a view to persuading us that the Chief Justice, who tried the case, did not adequately present some of the matters to the jury which were fit and proper for the jury to consider before the jury could come to the conclusion whether statements alleged to have been made by this Apellant were made by him or not. He denied that he had made such statements, although something rather like one of them is apparently to be found in a statement which the Appellant signed taken by police officers. It is suggested that the Chief Justice in summing up the case to the jury and having called attention to some of those statements as deposed to by police officers in the case did not give sufficient attention to denials which were made by the Appellant and indicated to the jury that they were statements which were not accepted by the defendant. Speaking for myself, with almost a lifetime of experience of jury trials in criminal cases, I am bound to say that when I sit in this Court and hear these arguments, they come to me I will not say with a sense of unreality but as being something very far divorced from what one usually finds at criminal trials, my experience being that juries pay the most careful and anxious attention to anything that is brought before them, that they not infrequently are able to ask questions which indicate how close their attention has been and how accurate is their recollection of evidence. However, be that as it may, I look at the suggestions which are made as to how the Chief Justice dealt with these matters and, speaking for myself, I can see nothing wrong with it, and that is the opinion of all the members of this Court. The matter was carefully put, adequately put and properly put by the Chief Justice, and it was then for the jury to decide Aye or No did they accept the prisoner's denials or did they accept the evidence of two witnesses who spoke affirmatively to statements made by the Appellant and, I think, another witness who was not able to give the main evidence but did depose to hearing the words or similar words spoken by somebody.

In those circumstances, it seems to me that the matter was essentially a matter for the jury to decide, and I do not think I need say anything more about it. In the opinion of the Court, the idea that there was a failure on the part of the Chief Justice to say anything short of what was required in putting that sort of case to the jury is entirely wrong.

The other point that is made is perhaps more interesting and perhaps rather more unusual. It is this, that it is said the Appellant had been arrested by the police officer on the roof of the Croydon building and that it was after he had been arrested by a police officer that the shot was fired by the other man or boy which killed the police officer Miles. The argument advanced about that is this, that whether there was a joint enterprise or not, a joint enterprise in which to the knowledge of both of them one of them was going to be armed – and the Appellant himself had some sort of armament upon him not of the nature which is in question with regard to this particular loss of life – the Appellant could not be held responsible for the act because the joint enterprise was at an end. That depends on what the jury thought was the joint enterprise. If they thought it was an enterprise to go and murder somebody and that was over and done with so that the joint enterprise was finished, they might very well have taken that view. I do not say it would have been the right view, but they might have taken the view that the enterprise was then finished as soon as one of them was arrested, but they might equally well have taken the view, and there was ample material for them to take it, and no complaint is made of the summing-up with regard to this, that the enterprise was not merely a burglarious enterprise but an enterprise in which they were to secure themselves against the possibility of arrest by arming themselves against those who came to apprehend them. In those circumstances the jury might very well have taken quite a different view as to whether the enterprise had finished or not. It is a little difficult for Mr Cassels because his own client was asked specifically at the hearing whether he was under arrest at the time when this shot which killed Miles was fired. He would not have it. He said he had not been arrested, that he was not under arrest, that the police officer had not detained him, and all the rest of it. In the face of that it seems to us that it is idle to suggest that this point, if it be the point, about the arrest is one which the jury could take into consideration and about which the Chief Justice ought to have directed the jury. The answers given in cross-examination by an individual on trial do sometimes have the result of destroying the possibility of a good point of law being persisted in which the learned counsel has endeavoured to get on its feet before a jury, and it seems to us that there is nothing in this point on either of the two grounds. In our opinion this is nothing more than an ordinary appeal in a murder trial, an ordinary appeal which is, in our judgement, without foundation and which is accordingly dismissed.

Selected Bibliography

BENTLEY, William George. *My Son's Execution*. London: W. H. Allen, 1957.

BRESLER, Fenton. *Lord Goddard: A Biography*. London: Harrap, 1977.

BRESLER, Fenton. *Reprieve: A Study of a System*. London: Harrap, 1965.

COBB, Belton. *Murdered on Duty*. London: W. H. Allen, 1961.

DU CANN, C. G. L. *Miscarriages of Justice*. London: Muller, 1960.

FATTEH, Dr Abdullah. *Medicolegal Investigation of Gunshot Wounds*. Philadelphia: Lippincott, 1976.

FURNEAUX, Rupert. *They Died By a Gun*. London: Jenkins, 1962.

GATTEY, Charles Neilson. *The Incredible Mrs Van der Elst*. London: Frewin, 1972.

GRIMSHAW, Eric and JONES, Glyn. *Lord Goddard: His Career and Cases*. London: Wingate, 1958.

HUMPHREYS, Christmas. *Both Sides of The Circle*. London: Allen & Unwin, 1978.

KILMUIR, Earl of. *Political Adventure*. London: Weidenfeld & Nicolson, 1964.

PAGET, R. T., SILVERMAN, S. S. and HOLLIS, Christopher. *Hanged and Innocent*. London: Gollancz, 1953.

PARRIS, John. *Most of My Murders*. London: Muller, 1960.

PIERREPOINT, Albert. *Executioner Pierrepoint*. London: Harrap, 1974.

SCOTT, Sir Harold. *Scotland Yard*. London: Deutsch, 1954.

SMITH, Arthur. *Lord Goddard: My Years With The Lord Chief Justice*. London: Weidenfeld and Nicolson, 1959.

YALLOP, David A. *To Encourage The Others*. London: W. H. Allen, 1971.

Index

Adams, J. 43
Alderson, PC James Leslie 16, 91, 108
Allsop, Kenneth 149
Antiquis, Alec de 1
Appleby and Ostler case 87–8
Attlee, Clement 56

Ball, Rev. (Prison Chaplain) 145
Barlow & Parker warehouse 9–12, 22, 59, 62, 75, 102; *see also* attempted robbery *under* Bentley, Derek
Bartley, Mrs Sarah 123
Bass, John 59, 64–5, 112
Beard, PC Charles 62
Beckman, Albert (Prison Officer) 143, 145
Bennet, J. W. (Coroner) 25–6
Bentley, Albert (uncle) 18, 19, 45–6, 109, 142
Bentley, Denis (brother) 3, 7, 37, 38, 99, 101, 142
Bentley, Derek William vii–viii; family background 3, 35–43; mental and physical status 4–6, 28, 30–47, 51–3; approved school and early career 4–6, 41–7; friendship with Craig 6, 47–50; attempted robbery at Barlow & Parker warehouse 6–12; shooting of PC Miles 12–15, 24; arrest and interrogation 16–21; statement 19–21, 29; custody and pre-trial events 22–3, 25–9; Dr Mattheson's Report on 30–5, 178–83; trial 3, 54–97; summing-up 93–7,

184–93; verdict and death sentence 3, 98–101; public controversy 25, 101–5, 107–10; condemned prisoner 105–7, 120, 135–45; appeal 111–19, 194–7; campaign against execution 120–35, 140–1; execution vii, viii, 145–9; reasons for execution 150–5, 157–9; plight of family after his death 155–7, 160; miscarriage of justice 3, 24, 159–64; and abolition of death penalty viii, 159–61; clearing of name vii––viii, 161–4
Bentley, Iris (sister) vii–viii, 3–4, 6–7, 17–18, 25, 35–8, 40, 74, 93, 99, 101, 106, 129, 135, 139–42, 145, 148–9, 157, 162, 164
Bentley, Joan (sister) 35, 37
Bentley, Lilian (mother) 3, 5, 17–18, 25, 35–41, 45, 47–50, 58, 64, 74, 93, 98, 101, 106, 109, 120–1, 124–8, 135, 138–42, 145, 148, 155–6
Bentley, Roger (brother) 41
Bentley, William (father) viii, 3, 5–7, 17–19, 25, 32, 35–45, 48–50, 58, 64, 70, 74, 92–3, 98–9, 101, 103, 106, 107–9, 116–17, 120–9, 134–5, 138–42,, 144–5, 148, 155–6, 164, 178, 179, 181
Bevan, Aneurin 133–4, 140
Binet, Alfred 42
Bodley, DI 1
Both Sides of the Circle (Humphreys) 157
Bradbury, Rita 137–9, 142

Bresler, Fenton 97, 110, 153–4, 159
Brett, Mr Justice (later Viscount
    Esher) 93–4, 187
Brown, PC 167
Browne, Clifton 132
Browne, Frederick Guy 143, 166n
Burt, Sir Cyril 42
Byng, Admiral John 153

Cassels, Frank H. (Bentley's barris-
    ter) viii, 54–7, 60, 63–5, 69, 70–1,
    80–3, 85, 89–92, 103, 110–15,
    117, 157, 195–6
Cassels, Sir James 54
Churchill, Sir Winston 56, 121
Close, DI 17
Collinson, Mr 43
Craig, Christopher vii, 7; friendship
    with Bentley 6, 47–9; family
    background 8, 23; attempted rob-
    bery at Barlow & Parker ware-
    house 8–12; shooting of PC Miles
    12–15, 33; injury, hospitalization
    and arrest 15–17, 21–2, 26, 31;
    Bentley's statement 20–1; too
    young to be tried for murder
    23–4, 151, 153; preliminary
    court hearing 26–7, 163; fire-
    arms evidence 28–9, 34, 62,
    74–9, 101–3, 126–7, 165–77;
    hatred of police 50, 122; trial
    54–97, 157; summing-up 92–7,
    184–93; prison sentence 98–101,
    111; family reaction 104–5, 126;
    controversy over verdict 25, 107;
    and Bentley's appeal 112–17;
    denial of Bentley's alleged order
    ('Let him have it, Chris') 126–7,
    129, 159; rehabilitation 154
Craig, Edith (mother) 8, 58, 99,
    103–5, 126–9
Craig, Lucy (sister) 58
Craig, Miles (brother) 23
Craig, Niven (brother) 8, 47–8, 50,

184
Craig, Niven (father) 8, 57–8, 62,
    99, 104, 107
Croom-Johnson, Mr Justice 112–19;
    Appeal Court judgment 194–7

Denham, PC Vincent 21, 70
Donnelly, Desmond 133–4
Dors, Diana 140
Drummond, Edward 51
Du Cann, C. G. L. 159

Edgar, PC Nathaniel 2
Eden, Sir Anthony 140
Elizabeth II, HM Queen 111, 121,
    131, 150, 152, 157
Ellis, Ruth 60
Elst, Mrs Violet Van der 145–7
Erskine May, Sir Thomas (author of
    the guide to parliamentary rules
    and precedents) 130

Fairfax, DC (later DS) Frederick
    ('Fairy') 11–15, 17, 26–7, 29, 59,
    60, 62–4, 66, 71, 75, 78, 81, 86,
    88, 89, 94–6, 100, 101, 103, 108,
    111, 115, 118, 159, 168–72,
    175–6, 184, 188–9, 191
Fatteh, Dr Abdullah 177
Fazey, Frank 7–8, 20, 49, 98
Fidoe, John 44–5
Freebody, Dr Douglas 16, 67
Fyfe, Sir David Maxwell (Home
    Secretary; later Lord Kilmuir)
    26, 110, 120–1, 124–7, 131, 134,
    140, 148, 150–2, 154–6, 158

George VI, King 1, 149
Gladstone Smith, Peter 2
Goddard, Lord Chief Justice Rayner
    28, 55–6, 59, 62–5, 67, 70–7,
    79–80, 82–5, 88–90, 92–101,
    103, 108, 110–16, 119, 122–3,
    153–4, 157–9, 163–4, 195–6;

summing-up at Bentley's trial
184–93
Gowers, Sir Ernest 160
Grimshaw, Eric 56, 158
Gutteridge, PC George 143, 166

Hale, Leslie 132–3
Haler, Dr David 22, 67, 146–7, 168, 176
Hanged and Innocent (Paget) 83
Harrison, PC Norman 11–14, 22, 27, 66, 86, 88, 95, 100, 111, 170–2, 176, 188, 191
Hatfield, Dr Gordon 68
Heald, Sir Lionel 122
Hilbery, Mr Justice 8
Hill, Dr (later Sir) Denis 31, 34, 44, 53, 123–4, 129, 148, 179
Home Office Standard Table of Drops 135–6
Howes, Mr and Mrs 49
Humphreys, Christmas (Prosecuting Counsel) 55, 57, 59–61, 66, 68, 71–3, 76–9, 82–7, 97, 112, 115–16, 157
Hutchins, Albert 46, 47
Hyde, H. Montgomery 108, 150, 152

Jaggs, PC Robert 14, 66, 111, 174, 189
Jaswon, Dr Nicholas 15, 66–7, 88
Johnson, Kenneth 129
Jones, Glyn 56, 158
Juvenile Delinquency (Pearce) 42–3

Kennedy, William Henry 143, 166n
King, Highmore 119–20

Law, Chief Inspector Percy 62
Lawton, Mr (Governor of Wandsworth) 120, 145
Levin, Bernard 56
Lipski, Israel 133

Lloyd George, Major Gwilym 159
Lord Goddard (Bresler) 159
Lowe, PC Stuart Stanley 14–15, 102
Lowther, Mr (Speaker) 133

McDonald, PC James Christie 11–14, 27, 29, 62, 64–6, 88, 90, 95, 100, 102, 111, 188, 191
McLoughlin, Madeline 58
McManus, Dr 38
McNaghten, Daniel 51
McNaghten Rules 51–2
Mattheson, Dr J. C. M. (PMO) 30–5, 43–4, 59; Report on Bentley 178–83
Maybrick, Florence 133
Medicolegal Investigation of Gunshot Wounds (Fatteh) 177
Miles, Mrs Catherine Elizabeth 17, 26, 104–6, 162
Miles, PC Sidney ('Milo') vii, 12, 16–17; shooting of 14–17, 21–3, 25–6, 28, 31, 54, 59–61, 63, 67, 72–3, 75–6, 79, 84–9, 93–4, 96–7, 101–2, 104–5, 106, 108, 111, 114, 117, 122, 126, 146, 153, 159, 162, 168, 170–3, 175–6, 185, 188, 192, 196; investigation of death and trial of Craig and Bentley: see under Bentley, Derek *and* Craig, Christopher
Miscarriage of Justice (Du Cann) 159
Morrison, William 128, 131–4
Most of My Murders (Parris) 102, 157
Munroe, Dr James A. 43, 44, 51–2, 178, 180
Murdoch, Dr James 145
My Son's Execution (W. Bentley) 92–3

Nelson, Edward Davis, and

Company (Craig's solicitors) 54
Newsam, Sir Frank 125, 129, 135
Nichols, Beverley 107
Nickolls, Lewis (Director, Metropolitan Police Laboratory) 27, 71–3, 88, 167, 169, 175
Notable British Trials (Hyde) 108, 150

Ormerod, Mr Justice 112–13, 115

Paget, Reginald 83, 132, 140, 150, 153
Pam 15, 137
Parris, John (Craig's barrister) 54–9, 61–4, 66–8, 71–6, 79, 82, 84, 87, 92, 96–7, 102–3, 117–18, 122–3, 157
Parsley, Norman 7–8, 17, 20, 49, 98
Pearce, Dr J. D. W. 42–3
Pearson, Mr Justice 112
Peel, Sir Robert 51
Pierrepoint, Albert (executioner) 107, 123, 130, 135–6, 144–7, 160
Political Adventure (Kilmuir) 152
Povey, D. (Prison Officer) 137
Procter, Harry 58

Reprieve (Bresler) 153, 159
Reynolds, Dr Doris 43
Richardson, R. L. 27
Roberts, Sgt Edward 15, 16, 27, 108

Samuelson, Anthony 97
Scott, Sir Harold 111
Shepherd, DS Stanley 16–17, 19, 21, 68–70, 170
Sheppard, PC Thomas 27, 167
Shooting to Live with the One-hand Gun 2
Silverman, Sydney (later Sir Sydney) 128–35, 140, 156, 159
Simon, Theodore 42
Smith, Arthur 158
Smith, DCI John 16–17, 19, 21, 22, 59, 69, 70–1, 91, 170, 172, 175
Smith, PC John 21
Stephens, PC Henry 16, 27, 108
Stevens, John (Bentley's solicitor) 25, 27, 54, 71

Thomas, George 2
To Encourage the Others (Yallop) 28, 153
Towes, C. F. 50, 178, 180
Tullett, E. V. 168

Ungoed-Thomas, Sir Lynn 128, 140

Voltaire, François 153

Ware, John 11
Ware, Pearl Edith 9–11, 22, 62, 102
Warr, Dowager Countess de la 154–5
Whitley, Mr (Speaker) 133
Wigan, C. R. 145
Wilde, Oscar 143–4
Winter, A. L. 33, 178

Yallop, David 28, 61, 97, 101, 108, 153, 161, 168, 174, 176
Yates, Victor 155

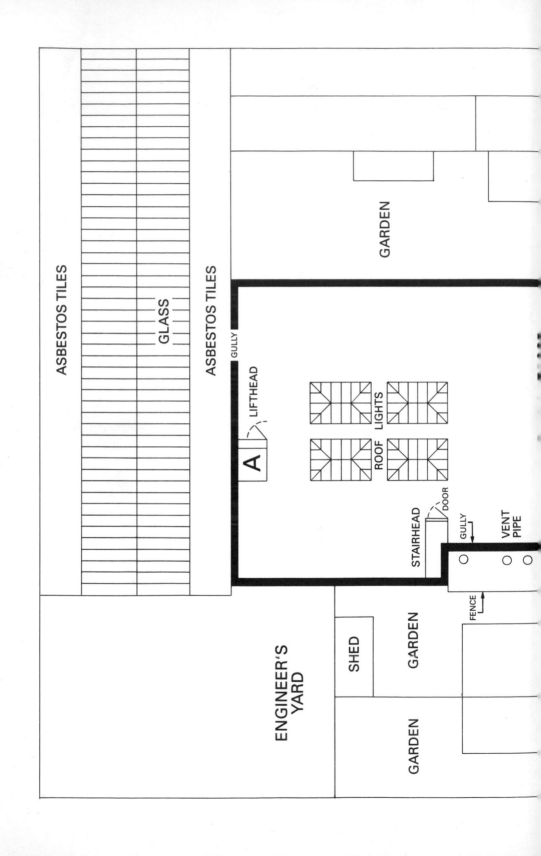